THE ANCIENT JEWS FROM ⁄ TO MUHAMMAD

This is an accessible and up-to-date account of the Jews during the millennium following Alexander the Great's conquest of the East. Unusually, it acknowledges the problems involved in constructing a narrative from fragmentary yet complex evidence and is, implicitly, an exploration of how this might be accomplished. Moreover, unlike most other introductions to the subject, it concentrates primarily on the people rather than issues of theology and adopts a resolutely unsentimental approach to the subject. Professor Schwartz particularly demonstrates the importance of studying Jewish history, texts and artefacts to the broader community of ancient historians because of what they can contribute to wider themes such as Roman imperialism. The book serves as an excellent introduction for students and scholars of Jewish history and of ancient history.

SETH SCHWARTZ is the Lucius N. Littauer Professor of Classical Jewish Civilization, and Professor of History and of Classics at Columbia University. He is the author of *Imperialism and Jewish Society, 200 BCE to 640 CE* (2001), which received the National Jewish Book Award and was a finalist for the Koret Book Award, and *Were the Jews a Mediterranean Society? Reciprocity and Solidarity in Ancient Judaism* (2010).

KEY THEMES IN ANCIENT HISTORY

EDITORS

P. A. Cartledge
Clare College, Cambridge
P. D. A. Garnsey
Jesus College, Cambridge

Key Themes in Ancient History aims to provide readable, informed and original studies of various basic topics, designed in the first instance for students and teachers of Classics and Ancient History, but also for those engaged in related disciplines. Each volume is devoted to a general theme in Greek, Roman, or where appropriate, Graeco-Roman history, or to some salient aspect or aspects of it. Besides indicating the state of current research in the relevant area, authors seek to show how the theme is significant for our own as well as ancient culture and society. By providing books for courses that are oriented around themes it is hoped to encourage and stimulate promising new developments in teaching and research in ancient history.

Other books in the series

Death-ritual and social structure in classical antiquity, by Ian Morris
978 0 521 37465 1 (hardback) 978 0 521 37611 2 (paperback)

Literacy and orality in ancient Greece, by Rosalind Thomas
978 0 521 37346 3 (hardback) 978 0 521 37742 3 (paperback)

Slavery and Society at Rome, by Keith Bradley
978 0 521 37287 9 (hardback) 978 0 521 37887 1 (paperback)

Law, violence, and community in classical Athens, by David Cohen
978 0 521 38167 3 (hardback) 978 0 521 38837 5 (paperback)

Public order in ancient Rome, by Wilfried Nippel
978 0 521 38327 1 (hardback) 978 0 521 38749 1 (paperback)

Friendship in the classical world, by David Konstan
978 0 521 45402 5 (hardback) 978 0 521 45998 3 (paperback)

Sport and society in ancient Greece, by Mark Golden
978 0 521 49698 8 (hardback) 978 0 521 49790 9 (paperback)

Food and society in classical antiquity, by Peter Garnsey
978 0 521 64182 1 (hardback) 978 0 521 64588 1 (paperback)

Banking and business in the Roman world, by Jean Andreau
978 0 521 38031 7 (hardback) 978 0 521 38932 7 (paperback)

Roman law in context, by David Johnston
978 0 521 63046 7 (hardback) 978 0 521 63961 3 (paperback)

Religions of the ancient Greeks, by Simon Price
978 0 521 38201 4 (hardback) 978 0 521 38867 2 (paperback)

Christianity and Roman society, by Gillian Clark
978 0 521 63310 9 (hardback) 978 0 521 63386 4 (paperback)

Trade in classical antiquity, by Neville Morley
978 0 521 63279 9 (hardback) 978 0 521 63416 8 (paperback)

Technology and culture in Greek and Roman antiquity, by Serafina Cuomo
978 0 521 81073 9 (hardback) 978 0 521 00903 4 (paperback)

Law and crime in the Roman world, by Jill Harries
978 0 521 82820 8 (hardback) 978 0 521 53532 8 (paperback)

The social history of Roman art, by Peter Stewart
978 0 521 81632 8 (hardback) 978 0 52101659 9 (paperback)

Ancient Greek political thought in practice, by Paul Cartledge
978 0 521 45455 1 (hardback) 978 0 521 45595 4 (paperback)

Asceticism in the Graeco-Roman world, by Richard Finn OP
978 0 521 86281 3 (hardback) 978 0 521 68154 4 (paperback)

Domestic space and social organisation in classical antiquity, by Lisa C. Nevett
978 0 521 78336 1 (hardback) 978 0 521 78945 5 (paperback)

Money in classical antiquity, by Sitta von Reden
978 0 521 45337 0 (hardback) 978 0 521 45952 5 (paperback)

Geography in classical antiquity, by Daniela Dueck and Kai Brodersen
978 0 521 19788 5 (hardback) 978 0 521 12025 8 (paperback)

Space and society in the Greek and Roman worlds, by Michael Scott
978 1 107 00915 8 (hardback) 978 1 107 40150 1 (paperback)

Studying gender in classical antiquity, by Lin Foxhall
978 0 521 55318 6 (hardback) 978 0 521 55739 9 (paperback)

THE ANCIENT JEWS FROM ALEXANDER TO MUHAMMAD

SETH SCHWARTZ

CAMBRIDGE
UNIVERSITY PRESS

CAMBRIDGE
UNIVERSITY PRESS

University Printing House, Cambridge CB2 8BS, United Kingdom

Cambridge University Press is part of the University of Cambridge.

It furthers the University's mission by disseminating knowledge in the pursuit of education, learning and research at the highest international levels of excellence.

www.cambridge.org
Information on this title: www.cambridge.org/9781107669291

© Seth Schwartz 2014

First published 2014

Printed in the United Kingdom by Clays, St Ives plc

A catalogue record for this publication is available from the British Library

Library of Congress Cataloguing in Publication data
Schwartz, Seth, author.
The ancient Jews from Alexander to Muhammad / Seth Schwartz.
pages   cm. – (Key themes in ancient history)
Includes bibliographical references and index.
ISBN 978-1-107-04127-1 (hardback) – ISBN 978-1-107-66929-1 (paperback)
1. Jews–History.   2. Judaism–History.   3. Jews–Civilization.
4. Palestine–History.   I. Title.
DS117.S48396 2014
909'.04924–dc23
2013045306

ISBN 978-1-107-04127-1 Hardback
ISBN 978-1-107-66929-1 Paperback

Contents

Preface

This book is in part an abbreviation, rethinking, updating and re-orientation of Schwartz 2001. If it is unusually argumentative for a Key Themes book, that is because the topic demands, I would argue, an argumentative rather than a magisterial style, but it is far less argumentative than its remote source. It is more concerned to present a historical narrative, as far as possible, and to give full accounts of various issues in political history, especially the Jewish rebellions of the Hellenistic and Roman periods, which were given short shrift in the earlier book. I have also made an effort to summarize the most relevant new archaeology of the past decade. Most bibliographical items cited in *The Ancient Jews* were published after 2000.

I could not have written this book without a year of leave, in 2012–13, a semester of which I owe to the happy arrival in May, 2012, of Jonah Margolin-Schwartz. I owe the rest to the goodwill and ingenuity of Mark Mazower and Margaret Edsall. I thank René Bloch for his comments on Chapter 2 and Beth Berkowitz for her comments on Chapters 5 and 7, though neither is responsible for any remaining defects. I derived immense benefit from numerous e-mail exchanges with Hannah Cotton; Walter Ameling and John Ma gave me important advice about Hellenistic Jerusalem, and John sent me in addition some not yet published papers which contain the most original ideas about the background of the Maccabean Revolt since Bickermann's. I am likewise grateful to Gil Gambash for sending me his manuscript on the British and Jewish revolts against Rome. My gratitude to Peter Garnsey and Paul Cartledge for their good-humoured encouragement and support should go without saying. Paul's editorial interventions were an education in themselves. Michael Sharp, the editor for Cambridge University Press, has been unfailingly kind and helpful. The emotional roller-coaster ride of parenthood has finally distracted me, now and then, from history (though it has, alas, completely deprived me of television, too), and for that I thank the aforementioned Jonah, his big sister Ayelet, and Judy. With any luck by the time I finish the next book I'll have the TV back.

Abbreviations

AJA	*American Journal of Archaeology*
ANRW	H. Temporini *et al.*, eds. *Aufstieg und Niedergang der römischen Welt*. Berlin, 1972–.
BASOR	*Bulletin of the American Schools of Oriental Research*
CEHGRW	W. Scheidel, I. Morris and R. Saller, eds. *Cambridge Economic History of the Graeco-Roman World*, Cambridge, 2007.
CHJ	W. D. Davies, *et al.*, eds. *Cambridge History of Judaism*, 4 volumes. Cambridge, 1984–2006.
CSEL	*Corpus Scriptorum Ecclesiasticorum Latinorum*
CPJ	V. Tcherikover, A. Fuks and M. Stern, eds., *Corpus Papyrorum Judaicarum*. 3 volumes. Cambridge, MA, 1957–64.
DOP	*Dumbarton Oaks Papers*
GLAJJ	M. Stern, *Greek and Latin Authors on Jews and Judaism*, 3 volumes, Jerusalem, 1976–84.
HSCP	*Harvard Studies in Classical Philology*
HTR	*Harvard Theological Review*
HUCA	*Hebrew Union College Annual*
IEJ	*Israel Exploration Journal*
INJ	*Israel Numismatic Journal*
INR	*Israel Numismatic Research*
JBL	*Journal of Biblical Literature*
JECS	*Journal of Early Christian Studies*
JJS	*Journal of Jewish Studies*
JQR	*Jewish Quarterly Review*
JRA	*Journal of Roman Archaeology*
JRS	*Journal of Roman Studies*
JSJ	*Journal for the Study of Judaism*

P. Murab.	P. Benoit, J. Milik and R. de Vaux, eds. *Les Grottes de Murabba'at* (*Discoveries in the Judaean Desert* 2), Oxford, 1961.
P. Yadin	Y. Yadin *et al.*, eds. *The Documents from the Bar-Kokhba Period in the Cave of Letters*, 2 volumes, Jerusalem, 1989–2002.
PAAJR	*Proceedings of the American Academy for Jewish Research*
PCPS	*Proceedings of the Cambridge Philological Society*
PLRE	H. M. Jones, J. R. Martindale and J. Morris, *The Prosopography of the Later Roman Empire*, 3 volumes, Cambridge, 1971–92.
REJ	*Revue des Études Juives*
SCI	*Scripta Classica Israelica*
Schürer-Vermes	E. Schürer, *The History of the Jewish People in the Age of Jesus Christ (175 BC–AD 135)*, revised and edited by G. Vermes, F. Millar and M. Goodman, 3 volumes, Edinburgh, 1973–87.
XHever/Seiyal	H. Cotton and A. Yardeni, *Aramaic, Hebrew and Greek Documentary Papyri from Nahal Hever and Other Sites* (Discoveries in the Judaean Desert 27), Oxford, 1997.
ZPE	*Zeitschrift für Papyrologie und Epigraphik*

Introduction

The administration of Ventidius Cumanus as governor of Judaea (48–52 CE) was, according to the historian Josephus, an ominous one for the Jews, featuring several cases of provocative military misbehaviour and the governor's anti-Jewish intervention in a civil mini-war between Jews and Samaritans, which ended badly for everyone, including the governor. On one occasion, though, Cumanus' decisive action forestalled what would otherwise have quickly degenerated into mass rebellion. Some Roman troops, on patrol in the western Judaean hills in the wake of an attack on an imperial slave, found in one village a scroll of the Law of Moses, and one of the soldiers cut it to pieces and burned the scraps.[1] News quickly spread, and the Judaeans, 'aroused as though it were their whole country which had been consumed in flames', marched *en masse* to the governor's palace in Caesarea Maritima, where Cumanus found the responsible soldier and had him executed. 'On this, the Jews withdrew' (*Jewish War* 2.228–31).

Is this episode self-explanatory, or deeply bizarre (Schürer-Vermes 1:456–7; S. Schwartz 2001:60–1)? We live in a world where group symbols are destroyed in acts of provocation which everyone seems to understand. Flag-burnings are routine and routinely cause outrage. The public burning of a copy of the Quran by an extremist Protestant pastor in Florida sparked violent protests in Afghanistan, but, perhaps more relevant to the pastor's stated intentions, offended enlightened opinion at home.[2] Public outrage at the provocative treatment of central Christian symbols is also familiar. Nearly twenty-five years after its creation, according to a story widely circulated on the Internet, Andres Serrano's notorious *Piss Christ* (a photograph of a plastic crucifix suspended in what was allegedly the artist's urine) was attacked and destroyed by pious Catholics in Avignon in

---

[1] In the alternative version, *Jewish Antiquities* 20.115, he simply – and more plausibly, if it was in fact a very large parchment scroll – ripped or cut it down the middle (διέσχισεν).
[2] Lizette Alvarez, 'Koran-Burning Pastor Unrepentant in Face of Furor', *New York Times*, 2 April 2011.

April 2011.[3] The fact that this story appears to have been at the very least greatly exaggerated suggests that whatever happened functioned primarily as a convenient peg on which to hang a larger debate on the embattled secularism of the French Republic.[4] Personally offended and wary of controversy, authorities in the late 1990s routinely banned display of Chris Ofili's *Holy Virgin Mary*, a painting composed partly of elephant dung; it was subsequently purchased by a collector and now hangs peacefully in Tasmania.[5]

On reflection, the idea that the destruction of a single copy of a book – admittedly, necessarily an extremely valuable item when considered merely as a commodity, given its size and the expense involved in its production (Haran 1983; 1985) – might cause a revolt, that in response to such a piece of misbehaviour a hard-headed (if none too competent) Roman administrator might execute one of his own soldiers, is very strange indeed. Modern nation states promote symbols which are inherently meaningless. Flag-burners are strictly speaking doing practically nothing beyond producing a bit of air pollution. They are engaging in a purely symbolic and also completely self-explanatory expression of hostility to a state – however complex the politics behind the act may be. A Torah scroll, or indeed a copy of the Quran, was to be sure a symbol in a somewhat similar sense, as Josephus observed. But it was something more specific, too, and more complex: the Jews argued to Cumanus that the perpetrator of such an outrage 'against their god and their law should not be left unpunished' (*War* 2.230).[6] The Torah scroll, then, stood not only for the Jews as corporate body, like a flag ('as though their whole country had been consumed in flames'), it also stood for God, that is, the Jews' god – who was both a universal divine principle (*ho theos*, or even *to theion*, without further specification) and a particular national patron god – its putative author, and 'the law', that is, it represented its own contents. The provocative soldier (if that is what he was, and not simply stupid)[7] and the provoked Jews actually had somewhat different things in mind: the soldier was insulting the Jews, the Jews understood this but also thought the soldier, who, like the Florida pastor (as he

---

[3] Angelique Chrisafis, 'Attack on Blasphemous Art Work Fires Debate on Role of Religion in France', *The Guardian*, 18 April 2011.

[4] A photograph at reuters.com demonstrates minor damage to the glass cover of the photograph, pretty clearly produced by a single hammer blow.

[5] 'Chris Ofili', *Wikipedia*.

[6] Slightly different at *Jewish Antiquities* 20.116: the Jews beseeched Cumanus to 'avenge not them but the god whose laws had been subjected to outrage; for they could not bear to live with their ancestral (laws) thus insulted'.

[7] The alternative version of the story, in *Jewish Antiquities* 20.115, makes the soldier's insolent intention explicit.

admitted to the press), presumably had little knowledge of the contents of the book he was destroying, had insulted God and the Torah itself. The scroll was indubitably a symbol but it symbolized different things to different people. This is why the soldier got more than he bargained for.

How did the contents of the scroll – a narrative of group origins and a collection of laws – and the scroll as a physical object come to assume such importance? Why, in this story, were 'the Jews', or some group of Jews, so swift to take offence at the isolated act of a small group of Roman soldiers? How and why did the news spread so quickly? However provocative the act of the soldier was, it is possible to imagine circumstances in which the Jews would have responded differently. Fifty years ago, who would have noticed if a small-town minister in the southern United States had destroyed a Quran? Indeed, why would he have bothered? Provocations occur and are effective in very specific circumstances, in our case, circumstances of growing tension over Roman rule in Palestine. Ostensibly spontaneous outbursts of public rage never fail to have a politics and a culture, which does not mean that they do not also embody and enact emotions. It is itself a political argument to represent them as pure and unmediated expressions of the popular will, as if the popular will does not need to be intentionally mobilized and organized in order to be expressed. In this case, though both the Roman act and the Jewish response have a familiar ring to them, they are in neither case self-explanatory: they too have a politics and a culture. Why did the Romans have more trouble imposing their rule in Palestine than almost anywhere else, as they demonstrably did? Why did the Jews resist, and why did their resistance take the specific forms it did? What led to the repeated breakdown of Roman–Jewish relations, which is foreshadowed in Josephus' account? These questions, how to account for the emergence of the Jews as a distinct and enduringly distinctive group, their impact on their social and political environment and its impact on them – to phrase them differently – are the core concerns of this book. I will address an additional set of questions as well, which emerge from the first, about why and how these issues retain their urgency as objects of study, including for classicists and ancient historians. But the remainder of the introduction treats still more basic questions: who and what were/are the Jews and how do we know anything about them at all?

WHAT SORT OF A GROUP ARE THE JEWS?

Most people who think about this question take for granted the continuous existence of a distinctive group called the Jews from some period in the remote past down to the present,[8] while acknowledging that certain aspects of the character of the group changed over time. In its most basic version, this view is shared by Jewish and Christian traditionalists, and by many others as well. Many Christians believed that the Jews had once been a great and spiritually gifted nation that had condemned itself to suffering and eternal decline by its role in Christ's crucifixion and by its subsequent failure to accept him as Saviour and Son of God. The Jews, Israel according to the flesh, had been superseded in God's affection by a new, spiritual, Israel, the Christian Church. The Jews were thus heirs of the prophets but modern Judaism was not identical with prophetic religion. The Jews had become debased (Simon 1986: 65–97; 135–78; 202–33).

The Jews had a somewhat similar view of the shape of their past. They, too, traditionally believed that their ancestors had once constituted a great nation which for its sins (not including the execution of Jesus) had been expelled from its land and deprived of its holy temple, on which Judaism had once strongly focused. But for Jews who retain traditional ideas the Jews never actually lost divine favour and access; God continued to speak, in however mediated a form, through the rabbis of the Talmud (70–600 CE) and through the writings and teachings of their successors and interpreters down to modern times. Jewish traditionalists awaited and await the restoration of the Jews – a dead letter in Christian thought unless the Jews converted to Christianity, at which point in the view of most theologians the question of their *corporate* restoration would be rendered moot: there would be no separate Jewish people after the Second Coming. In fact the idea of corporate redemption or restoration remained important in altered form even for those Jews who abandoned or modified traditional ideas –mainly after 1800 – inspiring and energizing modern nationalist and utopian political movements like Zionism, territorialism, socialism and communism (the latter two in their Jewish versions aspired to redeem the Jewish people by redeeming all the oppressed peoples of the world).[9]

The *idea* of a continuous Jewish history thus was in no need of invention by the first professional Jewish historians, who lived mainly in German states and the Habsburg Empire in the early and mid-nineteenth

---

[8] This is why a book like Sand 2009, which argues against this view, has the power to shock. On 'Jewish genes' see Ostrer 2012; Abu El-Haj 2012.

[9] Territorialism was the view that the Jews should possess an autonomous or partly autonomous national home: it was Zionism without Palestine. Specifically Jewish branches of the socialist and communist movements survive only vestigially, but from the late nineteenth through to the mid-twentieth centuries were significant movements in eastern Europe, the United States, and Palestine/Israel. On these movements and their complex interrelations see J. Frankel 1981, with updating in J. Frankel 2009.

century. But the *content* of such a history had to be laboriously mined out of obscure and neglected texts and documents, among other things, since corporate memory, Jewish, Christian and Muslim, had failed to preserve more than snippets of the past (Yerushalmi 1982; Schorsch 1994). Such investigations only added fuel to debates about the essential character of Jewish group identity – were/are the Jews a nation? Or are they a religion or rather an ethnicity or a 'race'? Are the Jews bound together by shared descent? Religious belief and practice? Culture? Are they bound together at all? These were all debates, among the Jews themselves and between the Jews and the leadership and intelligentsia of the countries they lived in, driven by contemporary ideological and political concerns about the status and role of the Jews in the emerging nation states of Europe, in which traditional modes of Jewish life and long-standing arrangements with political and religious authorities no longer seemed relevant (Rechter 2002). Though the nation state is by now a well-established concept, the questions it raises about the nature of Jewish identity, sharpened by the success of one of the responses, Zionism, remain unresolved; the debates persist. Scholarship is inevitably entangled in contemporary concerns.

This means that to write in a synoptic and summary way about the ancient Jews is to tread through a minefield. It will be best to begin by confronting some of the points head-on: what sort of group were the ancient Jews and what is their relation to modern Jews? What categories can we use most productively to think about them? What was the nature of their relationship to their social and cultural environment in antiquity? Let me open the discussion with a provocative soundbite before moving on to more systematic examination: if you were to stop a man on, say, West 86th Street in Manhattan and ask him if he is Jewish he is not unlikely to respond, 'Yes, but I'm not religious or anything.' What happens if you replace the word 'Jewish' in the question with 'Presbyterian' or with 'French'? The man's response is reduced to nonsense. In other words, Jewishness nowadays does not quite fit into our standard categories of religion or nationality, but straddles the border (Gitelman 2009); even people who have pared their Jewishness down to one or the other category – usually ethnicity – retain, like the New Yorker in the vignette, the sense that it is not really just the one. Did it work in a similar way in antiquity, too?

ANACHRONISM

Anachronism entails assuming that what is true now has always been true. If Jews are thought nowadays to have a special disposition towards commerce or the professions, or to have a preference for liberalism in politics (true in the USA but not the UK), then one might automatically assume this to have been the case in the past as well. Even historians can fall prey to such assumptions, but they have known since the birth of modern historiography in Renaissance Italy that they should not (Schiffman 2011), that one of their jobs is precisely to expose and criticize such thinking as unhistorical in failing to recognize that things change and that groups like the Jews do not (necessarily) have stable essential features. It is easy to show that Jews developed their orientation towards trade only in the Middle Ages, and their orientation towards the professions and liberal politics only in the nineteenth and twentieth centuries (Penslar 2001). The 'Jewish sensibility' – let's say a predisposition to self-ironizing gallows humour – traces of which survive to the present, is manifestly a response to the dislocations of modernity; we should not expect to find it among ancient or medieval Jews.

Admittedly, some anachronisms of this type are much harder to locate and eradicate. On the most basic level, the fact that ancient Jews were overwhelmingly rural and agrarian, not urban and mercantile, has profound cultural implications that scholarship has been struggling to come to terms with. For example, it implies that most ancient Jews, like most of their neighbours, were not literate. This fact not only flies in the face of modern stereotypes, in this case shared by Jews themselves and many others, about the Jews' predisposition to higher education, their being 'the people of the book' (originally a metaphorical extension but later a vulgar misunderstanding of an expression which originated as a description of the technical status of Jews *and Christians* – as opposed to pagans – in Islamic law – they are the *ahl al-kitab*, the people of the Book [the Bible], not the book (M. Cohen 1994)); much more importantly, it crucially affects the way we understand the literature they did produce, among many other things. Not all anachronism of this sort involves crude stereotype. One of my goals in this book is to produce an account of the ancient Jews which resonates oddly because so much of it (like so much of classical antiquity in general) is simultaneously uncannily familiar and completely unrecognizable.

Some regard the use of modern categories as tools of analysis as an additional and equally objectionable type of anachronism. Such scholars think that past societies should be described only in their own terms, using their own thought categories. Some anthropologists apply the same stricture to the contemporary or recent societies they study: to use non-native categories of analysis in this view is to engage in ethnocentrism, the anthropologist's equivalent of historians' anachronism. But I disagree. In fact I believe that this type of anachronism or ethnocentrism can be an essential item in the historian's or anthropologist's toolkit (this does not mean that every modern category is equally useful). To take as an example a concept especially relevant to this book, it has been argued that the term 'religion' as we now use it is shaped by the concerns of the European Enlightenment of the eighteenth century, and so is invalid if applied to earlier cultural practice, or outside areas that are part of the European cultural sphere. This is because the word is too freighted with modern baggage to use without misleading, but also because the abstract concept 'religion' allegedly did not exist in any meaningful way before the Enlightenment. Now this second point is inaccurate, since medieval Christians – and Muslims and Jews – indubitably had the term, and it indubitably had a meaning related, though not identical, to its post-Enlightenment meaning. On the other hand, it is demonstrably true that extremely cautious and sophisticated scholars (even of the stature of the celebrated anthropologist Clifford Geertz [1926–2006]) sometimes allowed the modern sense of religion to interfere with their understanding of the phenomenon in premodernity or outside Euro-America, demonstrating the contention that anachronistic/ethnocentric concepts have tremendous power to mislead and certainly should never be used thoughtlessly (Asad 1993).[10] In any case we may admit that in Greco-Roman antiquity there existed no term or conceptual category which corresponds to 'religion' (Nongbri 2008).

It can be argued that while 'religion' is applicable to some varieties of modern Judaism (Reform – truly a religion of the Enlightenment; Ultraorthodoxy; 'Renewal'; but not Zionism or Yiddishism, which may contain 'religious' elements but are essentially versions of romantic nationalism), no version of premodern Judaism can validly be understood as a religion, that, indeed, since the very English words 'Jew' and 'Judaism' have religious, as opposed to ethnic or cultural, denotations, even these words we must replace, when referring to antiquity, with the ethnic or geographical term 'Judaean' (person from the land of Judaea), and with a periphrastic phrase referring to the latter's culture (also a fraught modern concept, see note 10!), respectively (Mason 2007; cf. Boyarin 2009).

[10] On the enduring conceptual utility of certain observers' categories, e.g., culture, see Brumann 1999, with responses following especially of Lila Abu-Lughod and Ulf Hannerz; for critiques of religion, culture and ethnicity, see, respectively, Asad 1993; Ortner 1999; Ortner 2006: 11–16; 107–28; Hall 2002: 9–19. See also de Vries 2008. For all his show of epistemological caution, though, de Vries' discussion seems mired in empirically dubious presentist presupposition.

But 'religion', if understood to refer simply to practices, social and cognitive, which embody people's relationships with their god(s), is too useful a term to discard, even if it admittedly has a dangerous tendency to mislead. Those who advocate the abolition of such terms, as opposed to their cautiously sceptical and self-aware analytical deployment, are forgetting that historians' primary job is translation or explanation, and that we can begin to make sense of worlds which are different from our own only by using concepts familiar to us with all due caution and self-consciousness. 'Religion', 'culture', 'nation', 'ethnicity', all terms which bear heavy modern baggage, all terms which have on occasion been used with aggressive intent by the dominant, all nevertheless have a place in making sense of the ancient Jews (S. Schwartz 2011).

What we must not do, though, is assume that they were a lot like modern Jews. I would insist, in fact, that we cannot assume that ancient Jews were necessarily even recognizable to us as such. This tremendously complicates our attempt to recover a satisfactory account of the ancient Jews from fragmentary and opaque sources.

DO WE KNOW A JEW WHEN WE SEE ONE?[11]

In most places in the world in the early twenty-first century Jewish identity has become ineffably complex; one could say that it has fractured. Some Jews, mainly but not only among the orthodox, live lives of complete immersion in a demanding version of the Jewish religion and have meaningful connections only with others who share their dedication. For others, Jewishness has no meaningful religious components, its cultural component has been reduced to a matter of sensibility or inner state, and even as a mode of sociability it no longer holds sway (by contrast, the parents or grandparents of such Jews might also have lived a highly attenuated type of Jewishness but socialized exclusively with Jews: Endelman 2009). Furthermore, even for people with a 'thick' Jewish identity, what counts as 'Jewish culture', or indeed as Judaism in the religious sense, has become, in true postmodern style, hugely various. In the twenty-first century, even positivists and essentialists would have to admit that Jewishness is a constructed identity, so much so that one begins to wonder whether

---

[11] Shaye Cohen's answer to this question for antiquity was more or less 'no', but his treatment is rather simplifying. The answer must be that some (non-Jewish) people sometimes could. This is a straightforward sociological corollary of the fact that some Jews strove to maintain some measure of separation from their neighbours. Whether we can spot them in the evidence is a different question; see S. Cohen 1993.

it has any real implications at all, whether, that is, there is any sense, however remote or symbolic, in which all or even most of the people who call themselves Jews constitute a meaningful category, let alone a group. We begin to suspect that 'Jewish identity' is losing its meaning as a term of sociological analysis (Brubaker 2004: 7–63).

This was not the case for medieval and early modern Jews (M. Cohen 1994). Whether they lived under Christian or Muslim rule, Jews in the medieval and early modern periods belonged to a religious community which was defined by laws. Its institutions of governance, furthermore, were generally authorized by the state, implicitly or explicitly. To be Jewish meant to belong to a distinct legal category and to live your life according to a well-defined (if not always and everywhere uniform) set of rules. It required at very least conformity with the laws of the Torah as refracted through the Talmud and interpreted by contemporary rabbinic legal experts. It is true that Jews lived then in widely scattered communities. Each one individually was a very strongly marked and extremely tightly integrated group, and in some times and places there emerged structures which constituted or facilitated integration on the regional level, like the Council of the Four Lands (*Va'ad Arba' Ha'aratzot*), based in Lublin and Jaroslaw, in early modern Poland, or even transregionally, like the Leipzig Fair (*Leipziger Messe*), which brought together Jewish merchants, among others, from eastern and western Europe (Rosman 2010: 83; Carlebach 2011: 141–59). The question of intercommunal integration, which applies to all periods of Jewish history, even the very earliest ones (because even then there was a Jewish 'diaspora'[12]), and has a great multiplicity of responses depending on the historical specificities, is one of the factors which has always complicated the 'groupness' of the Jews. But two things are certain about the medieval and early modern experience of the Jews: wherever they lived they constituted a strongly marked separate group, and whatever patterns of intercommunal integration prevailed in reality, Jews at least *thought* that they all were a single group, because of both shared descent and shared dedication to a religious system, wherever they lived (a subjectivity which facilitated intercommunal integration when external circumstances enabled it). They exemplified in an eccentric way Benedict Anderson's (1983) notion of the imagined community – which is not to say that they were a precocious nation.

Where on this spectrum of modes of identification should we place ancient Jews? Scholarly consensus on this question has shifted dramatically

---

[12] 'Dispersion', a Greek word Jews used even in antiquity to refer to Jewish communities outside Palestine.

in the past generation. It used to be assumed that ancient Jews as a group resembled medieval Jews, possessing a thick, fixed identity, thorough dedication to the norms of Jewish law and belief, and a tendency to separate themselves as fully as possible from their social and cultural environments, to the point of having a tendency to resist foreign rule militarily (Moore 1927–30; Hengel 1974; 1989). In fact, at least until the destruction of Jerusalem and its temple in 70 CE, and possibly even long after that, the Jews had an even more strongly marked group identity since, unlike the medieval Jews, they possessed a country and an acknowledged religious centre which in some periods served to integrate them, even those scattered in the diaspora, in quite practical ways, for example through donation and pilgrimage. To be sure, there were outliers, as there were even in the Middle Ages. Aside from the famous sectarian groups discussed below, which older scholarship imagined to have been something like medieval heresies which had rejected a presumed Pharisaic or rabbinic orthodoxy, some Jews, it was thought, were 'hellenized', and this was often understood to mean that they were on the verge of disappearance as Jews, of merging into their Greek or Greco-Roman environment completely, or eventually of drifting off into Christianity (Niehoff 1999). A crucial figure in this category was Philo, scion of an aristocratic Alexandrian Jewish family who lived in the early first century CE. Philo wrote in Greek a long series of essays in which he interpreted passages of the Pentateuch (in Hebrew, the Torah), the first five books of the Hebrew Bible, allegorically and in accordance with the main ideas of Platonism and Stoicism. Some scholars regarded Philo as unrepresentative of the Jews of the first century. He was either an isolated eccentric, or he stood for a kind of Judaism which was very soon to die out among the Jews, both because it was compromised, a blind alley, and devoid of 'authenticity', and because the Jewish community of Alexandria was in any case doomed to extinction by the failure of the blood-soaked Diaspora Revolt of 116–17 CE (Lieberman 1975 [1948]). That Philo's nephew Tiberius Julius Alexander was an 'apostate' who worked for the Roman state in its most anti-Jewish phase, and that Philo's works were forgotten by the Jews until the age of humanism and preserved only by Christians – indeed some church fathers even regarded Philo as a kind of honorary Christian – seemed to prove the case against him (or for him, depending on the disposition of the scholar). Others defended Philo's Jewishness by arguing that his Hellenism was just window-dressing or spin meant to attract pagans or lapsing Jews, concealing authentic rabbinic theology and practice (Belkin 1940; Wolfson 1947). In any case, the popularity or persistence of varieties of Judaism in

antiquity which diverged from the presumed Palestinian Pharisaic or rabbinic norms was generally either denied or condemned; and these alleged
norms were regarded as totalizing and separatist. Jews, at least 'good' Jews,
lived apart.

In the 1960s and following, this consensus was practically reversed:
the very idea that there was a normative centre to ancient Judaism was
rejected, and eventually scholars adopted, or rather attempted to adopt,
a non-essentializing approach to their subject which made it sound more
like late twentieth- than twelfth-century Judaism. It was assumed that
Judaism was not any one thing, that there was no characteristic that Jews
shared, that for the most part little distinguished them from their neighbours – indeed, that the boundaries of Judaism were not simply porous
but ill-defined or even nonexistent (S. Schwartz 2011). To return to the case
of Philo, an early dissent from the old consensus, by the mid-twentieth-
century historian of religion Erwin R. Goodenough, claimed that Philo,
far from being marginal, was in fact the normative voice of the Judaism of
the Roman diaspora (Goodenough 1935; Goodenough 1953–68). Though
this view gained few (no?) adherents, it did help dislodge the old consensus, and helped legitimize Philo as a Jewish voice as 'authentic' as any
other. In other words, it began the systematic interrogation of ideas about
authenticity and normativity which became the hallmark of progressive
scholarship in the next generation. In general, 'Hellenistic' Judaism was
now given its due, and not only by Jewish reformers seeking precedent for
their laxism and Christian theologians who saw it as paving the way for
Christianity, and scholars increasingly imagined the ancient Jewish landscape as infinitely varied and decentred.

In its less extreme manifestations this view actually helped to clarify the
interpretation of much ancient evidence and also dislodged much accreted
scholarly dogma. That it was not *simply* a mechanical reflex of the intellectual mood of 'late modernism', but used conceptual tools provided by
late modernism in a serious attempt to come to grips with the peculiarities
of the evidence for ancient Jews and Judaism, is demonstrated by the fact
that there has never been any serious comparable move to de-essential-
ize medieval and early modern Jews. (There the comparable impulse has
found its articulation in scholars' attempts to break down some accepted
inner-Jewish boundaries, most importantly that between Rabbinites and
Qaraites; Rustow 2008.) The new scholarship effectively revealed the
theological and ideological underpinnings of the old consensus, its reliance on implicitly Christian, or Jewish orthodox, or romantic nationalist
assumptions about the existence of a single Jewish people unified by its

unswerving – or stiff-necked – devotion to 'the Law' and resistance to foreign cultural influence and political intervention. It advocated methodological self-consciousness and expressed a new awareness of the fact that ancient texts have to be *read* – treated with caution and scepticism and thoughtful respect and with full awareness of their textuality, not simply mined for information.

Nevertheless, the new scholarship, for all its vigilance and caution, was not infrequently blind to its own ideological motivations, or at least it avoided revealing them (S. Schwartz 2002a; 2007).[13] In the final analysis it produced a portrait which is after all a product of its own intellectual-historical environment – late twentieth-century liberalism (the orthodoxy–heresies model does not apply to ancient Judaism; rather, it was varied and had no normative centre), or radicalism (it had no boundaries, was eternally under construction, and finally, did not actually exist; no ancient artefact is discernibly either Jewish or not Jewish) – however successfully it exposed and avoided the pitfalls of earlier christianizing, or Jewish romantic, or Zionist scholarship and produced occasionally convincing re-evaluations of ancient texts and artefacts.

Inevitably, then, anti-essentialist social-constructivist and post-structuralist approaches have produced their own reductive and flattening clichés, and have also revealed that essentialism may be too powerful an interpretive tool to eliminate completely. Unless one surrenders in one's writing to paralytic self-doubt, it proves nearly impossible to write a non-reductive anti-essentialist account of anything because the very act of writing requires schematizing reduction, and the decision to write about something takes for granted an essentialist view a priori, unless the account is entirely critical and deconstructive. In the case of the ancient Jews, such

---

[13] Post-1970 scholarship was more zealous about methodological than about theoretical/ideological self-consciousness, though the latter was not completely absent and became more prominent probably after 1990. Along with it, some recommended and practised a personalized confessional style – something which academic Jewish historians resisted more than others, it has been claimed, perhaps because they were socially and intellectually closer to openly ideological readers of the past than most and felt more need to distinguish themselves (there is room for scepticism both about the claim and about the explanation). The confessional style is in any case inconsistent with anti-essentialism because underlying it is almost always the conviction or 'confession' that 'I have this view because I am who I am' – the causal link constituting the very definition of essentialism. But this only reveals the unresolved tension in some radical scholarship of the immediate past between strong structural determinism (true in its day of Marxism but more recently of work oriented toward identity politics) and the validation of agency as the only meaningful category of social analysis. This may in fact explain why the confessional mode is so much rarer than claims to anti-essentialism in Judaic scholarship: for most of its history academic Jewish studies has struggled precisely to distance itself from identity politics, though recent and contemporary trends in academic humanities have perhaps been exerting some countervailing influence.

approaches have led to the conviction that every Jewish artefact[14] must be interpreted first and foremost as an act of Jewish self-definition. But this turns out to be unhelpful. It may be true that this is what Jewish artefacts are, but it needs to be demonstrated that this is always the most hermeneutically sound or productive way to address them. If *all* Jewish artefacts are understood primarily as acts of Jewish self-assertion, then why does this point need to be repeatedly belaboured, and how are we to explain the artefacts' difference from one another? Such reading almost always ends in tautology: since the text is an act of Jewish self-definition, the best thing to say about the text is that the Jewishness that the text defines consists of the contents of the text. The fact that we have no idea how the mute majority of Jews (however they may have been defined) defined themselves imposes a paralysing additional constraint on the value of such an approach.

The anti-essentialist focus on self-definition involved a shift of emphasis from structure (what was ancient Judaism? What were its central institutions and how did they work? What were its core values and ideas?) to agency (how did Philo or Josephus or the rabbis or the Jews buried in the catacombs of Rome or Bet Shearim in Galilee understand and/or perform their own Jewishness?) and as such is more closely connected to the antifunctionalist tendency in postwar sociology and anthropology than to the spread of postmodernism from literary theory to other fields in the humanities. The pathbreaking series, *Jewish and Christian Self-Definition*, published by a group of scholars based in Canada, contained papers that had been written in the late 1970s, long before postmodernism had begun to make a mark on the study of ancient Judaism, indeed, just as Derrida was becoming famous in British and American literature departments (Sanders *et al.* 1980–3). Some members of the McMaster Self-Definition group had an interest in sociology and anthropology. Jacob Neusner, not a member of the group but an amazingly prolific author of books on rabbinic literature among other topics, whose influence as a decentrer and de-essentializer of ancient Judaism was much greater, absorbed postwar social theory not from antifunctionalist sociologists and ethnographers like Anthony Giddens and Pierre Bourdieu, but through the intermediation of the University of Chicago historian of religions Jonathan Z. Smith. Indeed, it was Smith who provided the theoretical foundation for Neusner's project in the late 1970s and the 1980s – an atomizing description of ancient

---

[14] Here is where the persistence of essentialism comes into play: how do we know after all what is and what is not a 'Jewish' artefact? Some ancient writings leave little room for reasonable doubt about how the author sees himself, but there are many uncertain cases.

Judaism based on an analysis of the separate 'Judaisms' allegedly embodied in the various rabbinic writings – in a famous presidential address to the American Academy of Religion in 1978 (Smith 1982). Smith advocated polythetic taxonomy in general and in making sense of ancient Judaism in particular (in other words, ancient Judaism can be understood as consisting of a multiplicity of different subgroups which may be contiguous with one another but need not share any essential features), and then sought to demonstrate the absence of a normative centre in ancient Judaism by citing texts that provide widely varying interpretations of the practice of circumcision. We should, then, speak, not of Judaism, as a single entity with a centre, essential features and clearly marked boundaries – with the Jews by implication constituting a fairly well-defined and integrated group whose members share a normative praxis – but of Judaisms, decentred, infinitely varied, with ever-shifting aggregations of definitive features. There is some validity to this after all, but Smith's illustration actually proves two things, neither of them intended by Smith. The first is the danger mentioned above of understanding ancient Judaism through concepts like 'religion'. Smith strikingly, embarrassingly and presumably unconsciously, christianized: the idea that theology is what mainly matters about a religion, rather than ritual behaviour, is after all a peculiarly Christian one, and it is a categorical error to describe other religions, including Judaism, by emphasizing theology over practice, as Smith did, by privileging the divergent ancient *explanations* of circumcision over its shared *practice*. So it emerges that the texts prove (my second point) that at least in this case one *can* tentatively speak of a normative centre in ancient Judaism. All Smith's texts endorse the practice of male circumcision, which is why they are so keen to discern its meaning, and none opposes it or regards it as optional (S. Schwartz 2011).

NEITHER MEDIEVAL NOR MODERN

Ancient Jews were not a chaotic disjunction bound – if only as an analytic convention, or as the political aspiration or religious hope of a minority of Jews – by the nearly arbitrary application of a term whose meaning is in the process of evaporation, as in the contemporary world. They were not infinitely diverse, boundariless, always and everywhere radically decentred. They were, to be sure, engaged in the permanent project of self-creation, but since everyone always is, this fact alone tells us nothing about the nature of their groupness. Nor were they a thoroughly segregated aggregation of subgroups bound internally and intercommunally by devotion to a corpus of texts and of rabbinically inspired practice, as well as by the interests of the states in which they lived in their eternal separation – a geographically discontiguous 'imagined community'.

What, then, were they? Without going into excessive detail about problems of periodization, which affect all historical accounts, we may begin by observing that 'antiquity' is not one thing. For the purposes of this book antiquity extends from the Battle of Issus, 333 BCE, to the Arab conquest of Syria and Palestine, 638 CE, with an inevitable focus, due to the nature of the sources, on what may be called the long first century, from the accession of King Herod in 40 BCE to the end of the Bar Kokhba Revolt in 135 CE, and on the relatively well-attested fourth century CE. Patterns of Jewish life shifted quite drastically at three points during this period: the Maccabean Revolt (167–152 BCE), the period of the anti-Roman uprisings (The Great Revolt, 66–73/4 CE; the Diaspora Revolt, 115–17 CE, and the Bar Kokhba Revolt, 132–5 CE), and the process of christianization which the emperor Constantine began when he converted in 312 CE. The first period was characterized by the emergence of important diaspora communities, by Jewish expansion within Palestine, by the growing importance of an institutional centre in Jerusalem, and by ever-increasing ideological ferment and cultural dynamism, all within the loose boundaries of a somewhat ill-defined and capacious but still discernibly discrete ideological system.

The second period was characterized by contraction and disintegration. The destruction of the centre was a symbolic blow, but it was much more than that – it altered patterns of expenditure (the temple had been a great magnet for silver and gold, and its priestly staff had been maintained by donations and a system of what amounted to taxation in kind), overturned an entire native Jewish political, social and cultural regime, and altered drastically the relationship between Jews wherever they lived and the Roman state. On the local level, the Jews of Palestine suffered a profound demographic blow, and those of Egypt – the largest and most ancient diaspora Jewish community in the Roman Empire – and Cyrenaica (part of modern Libya), probably something like extinction. Before 66 CE the central Jewish establishment had offered scattered Jewish communities not only a heightened sense of solidarity, but political aid and advantage as well; thus, even Jewish settlements in places unaffected by upheaval, like Ionia, or Greece or Italy, were thrown back on their own resources after the failed revolts, with results we are rarely in the position to evaluate.

The third period may have been preceded and accompanied by some demographic recovery. It too featured an alteration of the relations between Jews and empire. The Jews were now defined as a religious community, inferior to orthodox Christians, but still licit and certainly more privileged than either pagans, who had to endure the legal prohibition of their central religious ritual, animal sacrifice, and the closure of their temples, or heretical Christians, who were outlawed. The Jews' privileges also implied and eventually entailed a growing sense of political and social separation from their neighbours, but this was accompanied in the first century of Christian rule by the re-emergence of a limited though real institutional centre in Palestine. This consisted not, as it had before 66 CE, of temple, priesthood and kings, but of newly prominent dynasts called patriarchs, based in Tiberias, Galilee, who received extensive privileges from the emperor and retained contact with and claimed some control over the resurgent Jewish communities of the Roman diaspora. The first patriarchs were probably members of a family of wealthy and learned grandees in the second and third centuries (themselves perhaps descended from Gamaliel, a Jerusalem Pharisee whom the New Testament book of the Acts of the Apostles regarded as the teacher of the apostle Paul). The era of christianization saw the diffusion of other relatively new institutions and practices too – the rabbis with their peculiar intellectual and literary style, the local religious community centred on monumental synagogues and on charity collection and distribution, to mention only the most prominent items.

This book has several aims. The first of these is simply to provide information. But, as the attentive reader of the previous pages will have intuited, if she did not already know it, there is nothing simple about the provision of information, certainly not for anyone working on antiquity. The remains, literary and material, are not abundant, especially for the ancient Jews. The former consists largely of fragments for the first period, with the notable exception of the fortunately relatively voluminous works of Philo of Alexandria and Flavius Josephus, plus some of the more extensively preserved texts among the Dead Sea Scrolls. Many of the writings conventionally assigned to the period are undated and so difficult to contextualize that figuring out what to do with them at all constitutes their main interpretative challenge. For the following period the literary remains boil down to a handful of rabbinic texts – the Mishnah, Tosefta, and maybe some halakhic midrash collections – which would fill only a fraction of a library bookshelf (useful introductions: Strack and Stemberger 1996; Goodman and Alexander 2010). The final period was more productive, but much of the literature raises the same problems of contextualization as

Second Temple-period writing. Archaeology fortunately remains a growth industry, and is abundant for the first century and for late antiquity, but less so for the Hellenistic period and the two centuries following the revolts. For some periods there is no possibility of reconstructing anything like a standard historical narrative. In fact a tolerably convincing one can be provided, thanks to the detailed but tendentious and controversial histories of Josephus and some other brief texts, only for the period from the Maccabean Revolt (167 BCE) to the destruction of Jerusalem in 70 CE. Josephus' coverage of earlier periods is spotty and unusually unreliable, and his narrative comes to an end with the end of the Great Revolt; and he had no continuators, at least none whose work has been preserved. Like most ancient writing, ancient Jewish writing inevitably reflects the interests of an elite or sub-elite, what the historical sociologist Ernest Gellner called the 'clerisy' (priests, scribes, officials and courtiers overlapping but not coextensive with a landed aristocracy). This means that there is little chance of reconstructing a true social history, because the voices of the peasantry, the poor, women, and slaves are largely unrecoverable.

The remains that do survive have generated many controversies and problems of interpretation. So another aim of this book is to exemplify the proper deployment of models in an account which takes facts seriously – to lend structure and urgency to the presentation, help us to notice things we might otherwise have missed or have taken for granted, and even to understand the implications of informational gaps. The improper deployment of models or theories might entail reifying one – say, Marxism – and using it as a simple, all-purpose explanatory device in a way which inhibits detailed and intelligent reading and interpretation of the ancient sources. Used properly, models should *generate* intelligent reading.

The third aim of the book is to explain why classicists and ancient historians should know about the ancient Jews' history and texts. The humanistic organization of disciplines separated classics from theology; the history and literature of the Jews in the pre-Christian period were included in the latter, while the history of the Jews in the High and Later Roman Empire, and the largely rabbinic literature of the period, was of interest mainly to a handful of orientalists specializing in Semitic philology. Jewish studies per se had no real place in universities anywhere in the world until well into the twentieth century. Post-70 Jews were ignored both by classicists and by theologians, for whom the Jews ceased to matter after the *parousia* of Christ.

I fear it would be optimistic to say that by now most Hellenistic and Roman historians regard such segregation and neglect as a thing of the past. I know from experience that they do not, that, even if they profess to deplore it, there is little willingness to change – though there are some very noteworthy and distinguished exceptions. The simple and irrefutable fact that rabbinic literature is one of only three extant corpora of literature to have been written by culturally distinctive Roman subjects (the other two are the 'second sophistic' and the earlier patristic literature) has had little impact on the way Roman historians, or, it has to be admitted, rabbinists and Jewish historians, think about their field. This is an issue which goes far beyond the traditional question of 'the rabbis' attitude to Rome', so the problem cannot be solved by adding some topically appropriate snippets to the sourcebooks.

CHAPTER I

Beginnings to 200 BCE

HISTORY BEFORE THE JEWS: ISRAELITES AND GREEKS IN THE IRON AGE MEDITERRANEAN

The tendency to regard the Jews as a uniquely odd presence in the Mediterranean basin in antiquity provides an excellent reason to begin our account with a brief discussion of the ways in which the prehistory and early history of the Jews were absolutely typical for the physical and political geography of the central and eastern Mediterranean coast.[1] There is, in fact, an unexpectedly large number of points of similarity between pre-Hellenistic Greek and Israelite/Jewish history: stories of invasion, migration and colonization set at the transition between the Bronze and Iron Ages (*c.* thirteenth century BCE), a long and obscure archaic period in which subsequently central ideas and institutions took shape, periods of crisis in the sixth century and the powerful ideologies of highly particularistic but internally egalitarian citizen communities that emerged in the aftermath, and finally subjection to a single, though fissiparous, Greco-Macedonian empire (exploration of some parallels in J. P. Brown 1995–2001).

These parallels may or may not be the result of the diffusion of ideas and stories through contact; they are certainly the result of shared geographical proximity to regional and transregional political processes; to some extent they are also the result of a similar ecology. To be sure, it was

---

[1] I am following the old and correct convention of writing of Israelites before the first destruction of Jerusalem in 586 BCE, and Jews (= Hebrew, *yehudim*; Greek, *ioudaioi*) afterwards (C. Baker 2011). The primary meaning of the latter term is 'inhabitants of the district of Yehud/Judaea' (strictly speaking, the area centred on Jerusalem extending from Ramallah in the north to Beth Zur in the south, and from the Jordan River and Dead Sea in the east to the eastern edge of the coastal plain in the west). But the term almost always meant, from its first usages, people, wherever they lived, who combined a conviction of shared descent (by the second century BCE, sometimes self-consciously fictive, as in the case of converts) with a certain type of religious devotion; in other words, Jews. This distinction follows the practice of the biblical books themselves, and of Josephus, and also reflects the fact that what I am arguing in this section was a substantive shift beginning in the sixth century BCE in how the people in question imagined themselves.

highly consequential that Greeks gravitated to the coasts and Israelites to the hills. The modern idea that until sometime in the Hellenistic period the ancient Jews were somewhat isolated is not just due to reading later theological concerns back into antiquity. Ancient Jewish texts themselves mention it occasionally and ascribe it to the fact that Israelites/Jews did not live on the seacoast, which was the land of the Canaanites (= Phoenicians) and the Philistines, and later on the latter's cousins, the Greeks (Numbers 23.9; Josephus, *Ag.Ap.* 1.60). The hill country felt isolated, but the point should not be exaggerated. The line of ridges which constituted the heart of the biblical kingdoms of Israel and Judah was nowhere more than about 45 miles from the coast, an easy enough three-day walk even uphill, and the hills themselves, though challenging for large armies to penetrate and control, were in most places not very forbidding. Only at two points, in the Meron massif in Upper Galilee and Mount Hebron in southern Judaea/Idumaea, do the hills rise higher than 1000 metres; Jerusalem is 700–800 metres above sea level (Baly 1984; Mount Hermon in southern Syria is much higher but historically outside biblical Israel). The same biblical texts which declare Israel to be 'a nation dwelling alone' express extravagant concern about the frequency of the Israelites' contacts with outsiders.

It is true that Israelites and Jews had little or no mercantile tradition, unlike Greeks and Phoenicians, and also true that widespread cultural developments (for example, iron; syllabic [often misnamed 'alphabetic'] script, adopted by the Israelites slightly after the Phoenicians; use of coined silver; popular imported goods like decorated Greek pottery) reached the Palestinian hill country more slowly than the coast, though they did invariably reach them.[2] (By the Roman period roads among other improvements in communications had rendered the Jews' remoteness culturally far less significant.) Nevertheless, there remained crucial ecological commonalities: both Greeks and Israelites for much of their history shared a dry-farming, low-surplus, grain-, olive- and grape-dependent agricultural regime (Feliks 1990; Pastor 1997: 1–12) – the so-called Mediterranean triad – which kept both groups relatively small (in the case of the Greeks, divided into small units) and weak, subject to the imperialistic whims of the great, irrigation-based, river valley civilizations to their south and east – though the mainland Greeks (as opposed to those of Asia and of some of the islands) were relatively remote, so the impact of these civilizations

---

[2] Material culture: E. Stern 1982; writing, Saenz-Badillos 1993:62–8, acknowledging the difficulty of determining what counts as Hebrew.

on them was less direct than on the Israelites, until the Achaemenid era (539–332 BCE). The demographic dislocations of the thirteenth century, dim recollection of which was preserved in Greek and biblical tales, were in both cases the result of crises in Egypt, Mesopotamia and Asia Minor, which accompanied the transition from the Bronze to Iron Ages. The 'sea peoples' mentioned in Egyptian texts of the time as invaders of Egypt and of Egyptian imperial holdings in Phoenicia and Palestine, one group of whom was perhaps the biblical Philistines, may have been related to Mycenean Greeks.[3] But the Israelites remembered themselves, too, as having been among the invaders of that era, just as Greeks later told stories of Ionian and Dorian invasions. The archaic Greek cities, which began to emerge in the ninth and eighth centuries BCE, were perhaps nearly as much an artefact of the temporary recession of influence of the river valley empires as the small kingdoms of Judah, whose capital city was Jerusalem, and Israel, centred on the city of Samaria (Sabastiyyah, on the West Bank), which began to flourish in the same period (and whose kings employed east Greek mercenaries, among others, according to both biblical sources and archaeologists: Niemeier 2001; Luraghi 2006). These kingdoms, which shared stories of origins, a sense of close kinship, a language, and a set of religious practices focused on a shared god, had perhaps been founded as early as the eleventh or tenth centuries.

To reach such a conclusion we must adopt a critical but not altogether dismissive approach to the 'historical books' of the Hebrew Bible. These texts were edited as a five-book unit, extending from Judges to 2 Kings, perhaps around 500 BCE, beating Herodotus by a generation or two.[4] They contain our only narratives about the Israelite kingdoms (a narrative based on Kings appears in the biblical books of Chronicles). To be sure, the biblical histories are unreliable in very fundamental ways when it comes to

---

[3] Or Illyrians or Luwians: Dothan 1982; more scepticism in Ehrlich 1996: 1–22. Or perhaps they experienced a 'revival' of Hellenic consciousness only in the sixth century BCE, when Greek commercial imperialism began to make it fashionable in the Levant: Yadin 2004.

[4] For useful discussions of many of these issues – especially the 'maximalist–minimalist debate' see Grabbe 2011. I am unsympathetic to the most extreme minimalism, which regards *all* biblical texts as evidence *only* for the ideological positions of their early Hellenistic-period authors and so denies or professes agnosticism about the existence of an early Iron Age Israel altogether. This view seems to me far too simple and also pretends to be far too well informed about a period of Israelite-Jewish history at least as obscure as the eighth century BCE. My position is roughly Wellhausenian: the biblical authors painted a heavily ideological picture of the Israelite past but did not always simply invent it out of whole cloth. So the texts tell us both about the ideological positions of their authors and about an actual Israelite past, though these cannot be easily disentangled. There is also a positivist tradition, which regards the biblical histories as basically reliable, perpetuated in different forms by conservative Protestants and by the usually Israeli followers of the pioneering Zionist Bible scholar Yehezkel Kaufmann.

the eleventh-century kingdoms of David and Solomon, however magnificent and uncannily modern-sounding a piece of prose the David narrative in 2 Samuel may be. To make matters worse, they are exercises in theological argumentation, in a way which complicates their historicity: the writers chose to confront a tremendous problem. Since the eighth century some Judahite and Israelite prophets[5] had been exhorting their constituents not only to cease their wicked and oppressive behaviour, but also to worship only the national God, Yahweh. These exhortations inform us, incidentally, that traditional Israelite religion, which the prophets were urging the Israelites to abandon, was structurally the same as those of the Israelites' neighbours. There was a shared regional pantheon of gods, many of them Canaanite, like Baal, Astarte, and El Elyon, but others more broadly popular, like the Egyptian deities Isis and Osiris; but kingdoms and cities by the eighth century had begun to have special patron deities, increasingly viewed as national gods – Yahweh for the Israelites, Kemosh for the Moabites, Milkom for the Ammonites, Qos for the Edomites, Baal King of the City (Milk-Qart) for the Tyrians, etc. Initially, the Israelites worshipped Yahweh together with his consort, Asherah, but eventually abandoned the practice. We cannot even exclude the possibility that some non-Israelite peoples had extremist priests or prophets who insisted on the worship of the national god alone (Morton Smith 1952, 1971; Mark Smith 2000).

Be this as it may, according to the book of Kings itself, the first king to undertake a comprehensive reform of the religious life of Judah along the lines recommended by prophets like Jeremiah – most importantly, eliminating the shrines of all deities except for Yahweh, and, even more radically, shutting down all shrines of Yahweh except for the central temple in the royal city, Jerusalem – was Josiah (reigned 639–609). This was motivated by the 'discovery', in the course of maintenance work in the city's temple, of a scroll called 'The Book of the Instruction of Moses' (Hebrew: *Sefer Torat Moshe*), probably related to the pentateuchal Book of Deuteronomy (2 Kings 22–3; see Ben-Dov 2008). But it was not bad enough that Josiah himself died ignominiously in battle; shortly after his death, first in 597 BCE and then again in 587 BCE, the Babylonian king Nebuchadnezzar, who was the overlord of the Judahite kings, quelled rebellions at Jerusalem first by exiling a portion of the landowning and

---

[5] The word has come to mean 'foretellers of the future' but for the classical biblical prophets this was only a peripheral part of the job: they were vectors of divine communication, in practice preachers trying to convince their audience to do as God – or the gods – wished: Gordon 1995.

bureaucratic classes of Judah, and then by destroying the city and crush-
ing the kingdom, and exiling still more Judahites and establishing direct rule over the remainder. Yahweh had thus failed to keep his part of
an agreement (or 'covenant'; Hebrew: *bʳrit*; Greek: *diatheke*) with the
Judahites which had been touted by the reformist prophets and priests:
worship him in the proper way and he will guarantee his people's prosperity. They had done as he demanded, but he allowed the Babylonians
to destroy and exile them anyway (Jeremiah had said that God wanted
Judah to remain loyal to the Babylonians). The biblical books of Judges,
Samuel and Kings told their stories so as to explain how God had allowed
this to happen, how it was in fact the Israelites who had failed, not God,
and how the destruction and exile confirmed, not contradicted, the reliability of God and his prophetic intercessors.

EXILE AND RETURN, OR 'EXILE' AND 'RETURN'? FROM ISRAELITES TO JEWS

The political and religious regime that gradually emerged in the Persian
province of Yehud, which corresponded to the northern half of the kingdom of Judah,[6] was drastically different from anything described by the
Books of Kings. In brief, Kings describes Judah and Israel before the
Assyrian and Babylonian invasions of 722 and 587 as two little royal states
which were scarcely distinguishable from their neighbours, including in
religious terms, and largely lacked the defining features of what came to
be Judaism: they did not worship a single god in a single temple according to the laws set forth in the *Torat Moshe*, except at most during part
of the reign of Josiah. The initially tiny polity fostered by the Persians
after their conquest of the Babylonian Empire in 539 gradually embraced
all these features and so is the first political entity which we can designate Jewish. This is by no means a matter of imposing modern categories
on a recalcitrant ancient reality. The actors themselves brought about the

---

[6] The southern half, from Beth Zur to the Negev desert, was gradually infiltrated by the Edomites,
who had been displaced from their original home, the biblical land of Edom south-east of the Dead
Sea, by the Babylonians, and by Arabic-speaking groups, among them the Nabataeans, wander-
ing north out of the Arabian peninsula. Basic studies of Jews in the Achaemenid period are *CHJ*
1 and Lipschits and Oeming 2006. The latest survey is Gerstenberger 2012. There is a vast and
ever-expanding publication industry about the Jews and Judah under the Achaemenids, a rather
mysterious circumstance given that the evidence consists mainly of a few of the shortest books of
the Hebrew Bible, a handful of documents, and some unimpressive archaeological finds. In reality,
the period remains almost as much a blank for us as it was for the ancient rabbis, who simply eliminated it from their chronology.

terminological shift. Jews have never stopped calling themselves 'Israel' but in the Persian period they first began calling themselves 'Jews' (*Yehudim* [Hebrew], *Yehuda'ei* [Aramaic], *Ioudaioi* [Greek]).

Admittedly, we know about these changes in political and religious regime primarily from the biblical books of Ezra and Nehemiah, which are as theology-driven as Kings.[7] These books describe episodically and in confused order a set of events said to have occurred in the reigns of Cyrus (539–530 BCE), Darius I (522–486 BCE) and Artaxerxes I (464–423 BCE). But the regime whose origins these books purport to describe – Judaism – is itself quite reliably attested in the later fourth and third centuries BCE, and the biblical books, if read cautiously and critically, reveal in a plausibly lifelike way some of the tensions which may have accompanied the establishment of Judaism.

It is certain that at least one group of Judahites was exiled to Mesopotamia. Many of the names mentioned in the fifth-century BCE Murashu archive, a set of cuneiform tablets discovered in the Babylonian city of Nippur concerning financial transactions, are distinctively Judahite – a fact which also confirms what the biblical books presuppose, that at least some exiles retained a sense of separate identity in their new Mesopotamian homes.[8] Indeed, scholars have often supposed that it was in exile that the Jews 'became Jewish' – that they switched from polytheism to monotheism, and that they as a group began to live by the rules of the *Sefer Torat Moshe*. This is largely speculative, though the speculation is not wholly idle: the poet who wrote Isaiah chapters 40–9, the earliest and strongest identification of Yahweh as sole god of the universe, a foundational text of Jewish monotheism, lived in Mesopotamia (probably) at the transition from Babylonian to Persian rule (Blenkinsopp 2009: 117–22).

Though no cuneiform text specifically mentions what the Persian king Cyrus did to the Jews when he conquered the Babylonian Empire in 539 BCE, 'Isaiah''s declaration that the new ruler is the 'anointed of Yahweh' (*meshiah YHWH*), and the book of Ezra's somewhat dubious royal letters granting the exiled Judahites the right to return to their homes, both resonate strongly with the language of the 'Cyrus cylinder', a cuneiform text discovered at Babylon in which Cyrus claims to have been chosen by Marduk, the chief Babylonian god, and poses as a restorer of gods, temples and cities following the alleged depredations of the last Babylonian king, Nabonidus (Pritchard 1969: 308–16; Wiesehöfer 1996: 42–55). Slightly

[7] Sensible reflection on the historical value of these books: Blenkinsopp 2009.
[8] Basic study of Murashu: Stolper 1985. Judaeans: Coogan 1976; Bickermann 1978; 1984. Recent bibliography with discussion of recently published texts from outside Nippur, see Pearce 2006.

more reliable information about a possible restoration pertains, though, to Darius I. He is said to have permitted a group of exiles to return to Yehud under the leadership of Joshua, a descendant of the Zadokite family, who were the chief priests of the Jerusalem temple before its destruction in 587, and Zerubbabel, purportedly a member of the former royal family of Judah. Zerubbabel was praised by the prophets, but quickly disappears from the record, and no royal figure ever replaced him in the governance of Yehud (Ezra 2–3; Zechariah 3). This points towards a significant change. The old Jerusalem temple had enjoyed royal patronage, and its staff won a significant if short-lived victory when Josiah in effect granted them a monopoly over Judahite religious life, but the high priest had never been more than a minor functionary in the kingdom of Judah, whereas from now until the onset of Roman rule the high priest would be the de facto ruler of the province (Dandamaev and Lukonin 1989: 360–6; Gussmann 2008).

High priesthood means little without a temple and a sacrificial cult, and these were in fact restored, whether under Darius, as Ezra 3 and some of the later prophets say, or somewhat later. Zechariah 3, an op-ed (opinion) piece in the form of a prophetic vision, indicates that Joshua was initially a controversial figure among the returned exiles, who regarded him as impure (because he had been faithful to the idolatrous practices of traditional Israelite religion?), but that an agreement was reached: if he observed God's laws *properly*, God would allow him to rule the temple and, implicitly, to refound a high priestly dynasty. In this way the reforms of Josiah were finally made permanent: there is no evidence of any temple in Yehud but the one in Jerusalem, and its chief priest was a Zadokite who had committed himself to the laws of the *Torat Moshe*. One of the pillars of the new regime was in place.

But it is important to retain a sense of proportion. In its last days the kingdom of Judah and its main city Jerusalem had reached a peak of populousness and prosperity. The Babylonians are said to have carried over 40,000 Judahites off into exile, and these were only the wealthiest and most influential members of the nation, the peasantry having been left behind. We may at least guess that Jerusalem's population approached 10,000, and that of the kingdom as a whole may conceivably have been as high as 100,000.[9] By contrast, fifth-century BCE Jerusalem covered a fraction of its former area and the most responsible guesses place its population

---

[9] Broshi and Finkelstein 1992 estimate the population of Jerusalem as 7,500 in the eighth century, before it reached its peak. By Iron Age standards it was a very substantial place, as is clear even from the aporetic discussion of Van de Mieroop 1997: 95–7.

at 500–1,500; Yehud as a whole, which was considerably smaller than the old kingdom, is likely to have had fewer than 15,000 inhabitants, most exiles having apparently remained in Mesopotamia and the size of the peasantry having contracted in the wake of Babylonian conquest.[10] The second Jerusalem temple was correspondingly a much smaller and shabbier structure than the first one and much poorer as an institution; one reason none of the other predestruction Judahite shrines was rebuilt may be that there simply was not enough available surplus capital to do so. The Judahites were certainly not all automatically loyal to the new temple and its priesthood, and the returned exiles may even have tried to exclude the peasantry from involvement in its rebuilding, in the short term; certainly Ezra and some other texts – all relevant biblical texts reflect the interests of the returned exiles – regard the 'people of the land' (as opposed to the 'children of the exile' – that is, the returnees) with suspicion and hostility, possibly generated by the tensions involved in having exiles return and reclaim their old land, possibly, also, associated with religious or other differences between the groups (Ezra 3–6).[11]

Though so many of the specific circumstances were different, the socio-economic situation which emerged in Yehud in the course of the fifth century bore a close family resemblance to those which affected so many other cities and districts in the eastern Mediterranean under Persian rule or in its penumbra. The Persians fostered oligarchy in their western holdings, but in these same areas a heightened sense of egalitarian or communitarian citizenship had been developing, so that the standard ways of solving the problems endemic in inegalitarian, oligarchic, dry-farming communities – for example through the proliferation of ties of social dependency between wealthier and poorer farmers – were no longer effective. The poor were increasingly available to be mobilized politically by anyone who stood for the interests of the state/collectivity against the oligarchs: hence, tyranny (Lewis 2006; especially Morgan 2003: i–xxvi). Historians have tended to provide internalist accounts of these developments, with

---

[10] Figures provided in the biblical text – for example 42,360 returnees under Zerubbabel (Ezra 2.1; 2.63) – are unreliable. Finkelstein 2008 emphasizes the absence of archaeological evidence for a wall at Jerusalem, and suggests that Nehemiah 3 is a retrojected description of the Hellenistic wall. On population size see Finkelstein 2008 and Lipschits 2006. Gerstenberger 2012: 104: 20,000–30,000. Scholars who overlook archaeology paint rosier pictures of Achaemenid Yehud, e.g., the otherwise illuminating Blenkinsopp 2009: 46.

[11] Following the 'classical' view summarized by Grabbe 1998: 138. The 'revisionist' view that no such tensions existed is implausible: why would they not have existed? The 'people of the land' who competed with the 'sons of the exile' were presumably more or less their social equals – prominent, by the standards of a tiny, impoverished province: Fried 2006.

Greek historians emphasizing the role of the rise of the hoplite class (Snodgrass 2006: chapter 17) and Jewish historians adducing the allegedly community-building experience of exile (Blenkinsopp 2009: 80–5).[12] But the development was regional, not local, though the details varied locally, and so structural explanations must supplement internalist ones.

That the establishment of the pious religious community of Torah-observant Jews in the Persian province of Yehud was a by-product of the local modulation of tyranny, and that those whom their eponymous biblical books describe as responsible for this development, Ezra and, especially, Nehemiah, are very similar to the classical model of tyrants, is on the face of it surprising, but is hard to deny (Smith 1971: 126–47). At any rate the book of Nehemiah describes its hero as a very typical tyrant, indeed, with several peculiar twists, one of which is that much of his proto-democratic legislation he ascribed to Moses, since it was to be found in his version of the *Sefer Torat Moshe*. Much of the Book of Nehemiah consists of a first-person narrative which many scholars have regarded as an excerpt from a hypothetical 'Memoirs of Nehemiah' – perhaps a highly apologetic and self-aggrandizing report delivered to his Persian employers. Other scholars regard it as a fiction written much later, but a gripping and quite realistic one, if so (Blenkinsopp 2009: 90–116).[13] Nehemiah's memoir, and his mission in general, are reminiscent of those of his older Egyptian contemporary, the imperial courtier and physician Udjahorresnet, known from a long inscription (Blenkinsopp 1987). Nehemiah, according to the book of Nehemiah, was a Persian official, by background a wealthy Judahite exile – several biblical books are dedicated to the travails and triumphs of Jews, including Ezra, Daniel, Mordechai and Esther, in Persian imperial service – who was appointed governor of Yehud in 444 BCE by Artaxerxes I;[14] he had as one of his goals, as Ezra did also,[15] allegedly with the support of the king, the formal introduction of the *Sefer Torat Moshe* as the official law of the province. Darius I's commission, about fifty years earlier, of a group of Egyptian soldiers, priests and scribes to compile a code of Egyptian law to be published both in demotic Egyptian and

---

[12] Snodgrass, to be fair, provides one of the less Hellenocentric accounts, straying as far afield as Caria and Etruria.

[13] Gerstenberger 2012: 90–4 finds the 'memoir' unrealistic and therefore inauthentic, but what he objects to are its apologetic features, which actually confirm the apparent authenticity of the document, while detracting from its reliability – two separate issues.

[14] Johnson 2004.

[15] It is impossible to determine from the biblical narrative whether Ezra was thought to have preceded Nehemiah or followed him. His mission is dated to 'year seven of King Artaxerxes', but all three kings of that name ruled for seven years. Nehemiah served from year twenty to year thirty-two of Artaxerxes, who must therefore be A. I.

in Aramaic – the quasi-official language of the western Persian Empire – has been adduced as a parallel (Reich 1933; Manning 2003: 821; contrast Gerstenberger 2012: 59). His other main goals were to restore the allegedly ruined city of Jerusalem and to induce Judahite men who had married foreign women to divorce them; as in the Greek world, a heightened ideology of egalitarian citizen community was associated with intense particularism.

If Nehemiah's claim to have initiated the reconstruction of Jerusalem's walls, with each section assigned to a different Judahite village, is historical – which is in doubt, notwithstanding its prominence in the narrative, in the absence of any supporting archaeological evidence – a possible motivation was to create a sense of solidarity among the 'people of the land', and possibly between them and the 'exiles', by inducing them to cooperate on a project which demonstrated symbolically their common interests.[16] This communal division, which had dominated the narrative up to this point, henceforth disappears from Jewish history. He also cancelled debt (making much of the fact that he had debtors himself and so stood to lose), elevated the status of the low-ranking 'levitical' temple staff, against the interests of the priests, and gradually encouraged the adoption of the laws and rituals of the *Torat Moshe*, including the closure of markets on the Sabbath, and the celebration of the biblical festivals, like Passover and Tabernacles, which had previously either been completely unknown, or had long since fallen into desuetude. Finally, Nehemiah fostered an ideology of extreme ethnic separatism, which went far beyond the milder particularism of the earlier biblical books, indeed of the *Torat Moshe* itself (at least in our version): the Books of Ezra and Nehemiah describe the Jews as a 'holy seed' who must not be contaminated by association with foreigners, whereas other biblical books warn Israelites to keep their distance from their neighbours lest they learn their idolatrous ways. Marriage to foreigners is certainly frowned on but never prohibited absolutely, and if the foreigners in question can be induced to abandon idolatry, then the practice is hardly problematic at all. Indeed, some of the greatest figures of the Israelite past, such as King David, were descendants of such marriages (this is the position of the Book of Ruth). But Nehemiah was far more severe: idolatry was beside the point. The very foreignness of the foreigners was their disqualification, and Nehemiah wished to discourage not only marriage but also the interethnic, mainly elite, formal friendships (which often sealed the deal matrimonially) whose political, social and

---

[16] I tend toward an explanation rejected by Finkelstein 2008: Nehemiah 3 is a written-up account of some symbolic tinkering with the still partly extant Iron II wall.

economic importance in the Iron Age Mediterranean world in general has been explored primarily by Greek historians, though it is no less relevant to the Jews (Herman 1987; Konstan 1997; S. Schwartz 2010). Nehemiah's demand thus was not *functional*: that is, it was not meant to solve some practical problem, for example, the Jews' alleged 'assimilation'. Rather it was purely ideological, and its practical price was high, a fact of which the biblical books and later Jewish texts were all keenly aware. The Jews suffered for their separatism.

Nehemiah's administration was partly successful: a version of the *Torat Moshe* did become the provincial law-code of Yehud/Judaea; eventually it would become what Jews still call the Torah, the first five books of the Hebrew Bible, if it was not already substantially identical to it. The egalitarianism and the separatism Nehemiah advocated in rather extreme forms did both become hallmarks of Jewish practice, though greatly moderated, and in ways much more open to negotiation and accommodation than Nehemiah could have wished. Thus, the power of the priests was not broken until most of them were massacred and the temple was destroyed in 70 CE. The *Torat Moshe*, and Nehemiah, wished the priests to be simply a clergy, landless and without political power, but the priests were too well established as landowners (and Nehemiah never took the final tyrannical step of redistributing Judahite landholding); there remained a priestly aristocracy. Yehud/Judaea was thus more typical in its social stratification than it was supposed to have been. Similarly, the Jews never paid the full cost of Nehemian separatism – impoverishment and complete political marginalization – because they found ways, however limited, to continue the practice of interethnic elite friendship despite the religious problems it raised. Conversion to Judaism, first attested in the second century BCE, may have been introduced to serve this purpose (S. Schwartz 2007).

MACEDONIAN CONQUEST: WERE THE JEWS 'HELLENIZED' BEFORE THE MACCABEES?

Narrative history of the Jews fails us for 250 years after Nehemiah, assuming his book contains reliable information. Our most important source for the history of the Jews before 70 CE, the Jewish writer Flavius Josephus (37–*c*.100 CE), had next to no information on this period – a few dubious or historically impossible tales. Archaeological excavation and the antiquities trade have revealed tantalizing fragments. These suggest that two processes, judaization and hellenization, existed concurrently (Grabbe and Lipschits 2011). Yehud had a small-denomination silver coinage starting around 400 BCE, inscribed in archaic Hebrew letters with the high priest's name (telling us something about provincial governance) and decorated with Hellenic-style images. One coin features a Zeus-like divine figure some have identified as a rare figurative depiction of Yahweh – a fact in some tension with the Pentateuch's prohibition of the figurative representation of God (Meshorer 1982: 1:115–17).[17] Similarly complex are the religious implications of Aramaic papyri from a Judahite military settlement on the upper (= southern) Nile island of Elephantine (Porten 1996: 125–6; 139–51). These show, among other things, how that remote colony, about twenty years after Nehemiah's governorship, was encouraged by the Persian authorities to adopt elements of religious practice based on the *Torat Moshe*. Apparently, the code was meant to be valid for Judahites wherever they lived in the Persian Empire, not just in Yehud, though the process of its dissemination was slow and incremental. On the other hand, many small finds demonstrate the gradual hellenization of Palestinian material culture in the century *before* the Macedonian conquest (E. Stern 1982). Less surprising evidence exists for the intensification of the process of cultural change – extending now, for example, to some extent to language – in the century after the conquest (Eshel 2007; Kloner, Regev and Rappaport 1992). Finally, often overlooked but potentially important is evidence from surveys and excavations for some limited growth in number and size of settlements in Yehud/Judaea in the last century of Persian rule and the first century of Macedonian.[18] Despite the violence of part of the period in the world around it, Yehud/Judaea experienced these centuries as unprecedentedly peaceful ones: Macedonian conquerors, Persian resisters, diadochic generals and their descendants who went to war over Palestine five times in under a century, restricted their activities to the coastal plain, leaving Yehud/Judaea entirely in peace; the few generals to consider Jerusalem worth a brief detour arrived calmly and were given a friendly reception. The modest demographic and economic growth which resulted contributed to the dynamism and eventually the chaos of the period which followed.

Alexander of Macedon defeated the Persian king Darius III at Issus in south-eastern Asia Minor (Turkey) in 333 BCE and immediately thereafter subdued Syria–Palestine, conquered Egypt, and then headed east, to

---

[17] For the argument that the latter coin is not from Yehud but from the (non-Jewish) coast see Gitler and Tal 2006: 230.

[18] Grabbe 2008: 48–50; some or all of the growth may have occurred after the third century. The guess of Aperghis 2004: 49 that pre-Maccabean Judaea had 200,000–250,000 inhabitants is based on extrapolation from the impossible troop figures in 1 Macc.

Mesopotamia, Iran and India. Josephus (*Ant.* 11.304–45) and the Talmud (B. Yoma 69a) both tell the story of Alexander's visit to Jerusalem and his reverence for the temple and the high priest (called Iaddus by Josephus and Simon in the Talmud); in Josephus' account, the episode culminates in the conqueror's permission to the Jews to continue to live 'according to their ancestral laws'[19] – a bit of Hellenistic political jargon probably understood as referring to the Torah as interpreted by the high priest and his entourage.

We can be certain that this event never happened. We know Alexander's itinerary in some detail, and he had no time for a detour that none of the standard sources describe him making (Tcherikover 1959: 42–50). At most Alexander dispatched a general to the hill country to receive the Judaeans' obeisance; there is no indication they resisted. One of the problems faced by a comparatively non-interventionist empire like the Persian – which worked through local intermediaries embedded in local societies, and never tried to integrate their realm into a state, being concerned mainly with relatively efficient extraction of revenues – was that though they generated little opposition, they also won rather little loyalty from the mass of the people they ruled (Briant 2002: 855–7). That Alexander or one of his successors affirmed the Judaeans' right to their traditional constitution is not unlikely, though the earliest more or less reliable evidence for a Hellenistic king granting them this right consists of a document Josephus quotes, allegedly issued by Antiochus III after Jerusalem's capitulation to him during the Fifth Syrian War, 200 BCE (*Ant.* 12.138–44; Bikerman 1935).

After Alexander's death in 323, Palestine and Phoenicia became a bone of contention among his successors: both Ptolemy son of Lagos, who controlled Egypt, and Seleucus Nicator, who controlled, loosely, the vast eastern part of Alexander's empire but was based mainly in Syria and Mesopotamia, claimed it, and the area was also briefly ruled by Antigonus Monophthalmus, who for a time claimed the entirety of Alexander's realm as his own. In 301 Ptolemy won the area decisively, and, though his descendants and the Seleucids constantly fought over it, the Ptolemies continued to rule it for a century (Will 2003: 19–83). In 200, the Seleucid king Antiochus III seized the territory, but his dynasty was already on the verge of decline. Its slow unravelling had an exceedingly important impact on Jewish history, which will be explored in the coming pages.

---

[19] So too the Egyptians, Babylonians, Sardians, Phoenicians and Ionian Greeks, according to the generally propagandistic historiographic tradition, describing Alexander as if he were Cyrus: Briant 2002: 852–4.

What difference did Macedonian rule make to the Jews? Much recent Hellenistic history has focused on the continuities between Persian and Macedonian rule (Briant 2002: 2–3; Sherwin-White and Kuhrt 1993; Manning 2010: 19–28), and what little information we have about the short-term impact of the shift on the Jews more or less confirms this: life in Hellenistic Judaea was significantly continuous with life in Persian Yehud. Both empires ruled by bolstering local institutions and elites, combined with mild (compared with the Romans) tinkering especially to secure the flow of revenue, and slight intimidation produced by the presence of garrison troops and/or occasional visits by armed representatives of provincial governors (Ma 2000a: 106–78; Briant 2002; Wiesehöfer 2009). Both recognized the Jews as a nation – *'ama* in Aramaic, *ethnos* in Greek – which consequently had the right to use its own laws. That is, both endorsed, directly or indirectly, the legal validity of the Torah and the right of the priests to impose and interpret it.[20]

Evidence for cultural and religious continuity confirms this general picture. At one time a debate raged between those scholars who argued that the Jews became 'hellenized' very thoroughly very quickly, which helped explain the emergence of an apparent 'hellenizing' or reformist party among elements of the priesthood by around 200 BCE, and the development of an extreme anti-Hellenic reaction (Bickermann 1979/1937; Hengel 1974), and others who thought the Jews as a group resisted hellenization, aside from a few outlying collaborationist types (Tcherikover 1959; Feldman 1993). Developments in the field of Hellenistic cultural history in general have now softened the edges of this argument, with no one any longer accepting the extreme versions of either view. Much of the cultural change in the Near East that used to be attributed to the Macedonian kings now appears due to Roman rule, much later. The Macedonian kings did, to be sure, have novel practices, like building new Greek cities from scratch, or granting Greek constitutions to old non-Greek cities. They encouraged Greek language and culture in other ways too. Their own Greekness was of relatively recent vintage and not universally acknowledged (Engels 2010), yet they ruled the Near and Middle East precisely because Alexander the Great had been the most successful protector Hellas had ever had; they were zealous about Greekness but also, in the classical style, quite particularistic – despite having barely slipped in through

---

[20] But Baltrusch 2002: 42–58 argues that the Achaemenids actively supported Judaean institutions, which they used as part of their administration, while the Hellenistic kings merely granted Judaeans the right to use their institutions as a reward for their loyalty.

the gates themselves, they did not want them thrown open to everyone: they did not want to turn the Persian Empire and its subjects into Greeks, but did want to enable Greeks to rule over and enjoy privileges in the former Persian Empire. They thus tended to favour Greeks politically, in a blatant way in Egypt, with more subtlety elsewhere, to patronize Greek institutions, and to conduct court lives which were adamantly Greek in both language and culture. By contrast, the Persian kings may have lacked the basic idea that 'culture' is something that can be assumed and shed, and thus that there was a Persian culture which could be fostered. Thus, however complex and controversial it is to speak of 'hellenization', hardly anyone speaks of 'persianization' or 'iranization' at all;[21] only the classical Greeks, who mostly were not under Persian rule, or rather small numbers of aristocratic individuals, 'medized' or were accused of medizing, perhaps because they alone assumed that (spotty and selective) cultural practice could serve as political currency or as proxy for factional affiliation, or conversely that political alliance entailed cultural approximation.[22] The Persian kings did foster significant cultural change, as it happens: by their elevation of the status of a scribal *lingua franca* – a North-west Semitic language, unlike their native Old Persian, in the distant past spoken in parts of Syria, but transformed already by the Assyrian kings into a documentary language – they transformed the linguistic geography of the Near East and caused the replacement of dozens of local languages by Imperial Aramaic (S. Schwartz 2005).

The preferences and policies of the Hellenistic kings were thus not as blatant in their cultural effects as some used to think, but they were significant nonetheless and somewhat different from the basically linguistic changes fostered by the Persians, however unintentionally. Though some documents were written in local languages, most government business, even in small remote villages, was conducted in Greek, and the Hellenistic kings tended to be more document-oriented and bureaucratic than the Persians had been. Thus Greek quickly came to compete with Aramaic, though except in some coastal areas it never totally supplanted it, even a millennium later. But the cultural preferences of kings and officials, even quite far down the scale, had more profound consequences: even aside from the enhanced prestige that Greekness, sometimes in the form of the

---

[21] Except, in the best cases, to dismiss it: see the incisive Tuplin 2011. Even at Achaemenid Sardis, the evidence for Persianization is slight: Dusinberre 2003.

[22] The *locus classicus* is the Medism of Pausanias, victor of Plataea: Thucydides 1.95.128–34: see Graf 1984.

new Greek cities, now enjoyed due to royal patronage, anyone dealing with officials could find it highly disadvantageous not to know how to act – not just speak – like a Greek (Hopkins 1991).

THE NEW LITERATURE; THE TOBIADS

We have just enough information to be able to trace the impact of some of these changes among the Jews. The evidence for cultural continuity consists in the fact that in the third century literate Jews connected with the central Judaean institutions continued to write in traditional ways, in archaizing Hebrew for the most part, and in traditional genres, just as priests in Egypt and Mesopotamia continued to write texts in hieroglyphic Egyptian and cuneiform Akkadian well into the Hellenistic period. No tradition is ever actually unchanging, however much its preservers may insist that it is; Jewish literature plausibly datable to the third century is actually very varied, some compositions being difficult to distinguish from earlier works in the same genre, and others quite distinctive and novel. Thus, many of the 150 poems in the collection of biblical Psalms could have been written at any time between the late Bronze Age and the early Roman period; the genre may have changed over time, but the changes are so subtle that they have to be laboriously teased out by experts. The book of Chronicles, probably written in the later fourth or third century, is written very much in the style of the much earlier deuteronomic history on which it is based, but introduces some contemporary religious ideas; histories in the biblical style – for example, the first book of Maccabees – continued to be written at least until *c*. 100 BCE.

Other genres, though, were more novelty-prone, perhaps especially wisdom literature. On the one hand, wisdom sentences often have, and were constructed to have, a timeless, universal, feel; on the other, Israelite wisdom had a long tradition of being open to wider innovatory currents of thought expressed in unusual and striking language. The conventional-seeming piety of the pre-Hellenistic book of Proverbs was already criticized in the (probably also pre-Hellenistic) book of Job, which insists on the utter transcendence of God (probably a novel idea among the Jews in the sixth or fifth century BCE) and so on the inscrutability of his will. What is certain is that the bland reassurances of the deuteronomic tendency in Israelite/biblical religious thought, that God can be counted on to reward the righteous and punish the wicked, are wrong. But still more radical critics of traditional religious thought wrote in the third century.

The anonymous author of Kohelet (Ecclesiastes) takes Job's critique a step further: God's will is not so much inscrutable as irrelevant. The entire universe, both natural and human, is in thrall not to divine foresight, but to wearisome amoral regularity, which even the wise and the righteous cannot escape. Around the same time the author of the non-canonical book of Watchers (1 Enoch, chapters 1–36), many fragments of which turned up among the Dead Sea Scrolls, but which was preserved in full, in translation into Ge'ez, only in the Ethiopian Church, offered a different and in some ways more influential critique of the traditional piety, founded, like the others, on Jobian pessimism. This work provides a mythological narrative, based on Genesis and also on Israelite and Babylonian wisdom and cosmological traditions, of a partly failed creation, divine withdrawal, the victory and domination of evil personified as rebellious angels, and of God's eventual return and triumph, at an unknown point in the future. In sum, 1 Enoch – often regarded as the earliest Jewish 'apocalyptic' book – restored cosmological myth, which the biblical authors had been careful to omit, to Judaism, having recognized that myth could be mobilized to solve philosophical problems caused by monotheism (if there is one benevolent God, why is there evil?).

What is noteworthy about these texts, both the traditional and the innovatory, is that they betray few or no traces of 'hellenization'. Herodotus, and *a fortiori* Thucydides, had absolutely no impact on the author of Chronicles, and there is no evidence that the sages responsible for Kohelet or Enoch knew that Greek thinkers had been treating similar issues for centuries too.[23] Thus, the handful of Jerusalemite literate elites, who were responsible for all the surviving writing in Hebrew and Aramaic, the people we would expect to show the strongest signs of early hellenization, fail do to so.

The Tobiads

There are better places to look, though, than in a high literary tradition produced by a clerisy, people, that is, who were utterly committed to the powerful institutional cultures of the Jerusalem temple and its holy books, situated in a province where it is very unlikely that any semblance of Greek higher education was yet available in the third century BCE. What we can

---

[23] The argument here follows S. Schwartz 2001; for updated bibliography: Grabbe 2008: 78–84; many scholars have argued for Greek influence on Kohelet. For Chronicles, Japhet 2009 (opting for a late Achaemenid date).

learn from the literature is something about the enduring dynamism of these institutions under Macedonian rule. The kings supported them, they prospered, and continued to generate profound devotion among their constituents, who continued to think in novel and compelling ways about their national traditions.

Individuals among this clerisy – for example, the chief priests – may nevertheless have experienced the cultural pressures involved in working for Greek rulers. John, or Yehohanan, ben Hakkoz, the head of the Judaean embassy which had secured from Antiochus III the Jews' right to use their ancestral laws (2 Macc. 4.11), was a Jerusalem priest who necessarily had at least a rudimentary grasp of Greek rhetoric. There were others, at or beyond the fringes of the clerisy, who had a more direct experience of what a Greek empire meant. Over several centuries we have scattered bits of tantalizing information about a wealthy family called the Tobiads, after an ancestor Tobiah, who lived not in Judaea but in Ammon (Grabbe 2008: 293–7), in what is now Jordan (whose capital city Amman still bears part of its ancient name: Rabbat Benei Ammon, literally, 'capital city of the Ammonites'). It is not unlikely that the family began as Ammonite big-men, based in fortified houses near Amman, who due to their long history of marriage alliances with prominent Judahite families, and also to the fading of any sense of discrete Ammonite identity in the wake of the Babylonian and Persian conquests and the Nabataean incursion, came to identify as Jews. One early member of the family, called Tobiah the Ammonite (either because that is what he was or as an insult; Tobiah, not incidentally, means 'Yahweh is good', and so marks its bearer, or his parents, as worshippers of the God of Israel, not [or, not only] that of Ammon), turns up as an enemy of Nehemiah (Neh. 2; 4.1–8; 6), allied with and married into the leading Judahite families (Neh. 6.18), occupant of office-space in the Jerusalem temple from which Nehemiah had him expelled (Neh. 13.1–9).

About 200 years later, Zenon, a courtier of Ptolemy II, encountered one Toubias, a trans-Jordanian grandee like his ancient kinsman, while on a visit to the Ptolemies' holdings outside Egypt; some records of this tour survive among the thousands of documents and letters which constitute a collection of papyri called the 'Zenon Archive'. Toubias kept a private troop of mercenaries, infantry and mounted, from a wide variety of backgrounds, which the authorities wished to incorporate into the Ptolemaic forces; he also owned land and engaged extensively in trade (*CPJ* 1.1–6). He was in sum precisely the sort of local big-man ambitious governments like that of Ptolemaic Egypt must either co-opt or crush. Since Toubias was amenable to cooptation, he was in regular contact with Zenon when the latter was in the region, and we must suppose that the Ptolemaic authorities kept tabs on him at other times through lower-ranking officials. Toubias retained his Judaean name and probably – though this is less clear from the papyri than from literary sources about his kinspeople or descendants – his Judaean loyalties. But he employed a Greek secretary, and was pointedly careful to thank not God but 'the gods' – not a routine formulation – for his good health in an epistolary exchange of pleasantries with Zenon (*CPJ* 1.4; S. Schwartz 1993b).

The next truly reliable information about the family comes from the books of Maccabees, where we learn that, when Seleucus IV's finance minister Heliodorus tried to plunder the treasury of the Jerusalem temple, Hyrcanus son of Joseph son of Toubias (2 Macc. 3.11; probably but not certainly the Toubias just mentioned; in any case a kinsman) had private funds deposited there – reminding us of his ancestor's office in the temple and marriage alliance with the high priest. Later we learn that the Toubian troops – descendants of Toubias' co-opted private army – joined the Maccabean Revolt on the Maccabean side (Bar-Kochva 1989: 82–4; 508–15). Chronologically intermediate and far harder to parse is a peculiar tale Josephus relates about Joseph son of Toubias and his son Hyrcanus (*Ant.* 12.154–236; Wills 1995: 185–211).

Joseph, who is married to the high priest's daughter, travels to Alexandria to bid on the tax-farming contract for Palestine – an event not only political and financial in character, but also social – in competition with his in-law Onias, the high priest of Jerusalem. He wins, but gets into various highly sinful misadventures along the way. After many prosperous years he is succeeded by the youngest of his seven sons, who has adventures of his own but eventually flees to a castle across the Jordan (Josephus, having confused the chronology, muddles the reason for the flight – Antiochus III's victory – and also was unaware that Hyrcanus would have been fleeing to his family's country seat). These men are portrayed as dedicated to the prosperity and welfare of Judaea, and hostile to the new Greek cities of coastal Palestine, as socially part of the fabric of the Judaean upper class, but as lacking any sort of pious concern either for the temple or for the Torah. They illustrate the cultural pressures described above, because in order to maintain their positions they had to know how to behave like Greeks, but they also had to retain their Judaean ties, and even perhaps play them up, in a way which would convince their Alexandrian patrons of their ability to deliver both loyalties and revenues. Yet even in this family, with its long history of contacts with Alexandria and its kings and officials, hellenization could not be taken for granted; Josephus says that Hyrcanus' brothers could not succeed their father because their manners were too 'rustic', meaning that they could not function socially in the environment of the royal court.

CHAPTER 2

Maccabean Revolt and Hasmonean dynasty

A GREEK JERUSALEM?

The 'hellenization' of the cities of central and eastern Asia Minor and the Syro-Palestinian coast is an obscure process which had fatefully import- ant consequences (G. Cohen 1995; 2006). In the course of the third cen- tury BCE most cities in these regions were transformed from non-Greek to Greek cities. Most of them cultivated cultural and political traces of their pre-Greek past, now marginalized into what we may call 'local col- our', adding some special character to cities which otherwise aspired to be as similar as possible culturally and institutionally (Millar 1983; Sherwin- White and Kuhrt 1993). This development eventually changed the texture of life in the eastern Mediterranean and must be regarded as the most consequential process initiated by the Hellenistic kings. Yet we know very little about how and why this happened, and surprisingly little, too, about the short-term implications of the change: in what way, precisely, were these cities 'Greek' after the moment of transformation? Still, several points seem nearly certain: in most cases, these cities are to be distinguished from colonies, that is, Greek cities which grew from the practice of the kings of settling their (Greek) veterans or active troops in nucleated settlements, sometimes in or near pre-existing towns or villages, and granting them land and 'bodies' (*somata*; enserfed non-Greek natives). It seems unlikely that cities such as Sardis, Tarsos, Arados, Tyre, Sidon, Askalon and Gaza were ever colonized, though some or all could have received voluntary settlement by Greek immigrants. This implies that the initiative for the transformation came from the locals, presumably the leading classes of the towns, which in turn suggests that these hellenized cities may be under- stood as especially concentrated examples of the cultural and political pressures I described above.

We do, however, have somewhat sketchy information about one such city: Jerusalem. Somewhere in the background of the story of Jerusalem's abortive hellenization is the reorganization of, and imposition of enhanced government control on the finances of temple establishments in the Seleucid province of Koile-Syria-kai-Phoinike, which included Judaea, under Seleucus IV (187–175).[1] The inscription from which we have only recently learned about this provides a tantalizing glimpse, not a full account: at most it allows us to speculate that heightened financial pressure on the Jerusalem temple led to turbulence in the high priesthood. It may also enable us to historicize the miracle tale which opens 2 Maccabees: the viceroy (*ho epi tōn pragmatōn*) Heliodorus entered the temple treasury to plunder it but was struck down by heavenly hosts and escaped with his life thanks only to the intervention of the high priest: God, not the Seleucids, won the first round. A certain Olympiodorus, not Heliodorus, was the financial overseer or perhaps rather the provincial 'high priest' appointed by Seleucus; Heliodorus, according to the inscription, was his supervisor. If the tale has any historical foundation, and whoever its real-life villain was, there was necessarily both more administrative and political hassle and less portentous cosmology involved than 2 Maccabees indicates. Indirectly, the story informs us that what the official undoubtedly would have experienced as a bad day at the office, some Jews at least regarded as an unprecedented act of sacrilege and a profoundly alarming threat.[2]

Financial pressures also underlay the actual opening events of the crisis; the high priesthood could now be secured from the king for silver. Joshua, also called Jason, son of Simon thus induced King Antiochus IV to remove his brother Onias from the post and appoint him instead (*c.* 175 BCE), and he was soon replaced by a higher bidder named Menelaus, who, though a priest, apparently was not a member of the high priestly family. But there was much more to the episode. Jason, in return for the promise of an additional gift, secured from the king the right to establish a *gymnasion* and *ephebeion* at Jerusalem, and 'to enroll those at Jerusalem as Antiochenes', or 'draw up a list of Antiochenes in Jerusalem' (2 Macc. 4.8–14). The meaning of these concessions has been controversial, but perhaps unnecessarily so. They do not in themselves constitute the formal transformation of Jerusalem into a Greek city – with the district of Judaea, which hitherto

---

[1] Older scholarship adduced financial pressures created by Rome's imposition of an indemnity on the Seleucids following the Battle of Magnesia in 188: Gera 1998: 106–7.

[2] Cotton and Wörrle 2007, including an excellent discussion of the new text's relation to 2 Maccabees 3. Additional fragments of the text, discovered in excavation at Marisa/Tell Sandahanna, are published by Gera 2009. Internal plunder is a running theme in Maccabees' accounts of the Seleucid kings and their agents. Whether or not the tale of Heliodorus has a historical kernel, the theme is realistic: Ma 2007: 184.

was not constitutionally distinct from Jerusalem, transformed by extension into its territory – but they seem steps in that direction. I thus oppose the very recent tendency to interpret Antiochus IV's grant to Jason in light of an inscription recording the grant of *polis* status to the small settlement of Toriaion (or Tyriaion) in Phrygia by Eumenes II of Pergamon (reigned 197–159 BCE), notwithstanding the illuminating parallels between the two episodes.[3] The fundamental distinction between the cases is that Toriaion was a Greek settlement without political status, whereas Jerusalem was merely the main settlement in a recognized non-Greek *ethnos*, the *Ioudaioi*. Eumenes granted the Toriaians the right to use their *idioi nomoi* (own laws), a gift constitutive of their new status as citizens of a Greek city. The *Ioudaioi* – not the city of Jerusalem – already possessed authorized use of their *patrioi nomoi* (ancestral laws), as a gift from Antiochus III. Even if we were committed to interpreting events at Jerusalem in light of those at Toriaion, we would still have to conclude that Jerusalem needed a pre-existing Greek community in order to be granted autonomy and be transformed into a Greek city. Perhaps this is what Jason was trying to achieve, as Bickermann long ago argued. The most attractive alternative is that Jason was trying to found a city, Antioch-in-Jerusalem, which would exist alongside the still functioning polity of Jerusalem/Judaea, an arrangement attested elsewhere in the Hellenistic world (Ma 2012: 77–8).[4]

Jason had supporters. Although his reforms had no direct impact on the traditional cult of the Jerusalem temple, 2 Maccabees tells us that the young priests increasingly neglected their service there: 'setting at naught their hereditary distinctions, they put the highest value on Greek honors' (4.15) – a neat way of describing a shift in values. This, the author says, was the budding or flowering (*akme* – not 'high point', as often translated) of *hellenismos* – a process, then, near its start; it had not yet borne fruit. Jason and his supporters should not be seen as people who already conformed to some Hellenistic Greek ideal of *kalokagathia*, and were now acting on this change. Rather, the change was still aspirational. The envoys Jason sent with gifts for Herakles-Melqart, divine patron of Tyre's isolympic games, in the end were shocked by their brush with idolatry, and donated the silver to outfit the city's fleet instead (2 Macc. 4.18–20).

This implies that most things at Jerusalem and in Judaea in general remained unaltered, which may in turn explain why for all the

---

[3] Text: Jonnes and Ricl 1997; Ameling 2003 and D. Schwartz 2008 make the case for a tight parallel; contra: Mittag 2006: 235–44. For a different approach, Ma 2000b.

[4] I am grateful to Ameling and Ma for their comments to me, though neither would agree with every detail of my account.

denunciation of Jason by ancient Jewish writers, none can report any contemporary Jewish opposition to him. His reorganization of the province, if this is what he intended, never had the chance to proceed beyond its still uncontroversial early stages. Jason himself remained the traditional high priest of the Jerusalem temple, whose cult was as yet unchanged. The claim of 2 Maccabees that Jason abrogated Antiochus III's gift (*philanthropa*) to the Judaeans – that is, the right to follow the laws of the Torah – is probably not to be taken literally, or should be understood as proleptic: he began the process which ended in the abrogation of the Torah several years later (Ma 2012: 77).

In fact, Jason was soon deposed; his successor Menelaus has sometimes been thought a more radical hellenizer than Jason (Bickermann 1979/1937: 83ff., following the dubious report in Josephus, *Ant.* 12.240–1; 384), but Menelaus – who retained his position through several fundamental changes of regime and according to a document preserved in 2 Macc. 11.28ff. led the embassy in 165/4 asking Antiochus to rescind his decrees – comes across as an opportunist rather than an ideologue. Be this as it may, Jason did not depart peacefully, but led supporters in an uprising which led to a royally backed restoration of Menelaus. At this point (169–167 BCE) the narrative becomes murky. Two failed Seleucid expeditions in Egypt were followed by violent detours to Jerusalem by Antiochus IV on his return trips to Syria, including plunder, breaching the walls, and the imposition of a garrison in a fortified area in Jerusalem called the Akra (location unknown). These in turn were followed in late 167 by a remarkable royal decree, the reason for the issue of which scholars have struggled for centuries to understand, so far without success.[5] The Judaean ethnos was deconstituted, the Torah declared not simply no longer binding but illegal, observance of its rules punishable by death, and the temple of Jerusalem was rededicated to Zeus Olympios-Baʿal Shamim, with Menelaos continuing to serve as high priest. Finally, the Judaeans were compelled to offer sacrifices to Dionysos (1 Macc. 1.44–59; 2 Macc. 6.1–9).

This episode is the first known religiously based persecution of the Jews. In part because it had so many successors, and in part because of enduring prejudices, modern analysts of the episode have had to struggle

---

[5] Bringmann 1983: 18–25 argued for redating the decree to late 168, immediately following the second sack of Jerusalem, motivated by the king's humiliation in Egypt on the 'Day of Eleusis' – the occasion when C. Popilius Laenas intimidated Antiochus IV into withdrawing. This can contribute to an explanation of the decree. But his arguments have not been universally accepted: Gruen 1993: 245 n. 20.

to free themselves from the notion that it is self-explanatory. For some it seemed obvious that the Jews had earned persecution for their intransigence in the face of admirable Hellenic universalism; to others it seemed that gentiles automatically hated the Jews, and no specific manifestation of this historical rule required special comment. But in the early twentieth century some historians began to draw on their Enlightenment heritage to problematize the episode. Radical thinkers of the eighteenth century supposed that whatever their other faults may be, polytheists are naturally tolerant, since polytheism, 'by limiting the powers and functions of its deities ... naturally admits the gods of other sects and nations to a share of divinity'; it is monotheists who are narrow and uncompromising (Bickermann 1979/1937: 76–8).[6] This makes it all the more surprising that a polytheistic ruler, Antiochus IV, perpetrated one of the most notorious acts of religious persecution in history. But, David Hume notwithstanding, polytheists are not necessarily religiously tolerant; there is not always room in their pantheons for one more god, and they are as likely to have religious taboos and horrors as monotheists (Garnsey 1984). Nevertheless, it was more common in the ancient world to expel practitioners of foreign cults suspected of upsetting the *pax deorum* than it was to uproot the traditional worship of a local ethnic god, though this too is not unparalleled – think of Claudius' treatment of the druids in Gaul (if we follow Suetonius, *Divus Claudius* 25.5). So, whether or not Hume's view is universally valid, the question remains, what motivated Antiochus IV to uproot an established ethnic religion which had been supported by his father, and by all his predecessors back to Artaxerxes I, despite its having been from the perspective of the Greeks a peculiarly misanthropic religion which insisted on the uniqueness of its god and the separation of his worshippers? Antiochus IV promoted his patron god Apollo throughout his realm, but did not engage in religious persecutions elsewhere, so the answer probably lies not in his own religious preferences but in the events of the previous two years, which the author of our only source, 2 Maccabees, seems to have intentionally recounted in as confusing and obscure a way as possible.

The ancient historian Elias Bickermann (1979/1937: 76–92) notoriously argued that the royal decrees were initiated by a faction of extreme

---

[6] This idea was extant earlier and has had an important and highly charged post-Enlightenment afterlife – and not only in contemporary Indian politics with its tensions between Hindus and Muslims; the classic statement, and the source of the quotation in the text, is David Hume, *The Natural History of Religion* (1957: 48–51). Ancient historians might have absorbed the idea in addition from Gibbon.

hellenizers among the Jews, led by Menelaus, that these men aspired, more vehemently than Jason had done, to remove all obstacles in the path of the Jews' integration in the new world of the Hellenistic Greek cities, and so produced a radical revision of Judaism which syncretized the God of Israel with Zeus and with the Syrian god Ba'al Shamim, and eliminated all rules which imposed any sort of separatism on the Jews. It is in retrospect difficult to sustain Bickermann's excessively precise description of the totally unattested theology of the (hypothetical) radical reformers, and unlikely too that Menelaus was the chief villain of the story; the books of Maccabees focus on Jason, not on him. But Bickermann was right to insist that the reforms and the uprisings which followed, which quickly coalesced into a single rebellion, were all supported by *factions* among the Jews. The romantic version of the story, adumbrated to be sure by 1 Maccabees and by traditional Jewish liturgical texts, but worked out in full only by the incipiently nationalist Jewish scholarship of the nineteenth century and the Zionist scholarship of the twentieth (Tcherikover 1959), which imagined a nation united, except for a few quislings, in successful opposition to the first-ever example of anti-Jewish oppression, was completely unrealistic (but see now Ma forthcoming). The actual responses of the Judaeans to the royal decrees were varied, but the most common was probably compliance, however unhappy (1 Macc. 1.43). But the sources hint at a variety of other possibilities. Flight to the Judaean desert is attested (1 Macc. 2.28–38), as is flight to Egypt (Josephus *Ant.* 12.386, with some interpretation), but there were also enthusiastic supporters of the decrees (1 Macc. 1.52); one can imagine that Jason's faction split under the pressure of the decrees' radicalism, with some reverting to resistance, and others enthusiastically joining the royalist party. Both 1 and 2 Maccabees indicate that the royal garrison in the Akra was also home to many Jewish 'sinners' – supporters of the reforms – yet, as indicated above, in 164, Menelaus himself used his influence to convince the king to rescind the persecution; even among some of the pro-royal faction, conformity to the decrees was awkward and uneasy.

The resistance soon coalesced around the Hasmonean family, originally from the village of Modein, on the north-western edge of Judaea, or perhaps even beyond its boundaries. They were local big-men, who later claimed to be Jerusalem priests, but according to 1 Maccabees, a book otherwise strongly favourable to them and uncritical of their claims, they offered no resistance to the decrees until a royal official arrived in their village to induce the villagers to sacrifice.[7] After the death of the family's patriarch Mattathias around 166, the leadership of the faction and soon of the rebellion was assumed by his son Judah, nicknamed Maccabee (the word's meaning is unknown), who, with a growing band of guerrillas, won a series of victories over small Seleucid forces.[8] Within two years the king's commitment to his decrees flagged in the face of the aristocracy's loss of enthusiasm, and of Judah's agitation, and he cancelled the persecution. Judah briefly seized control of the Jerusalem temple (late autumn, 164), and had it restored to its previous state – this episode is familiar to Jews as the origins of the festival of Hanukah; the sacrificial worship of the God of Israel resumed, rather bafflingly still under the high priestly supervision of Menelaus; Judah did not rule the city (1 Macc. 4.39–61; 2 Macc. 10.1–8; 2 Macc. 11.28–33; 13.3–8).[9]

Antiochus IV's death was the beginning of the end for the Seleucid dynasty. For the next century there would be near constant civil or dynastic war, and the Seleucid realm quickly eroded, so that when Pompey invaded Syria in 65 BCE, there was little of it left for him to conquer. It was in this circumstance that a remote village-based band of successful guerrillas quickly remade themselves into rulers of a kingdom which steadily grew in size and importance. By 163 Judah had become a substantial military leader whom the advisers of Antiochus V had come to think deserved serious attention. He was nearly defeated by the regent Lysias in 162, but the latter was called away to deal with a civil war at Antioch, and to ensure his safe retreat he offered Judah significant concessions: the *philanthropa* of Antiochus III were restored; the renewed cult of the God of Israel was officially recognized, as opposed to tolerated; and the authority of the Torah as constitution of the Judaean ethnos was re-established (1 Macc. 6.59; 2 Macc. 11.22). Judah, who had been fighting precisely for this, had won, but continued fighting presumably because he had also always been fighting for the advancement of himself and his faction. In early spring 161 he won a surprising victory over a large army led by Nicanor, who had allegedly threatened to destroy the Jerusalem temple (2 Macc. 15); this episode ends the Second Book of Maccabees, which had begun with the threat against the temple by the royal minister Heliodorus about fifteen years earlier.

[7] The evidence for the priestly background of the Hasmoneans is fully surveyed though problematically analysed in Schofield and Vanderkam 2005; cf. S. Schwartz 1993a.
[8] Bar-Kochva 1989 provides a scholarly but positivistic account.
[9] For reconstruction of the correct sequence – cancellation of the persecution and Menelaus' apparent repentance *preceding* Judah's purification of the temple – see Habicht 1976, anticipated by Bickermann 1979/1937: 55–60, whose account is followed here; likewise, Ma 2012. Menelaus was still on the scene at least a year after the first Hanukah: 2 Macc. 13.

Every photographer knows that it's all in the cropping. 2 Maccabees gives the impression of an untrammelled happy ending, but this is highly misleading. The following year, a still larger Seleucid army under Bacchides finally crushed Judah's faction at Elasa, killing the leader and putting the few survivors, including his brothers Jonathan and Simon, to flight (1 Macc. 9.1–33). The Maccabean Revolt thus appeared to end with the defeat and humiliation of the Hasmoneans, following their successful restoration of the *status quo ante*: royal recognition of the Jewish nation, its laws and temple. 1 Maccabees, our only primary source for the episodes following Judah's defeat of Nicanor, has little to say about the eight years after Jonathan and Simon's flight across the Jordan, beyond reporting a few acts of brigandage, in the short term the only way warlike fugitives had of staying alive in the Syrian desert (1 Macc. 9.34–73).

But when the curtain rises again in 152 BCE, Jonathan has somehow succeeded in reassembling a substantial armed following and establishing a significant base of support in Judaea; though the reports of brigandage offer a tantalizing hint as to how he might have proceeded to re-establish himself, we can do no more than speculate.[10] What 1 Maccabees (chapter 10) tells us is that by 152 the rival claimants to the Seleucid throne, Demetrius I son of Seleucus IV and Alexander Balas, who claimed to be the bastard son of Antiochus IV, were each trying to mobilize support, and so each made offers to Jonathan. Jonathan backed Alexander, who reciprocated by appointing Jonathan high priest (the post may have been vacant for a few years), and his brother Simon *strategos*, or general (in practice, chief tax collector), of the Palestinian coast. Jonathan appears to have spent the next ten years as a faithful vassal of whichever Seleucid pretender he happened to be supporting, sending troops as requested and keeping his constituents in line. The Jews' reaction to Jonathan is nowhere reported (1 Maccabees, which is strongly supportive of the Hasmonean dynasty, would never have mentioned hostility, and even tries to pass off Jonathan's wars on behalf of the Seleucids as the heroic equivalent of Judah's wars against them) but it is hard to overlook the fact that in his own way he was as much a sinner as Jason and Menelaus. He had usurped the dynasty which had served as high priests since the days of Darius I, in fact, according to the holy books, since the days of David and Solomon, despite the fact that his own priestly lineage was questionable (Menelaus

[10] On Jonathan and Simon in general see Sievers 1990 and Shatzman 2007. Both follow Bickermann (1979/1937) in emphasizing that Jonathan and Simon were primarily Seleucid courtiers. Dąbrowa 2010: 42–66 outdoes 1 Macc. in piety towards Jonathan.

had been a sinner, but at least was a real Aaronide). Much more seriously, he persistently violated two important biblical laws: he left the temple compound, and even worse, he served as a general (1 Macc. 11.60–12.38), which inevitably meant that he was constantly in a state of 'corpse impurity' due to contact or the sharing of space with dead bodies. The combination of roles, high priest and military leader, was, as far as we can tell, unprecedented. Jonathan can hardly have been regarded as the ideal incumbent for the position, especially not by the pious traditionalists who had been part (though often a surprisingly ambivalent part) of the base of Hasmonean support, and it may be no coincidence that some of the sectarian groups which became a conspicuous part of Judaean life later on appear to have got their start as pietistic, in some cases priestly, opponents of Jonathan (S. Schwartz 2001: 32–6).

In any case Jonathan was assassinated in 142 by Diodotus Tryphon, a pretender whose patronage he was seeking (1 Macc. 12.39–13.24), and his surviving brother Simon immediately negotiated an alliance with Tryphon's opponent Demetrius II son of Demetrius I (1 Macc. 13.34–40). Simon was appointed high priest but also secured from the pretender a remission of tribute for his province (1 Macc. 13.41–2). If Jonathan had been a successful courtier, skilled at manipulating the deepening crisis at Antioch for his own advancement, Simon had different ambitions, perhaps having sensed that for the time being the Seleucids had little to gain by attempting any military intervention in Judaea. He presented the royal concessions to the Judaeans as tokens of their independence, and launched a series of successful campaigns against the remaining Seleucid fortresses in Judaea (1 Macc. 13.43–8). The garrison of the Akra – perhaps still constituting the city of Antioch-in-Jerusalem – was still in place in 140 BCE, still apparently populated in part by Jewish 'sinners'. Simon crushed them and razed the fortress, an act 1 Maccabees presents as packed with symbolic importance (1 Macc. 13.49–52); it allowed Simon to present himself to the Judaeans as their legitimate ruler – though not yet king – by the *ius gladii*, not by royal appointment. He then convened an assembly of Judaeans (1 Macc. 14.25–49 – presented as spontaneous: Sievers 1990), reminiscent of the assemblies Ezra and Nehemiah had convened to have the Judahites accept the *Torat Moshe* by public acclamation; this assembly passed a decree declaring Simon high priest, and his descendants high priests, and also secular rulers of Judaea. Whereas Ezra and Nehemiah's assemblies had ended in oral oaths taken by the assembled nation, Simon's ended with the text of the decree inscribed on bronze tablets and erected in the temple precinct, standard practice in Greek cities, and a fine symbol not only of the legitimacy of the Hasmoneans, but also of the progressive hellenization of these great enemies of Hellenism (Gruen 1998: 34–5; Rappaport 1990: 493–7).

THE HASMONEAN DYNASTY

The Hasmoneans had a brief run – under eighty years from Simon's self-coronation in 140 BCE to Pompey's arrival in Jerusalem in 63 BCE. As Tacitus already noted, their ascendancy coincided with the empire vacuum created by the collapse of the Seleucids (*Historiae* 5.8). But they had several highly consequential achievements. If the period from Artaxerxes I to Seleucus IV had been a stable one characterized by slow and steady growth, the Hasmonean period began one of more intensive growth and expansion. For the first time Judaea emerged as a player on the wider scene of the central and eastern Mediterranean. Several factors lay behind this development. First, that scene itself was characterized in this period by a tendency towards ever greater integration, and the only way for small states to survive was by learning to cope. This meant that the Hasmoneans, though they had fought for the restoration of the separationist Torah and against Jason and co.'s radical integrationism, in the final analysis had to get along in the world of Hellenistic Greek cities and hellenizing *ethne* and successor kingdoms every bit as much as he; but they succeeded in doing so while sacrificing relatively little of the integrity of the Judaean *ethnos* – a fact surely partly enabled by the rise of culturally hybrid post-Seleucid successor kingdoms and the receding importance of the *polis* as a political power-unit in Asia's and Syria's last century before the arrival of Rome (Gruen 1998: 1–40; Sartre 2001: 371–433; Sullivan 1990: 1–24)

Indeed, the Hasmonean principality was a flagship example of the culturally hybrid post-Seleucid kingdom. From a very early period the Hasmoneans adopted the practice of giving their children double names (at any rate their sons; of the three Hasmonean women known to us by name, one has a double name, one only a Greek name and one only a Hebrew name). The Hebrew name was invariably that of a known member of the family, one of Simon's brothers or his father, and the Greek name invariably one important in the circle of Alexander the Great – but not dynastic names like Antiochus or Seleucus (unsurprisingly) or even, more tellingly, Ptolemaios. Thus the three sons of John Hyrcanus (the latter a name of unknown but not Greek origin; a Tobiad connection – see above – should not be excluded) son of Simon (ruled 134–104 BCE) were named Judah Aristobulus (ruled 104–103), Jonathan (shortened to Yannai/Jannaeus) Alexander (ruled 103–76), and Mattathias (this is uncertain) Antigonus (murdered by Aristobulus in 104). It is assumed but not certain that Jannaeus' sons had Hebrew names, though they are called only by the names Hyrcanus and Aristobulus; the latter's son Antigonus (ruled 40–37), however, indubitably was called Mattathias (Ilan 1987; Rappaport 1990). This practice reflects not only hellenization but probably also something of the intensity of the family's quest for legitimacy, not of course fully secured by Simon's carefully orchestrated 'great assembly' of 140 BCE. By commemorating both their own family's heroic past and their connections with Hellenistic/Macedonian traditions, they were trying to appeal to different constituencies among their subjects, or rather to different though overlapping political tendencies among them; they were also trying to appeal to their peers in the late Hellenistic eastern Mediterranean and Near East.

A spike in the usage of Greek in Judaea and neighbouring districts is also attested in this period. The Hasmoneans themselves eventually issued bilingual or even trilingual coins, reflecting the same ideology as lies behind their naming practices. The Hebrew legend tends to be written in the same archaic Hebrew script (presumably by now almost completely illegible even to the literate) used on the coins of Persian Yehud, and refers to the ruler not as king but as *Ha-kohen Ha-gadol*, the high priest, whereas the Greek legend calls him *basileus*, just as in the unusual cases of coins with Aramaic legends the ruler is labelled *malka* (king).[11] These coins contain no image of any human or animal, only of inanimate objects like anchors and cornucopiae, implying the dynasty's public embrace of aversion to images. A strict version of iconophobia was becoming common among the Jews in the third and second centuries BCE. Greek, moreover, is increasingly the language used in public writing in this period, never supplanting Aramaic or less commonly Hebrew, but increasingly supplementing it. In this period too Palestinian Jews began writing literature in Greek, the first example, dating from as early as 159 BCE, being a history of the kings of Judah based on the biblical histories but written in the style of Hellenistic local historians in the non-Thucydidean tradition. The author of this book, named Eupolemos, is plausibly identified with the Eupolemos whom Judah Maccabee sent on a mission to the Roman Senate around 162 BCE; he was the son of John ben Hakkoz, who had been

---

[11] Some *perutot* (small denomination bronze coins) of Jannaeus designate him 'king' in Hebrew, and a rare issue has both *kohen* and *melekh*: Barag 2012; Rappaport 1990.

the Judaeans' envoy to Antiochus III after the Fifth Syrian War (Schürer-Vermes III.517–21).

The rulers tried, to the extent they could, to cultivate friendships with neighbouring kings and states (though they seem usually to have been hostile to Greek cities), but we know little about the family life of the Hasmoneans, and surprisingly little about their prosopography. Their successor and in-law Herod would foster marriage alliances with other client kings, but we do not know whether the Hasmoneans did the same, notwithstanding their friendships with the Ptolemies, and sporadically with the Nabataeans and others as well. They also followed standard practice in moving very quickly from an army of Judaean supporters to one consisting partly of Greek and Asian mercenaries (Josephus, *Ant.* 13.249; 374; Shatzman 1991; Rappaport 1990).

Josephus' account of these rulers gives the unmistakable impression that they were trying very hard to conform to what was expected of late Hellenistic rulers, in a way which was compatible with the retention of much native culture, though rigorists disapproved of the compromises (Gruen 1998: 1–40; Rappaport 1990; Rajak 2002: 39–60). Every Hasmonean experienced a rebellion by Judaeans, at least one of them, under Alexander Jannaeus, very serious and crushed with stunning cruelty – hundreds of rebels were reportedly crucified (!) in the central market of Jerusalem, and their wives and children slaughtered by the thousands, while the king looked on from the balcony of his palace (Josephus, *Ant.* 13.380). The compromised and complex cultural position of the Hasmoneans was probably most incisively evoked in modern times in a brilliantly intuitive poem, 'Alexandros Iannaios and Alexandra', by Constantine Cavafy.[12]

There were limits to the Hasmoneans' compromises. However problematic they were as high priests (Josephus, *Ant.* 13.288–92; 372–3), however much they encouraged the use of the Greek language and elements of Greek culture, and however much they sought to get along in the culturally Greek elite world of the eastern Mediterranean of the waning Hellenistic period, they seem not to have tampered with the cult of the Jerusalem temple, nor to have challenged the basic authority of the Torah. They also seem never to have adopted on a large scale the Hellenistic practice of founding cities and naming them after themselves or their relatives or friends (though the existence of a tiny desert village named Aristoboulias – more likely named

---

[12] C. Cavafy and Theoharis Constantine Theoharis, *Before Time Could Change Them: The Complete Poems of C. P. Cavafy*, New York: Harcourt, 2001, 336–7.

after a local proprietor than after a Hasmonean king[13] – and, more definitely connected with the Hasmoneans, fortresses named Alexandreion,
in Samaria, and Hyrcania, in Judaea, may require us to tone down any
sweeping assertions).[14] This is more interesting because, unlike in the case
of the use of images or changes in the temple service, it is at first glance
uncertain why they should have avoided this practice. One possibility is
simply finances; the Hasmoneans could never afford to found cities, and
so had to restrict themselves to rather small fortresses. This suggestion is
implausible, however, since they could have easily enough *refounded* cities,
and in any case in some periods at least they had a considerable income
from plunder. A close reading of Josephus' accounts of Herod's building
projects slightly later suggests a different motivation: the Judaeans traditionally had an aversion to, or ambivalence towards, or a tendency to
disapprove of, the practice of memorialization in monumental form,
indeed of many of the practices characteristic of Hellenistic and, later,
Roman euergetism and memorialization (S. Schwartz 2010). As we will
see, Herod's adoption of these practices was experimental and not entirely
successful.

EXPANSION

Also highly consequential was the Hasmoneans' territorial expansion.
When Simon died in 134 BCE, his realm was still restricted to Hellenistic
Judaea, the small district around Jerusalem. A few people who were or
said they were *Ioudaioi*/Jews were to be found elsewhere in the country,
but it seems likely that many of these were military colonists and their
descendants.[15] Some were people who had gravitated to the coastal cities.
By the time the expansion came to an end with the death of Alexander
Jannaeus in 76, the Hasmoneans ruled all of Palestine west of the Jordan
and probably some territory to its east as well, especially in the vicinity
of the Sea of Galilee. This process had begun late in the reign of John
Hyrcanus, around 110 BCE, with the conquest of Samaria and Idumaea
(*Ant.* 13.254–8, misdated to 129 BCE; 280–3), and then of the Jezreel val-
ley north of Samaria. It continued with the conquest of Galilee in the

---

[13] This village is first attested in XHever/Seiyal 69, a marriage contract dated 130 CE; the editors
(pp. 251–4) take this document as confirmation of Avi-Yonah's suggestion that the village was a
Hasmonean foundation, but it is hard to see why.

[14] And see Regev 2011 on the avoidance of architectural magnificence in the Hasmonean palaces of
Jericho; and Rajak 2002 on 1 Macc. as constituting an archaizing Jewish 'invented tradition'. Regev
2012 emphasizes the traditionalist self-presentation of the Hasmoneans.

[15] Very weakly confirmed for Galilee by Syon 2006.

very brief reign of Aristobulus – the first Hasmonean to assume the royal title – (*Ant.* 13.301–19),[16] and concluded with the gradual conquest by Jannaeus of the cities of the Palestinian coast (except Askalon, which was protected from conquest by the fact that it was the property of the Hasmoneans' allies, the Ptolemies) and the desert fringe. Our information about the fate of these districts is sketchy, but Josephus appears to indicate that Hyrcanus offered the Idumaeans the choice of becoming Jews or leaving their land;[17] in Samaria, Hyrcanus destroyed the Samaritans' temple of Yahweh on Mount Gerizim near Shechem and probably regarded this as sufficient to transform the Israelite Samaritans into Jews, loyal to Jerusalem (Shatzman 2005, following S. Schwartz 1993a). The valley, which was the most important wheat-growing region of the country, had probably been a royal estate inhabited by enserfed peasants; what became of them after conquest is unknown. Aristobulus offered the Galileans the same choice his father had offered the Idumaeans. Modern scholars often assume that these areas were colonized by Judaeans, but, plausible though this idea is, no ancient source says or implies as much; archaeology is suggestive – not surprisingly the strongest evidence comes from fortified settlements – but not probative (Leibner 2012). How Jannaeus disposed of the Greek cities depends on the reading of a single sentence in Josephus' *Jewish Antiquities*; some manuscripts have the word *ouk* (not) in the sentence, while others lack it, reversing the meaning: either Jannaeus did or did not normally insist that the cities convert (*Ant.* 13.395–7)!

CAUSES AND CONSEQUENCES

Modern scholars have been divided on the Hasmoneans' reasons for undertaking the project of territorial expansion and how in fact it proceeded. It has even been argued that it was not conquest and forced conversion at all, but the creation of a coalition of non-Greek Palestinians bound by the shared practice of male circumcision (and so perhaps a shared or shareable myth of Abrahamic descent) – an hypothesis sustainable only if the Greek cities were not judaized too (Kasher 1988). But Josephus unambiguously describes military campaigns and conquests, and though he was capable of grotesque inaccuracy it seems reasonable to give him some limited credit in this case. There was to be sure some element of volition in the

---

[16] Leibner 2012 demonstrates that it was an extended process likely to have begun before Aristobulus' reign.

[17] Most important in the massive bibliography on this episode: S. Cohen 1999a; Shatzman 2005. See also, S. Schwartz 2007; Eckhardt 2012.

submission and conversion of the Idumaeans *et al.*; their territories were not devastated, their great families retained their leading roles, and eventually rose to positions of influence in the kingdom in general; the conversion for the most part 'took'. To be sure, there was resistance both active and passive – we have evidence for example of an influx of Idumaeans into Egypt in the late second century BCE (Rappaport 1969) – but Idumaeans and Galilaeans, though not Samaritans, remained Jews for ever after. Nevertheless, the annexed territories were probably subjected to Judaea, not made its equal partners, and it is hard to see why and how the leaders of the territories would simply have yielded to the Hasmoneans without some element of violent force in the encounter. It may be best to think of the Hasmonean expansion as a miniaturized version of the Roman expansion; the territories were conquered – the Hasmonean principality was surely the most powerful and militarily experienced in the region aside from their rivals the Nabataeans – but their leaders were then invited into junior partnership, facilitated by the fact that the non-Greek peoples of Palestine did share many practices, and at least some of them probably claimed descent from the same ancient patriarchs as the Jews. Abraham and Isaac were the ancestors of the Idumaeans, too, and their traditional burial place, the Cave of the Machpelah in Hebron, was in Idumaean territory. The idea that alliance entailed (one-sided) cultural compromise may have been partly borrowed from the Greeks, though it may also have had a pre-Hellenistic history among the Jews. To the extent that the people of the conquered districts were willing to accept this arrangement, they were then entitled to participate in the next wave of conquests, their loyalty to the new dynasty thereby secured by plunder and gifts of land.

There was no precedent for such behaviour in Jewish history. The conversions of the Idumaeans, Galilaeans and possibly some of the coastal Greeks constitute the first historical cases of conversion to Judaism, though there are some earlier literary accounts which present conversion in a very different way – as an act of personal dedication on the part of someone who had come to recognize the unique power of the God of Israel (this is much closer to –indeed the source of – the models of religious conversion familiar to us). The territorial expansion is also difficult to parallel. These facts have led scholars to speculate about religious factors in the motivation of the Hasmoneans, which is certainly possible; for example, it is often stated that the Hasmoneans wished to purify the entire land of Israel of idolatry. Of course we may also consider more mundane explanations. The Hasmoneans expanded because they could; they were highly warlike and aggressive, stronger and better organized than the neighbouring districts, and there was no imperial authority to keep them in check. But they were not strong enough to impose on their neighbours a condition of absolute subjection, or had other reasons for refraining from doing so, and chose tense and unequal alliance instead. That non-Jews, by adopting the worship of the God of Israel, could become not simply pious but Jewish was an idea already extant in circles near those of the Hasmoneans, and had begun developing even earlier. The author of the book of Ruth believed its eponymous heroine could join the *'am* – people or clan – of the Judahites by leaving her father's gods and worshipping the God of Israel, without actually altering her technical 'citizenship' – she remained a Moabite while adhering to the people of Judah; likewise, the Idumaeans who 'became' *Ioudaioi* also remained Idumaean. Some scholars have seen behind the idea that a change in behaviour might lead to a formal change in status the influence of Greek ideas about citizenship. However, none of this explains why the Hasmoneans opted for this approach. There is perhaps something to the idea that alliance for the Jews had come to mean that the allies had to compromise their own religious practices ever more fully to accommodate those of the Jews.[18]

The consequences of the expansion were so fundamental that our main source, Josephus, a Judaean priest who was born a century and a half after the reign of John Hyrcanus, was largely blind to them, leaving us to speculate about how the expansion had changed things. But Josephus wrote about one of the consequences in great detail, and this was the swift rise in importance of some of the leading families of the annexed districts, the best known being the Idumaean family of Herod, whose grandfather Antipas is already described as an ally of Alexander Jannaeus only a few years after the judaization of his district (Josephus, *Ant.* 14.8–10) They surely had counterparts in other districts, but the meteoric rise of the Idumaean Antipatrids in the first century BCE has tended to eclipse the competition. We can in any case say that, whatever the Hasmoneans' intentions had been, they tended to rule the new districts 'patrimonially', that is, through a set of unequal 'friendships', or what the Romans would have called *clientela*, with their great men. These in turn are occasionally attested as generals serving the Hasmoneans, and soon enough as being in direct competition with their patrons when the dynasty began its collapse in 67 BCE.

---

[18] There is a thorough account with up-to-date bibliography (though it excludes items written in Hebrew, like the fundamental Shatzman 2005) in Dąbrowa 2010: 70–7. My account here follows S. Schwartz 2001 as elaborated in S. Schwartz 2007. The fundamental discussion of the early history of conversion to Judaism remains S. Cohen 1999a; Eckhardt 2012 provides some updating.

That the Idumaeans *et al.* were not simply subjected to the Hasmoneans but also became *Ioudaioi* implies that they were expected to submit to the authority of the priests and of other officials who administered the central Judaean religious institutions and, conversely, that they were expected to abandon their own. There is little evidence about how this proceeded; it is obvious that it was a gradual and for a long time partial process. Josephus mentions an attempt to revive the traditional Idumaean religion in the reign of the Idumaean Herod, nipped in the bud by the king himself, whose identification with Judaism was quite complete, notwithstanding his reputation as a Roman collaborator (*Ant.* 15.252–66; S. Cohen 1999a: 13–24; Eckhardt 2012). Private devotion indubitably survived, aided by the survival of the Edomite religion in Egypt and Nabataea. Furthermore, even Jewish-identified Idumaeans and Galilaeans showed clear signs of ambivalence. Many Judaeans regarded both Herod and Jesus of Nazareth as sinners, and tensions between the various ethnic groups sometimes led to violence, as we will see. Nevertheless, in the aggregate, one of the effects of the expansion was to swell the number of people technically under the authority of the priests, required to pay the taxes which supported them, and make donations and pilgrimages to the Jerusalem temple.[19] The Hasmonean expansion helped make Jewish Palestine more dynamic, and had a powerful, initially positive, impact on the economies of Jerusalem and Judaea. But it was probably a factor in raising tensions in the long term both within the Jewish community of Palestine and between it and its neighbours, whether they were country people who had avoided judaization or citizens of the eventually restored Greek cities of the coast and the Decapolis, which emerged as hotbeds of anti-Jewish feeling.

Like the process of judaization itself, these developments took several decades, and their impact was enhanced and complicated by the arrival on the scene of the Romans, who would rule the country with three very brief interruptions (one caused by native revolt, the other two by foreign invasion) from 63 BCE until the Arab conquest of Palestine in 638 CE.

CIVIL WAR AND THE ARRIVAL OF ROME

Before Alexander Jannaeus died in 76 BCE he did something common among Hellenistic kings but nearly unknown among Israelite and Jewish

---

[19] D. Schwartz 1990: 124–30 claims to identify a 'priestly' view that rejected the validity of conversion and refused sacrifices and some gifts from gentiles, including proselytes. Perhaps a rigoristic minority held such a view but it was not the 'priestly' view *tout court*, since the conversions were imposed by a priestly family and massively benefited the priests above all.

rulers: he left the throne to his wife, though he had two competent adult sons (Josephus, *Ant.* 13.398–404). The expansion ended with Salome Alexandra (76–67 BCE), because no further expansion was possible. To the south lay the desert, to the west the sea, to the east the powerful Nabataeans and to the north the terrifying Tigranes of Armenia, who ruled, in conjunction with his father-in-law Mithridates VI of Pontus, as far south as the vicinity of the current Israel–Lebanon border, having replaced the moribund Seleucids as the great power in the area (*Ant.* 13.419–21). Women were not permitted to serve in the Jerusalem temple, whatever their ancestry; Salome gave the job of high priest to her older son Hyrcanus, and tensions between him and his brother Aristobulus rose even before the queen's death. Both princes had alliances with leading families of the newly annexed territories (*Ant.* 13.405–32). Presumably they had other alliances too, with Judaean officials, priestly factions, etc., but curiously Josephus never mentions these. Hyrcanus was allied with Antipater, a leading Idumaean, and his sons (*Ant.* 14.8), and Aristobulus apparently with leading Ituraeans (an Arab tribe which dominated Galilee and the Beq'a valley of Lebanon; *Ant.* 13.427). Alexandra designated Hyrcanus her heir, but Aristobulus immediately rejected this arrangement, and a thirty-year war of succession/civil war began. When Pompey conquered Syria in 65 BCE both factions appealed to his representative M. Aemilius Scaurus for support (*Ant.* 14.29–33), and when he arrived in Palestine himself in 63, he recognized Hyrcanus, not as king but as high priest and ethnarch of a much reduced territory centred on Judaea and Idumaea. The rest of the country was restored to the Greek cities which had once controlled it or, in unurbanized areas, placed under direct Roman rule (*Ant.* 14.73–6).[20]

This arrangement was short-lived, because Roman rule in Syria proved highly unstable in a period when the Roman Senate was itself degenerating into a condition of civil war, a fact which revived and fostered the Judaean civil war for decades to come. Indeed, Roman rule in Palestine had a nearly two-century-long period of adjustment, and its beginnings were inauspicious. It began in betrayal: the Hasmoneans' alliance with the Roman Senate was almost a century old when Pompey seized and dismantled their kingdom. The general furthermore behaved in ways which reminded some Judaeans of the worst Seleucid misbehaviour, casually touring the innermost rooms of the Jerusalem temple, even the holy of holies which only the high priest was permitted to enter only on the Day

[20] Josephus, *Ant.* 14 provides the primary account of the Hasmonean civil wars; see Schürer-Vermes 1.233–86; D. Schwartz 1994; Bellemore 1999.

of Atonement. He then either did or (more likely) did not add insult to injury by plundering the temple treasury, depending on which ancient writer one chooses to believe (no: *Ant.* 14.64–73, supported by Cicero, *Pro Flacco* 28:67; yes: Cassius Dio 27.16.4). Pompey's new arrangements certainly are ominous in retrospect, since they reveal that the new rulers were willing to go farther than the Persians or the Macedonians, who, aside from Antiochus IV, rarely consciously did more than tinker with the status quo, while the Romans cavalierly created entirely new political realities.

In any case, the Jewish civil war continued until 40 BCE, during which period Antipater's sons emerged as leading figures, Antipater himself having been assassinated in 42 BCE (*Ant.* 14.280–4); but both sides were able to draw on Roman senatorial support as well as on local clienteles. This may in fact be our most important lesson from the civil war. Josephus and other ancient Jewish writers often implied or even claimed that the Jews were loyal only to God and to their religious institutions, and were immune to the attractions of mere social institutions like patronage. This view is implausible a priori – such social institutions were not usually optional in a premodern economy, and religious institutions could rarely compensate. In the case of the Jews, biblical charity could not do all the redistributive work that fixed relationships of social dependency could. On the other hand, there is some truth to Josephus' view as well; these relationships clearly were not as pervasive among the Jews as among some of their neighbours, and could often be quite fraught, as will be clear in our discussion of Herod in the coming pages. Yet in the account of the civil war Josephus breaks out of character and shows the Jews behaving, admittedly in an abnormally unstable situation, like everyone else in their world – constituting the entourages of armed grandees out of senses of personal loyalty which did not necessarily, notwithstanding the attempts of some modern historians to find religious elements in the choice of whether to support Hyrcanus or Aristobulus, have any further ideological components (Shaw 1993; S. Schwartz 2010).

In 40 BCE, the Parthians, who had long since taken over the Seleucid Empire east of the Euphrates river, invaded and conquered Syria and Palestine (*Ant.* 14.330–6). Both Judaean parties initially appealed for support to the Parthian general Pakoros, but, while the more powerful Roman factions had normally supported Hyrcanus, Pakoros chose Aristobulus' heir Antigonus, whom he named king of the traditional Hasmonean realm, and the Hyrcanian faction was destroyed (*Ant.* 14.337–64). Its aged leader was caught and his nephew bit off his ears (*Ant.* 14.365–6, with

Jewish War parallel), both to humiliate him and to make him ritually unfit to serve as high priest. He was then sent off to exile among the Jews of Mesopotamia where, according to Josephus, he was received with great sympathy and respect. Some of the Antipatrids died in battle, but Herod, who had been personally cultivating the patronage of Mark Antony for several years, fled to Rome (*Ant.* 14.379–80). There Antony and Octavian, in a temporary lull in hostilities, joined forces to introduce Herod to the Senate, which voted to appoint Herod king, though apparently without specifying a territory (381–5). Since Herod's native country was not ruled by the Romans at the time, what Herod's coronation meant in practice was that he accepted the job of helping the Romans reconquer southern Syria; presumably the details of Herod's territory would await the completion of the task.

CHAPTER 3

Herod to Florus

HEROD

Herod is perhaps the only figure in ancient Jewish history who has been loathed equally by Jewish and Christian posterity, because both Talmudic rabbis (100–600 CE) and evangelists and church fathers remembered him as bloodthirsty and tyrannical; the rabbis, for good measure, also recalled an episode of necrophilia. It does indeed seem not unlikely that Herod was on the whole an unlovable person, and even his court historian Nicolaus of Damascus could not conceal his degeneration into paranoid cruelty in old age.[1] Herod is the best attested of all ancient Jews, of all Roman client kings, probably one of the best attested of all Romans, Josephus having devoted over four books of his oeuvre to the king's life and career (*Jewish War* 1; *Ant.* 14–17), though some of the information is contradictory and probably much of the rest is unreliable. Still, we can say much more about him than bland expressions of unnuanced moral judgement.[2]

We should begin precisely by putting some of that moral judgement back in its historical place. Herod was ruthless and cruel, but he was the heir of such figures as Aristobulus I, who murdered nearly his entire family, and Alexander Jannaeus, the aforementioned king who drank cocktails on his balcony together with his concubines as thousands of his subjects were executed below; and he was the contemporary and client of such figures as Pompey, Julius Caesar, Mark Antony and Gaius Octavius (Octavian Caesar/Augustus) whose tendency to mass murder dwarfed anything to be found in the east. What all these men, including Herod, shared was a lack of legitimacy – all lived in a turbulent era of political realignment in the Mediterranean basin, in conditions which favoured the extremely violent.

---

[1] Nicolaus was Josephus' main source for the later Hasmoneans and especially Herod: Toher 2001.
[2] The basic account in English remains Schürer-Vermes I; landmarks in a massive bibliography: Otto 1913; Schalit 1969; Richardson 1996. Some recent work has been eccentric: Kokkinos 1998; Kasher and Witztum 2007; Rocca 2008; Günther 2005.

In the best cases such people might learn to overcome their tendencies, but a widely publicized potential to wreak havoc was certainly a powerful political asset even for the greatest state-builder of the time, Augustus.

Though his stage was a smaller one, Herod's role was still exceedingly complex and difficult. He had some inherited Idumaean clientele (*Ant.* 14.398) and had won some supporters in Galilee when he served as Hyrcanus' strong-arm there in the 40s (especially among the 'Syrians': *Ant.* 14.160; *Jewish War* 1.205; but cf. 14.395), but he would also rule a kingdom which included the highly resistant Judaeans, themselves divided by political loyalties and religious inclinations; the Samaritans, who were drifting back, possibly with Herod's help, into their traditional separation from the Jews; the inhabitants of the Greek cities which had been restored by Pompey; and the unurbanized 'Syrians' of the Golan and Trachonitis – the rough country south of Damascus. He had to return a country which had endured thirty years of civil war to revenue-bearing condition, and solve an especially severe problem of brigandage – endemic in the aftermath of long periods of disturbance, and endemic even in otherwise peaceful times in the marginal desert-fringe zones which are so important a feature of the ecology of Palestine, trans-Jordan and southern Syria. Most crucially of all, he also had to retain the 'friendship' of his frightening *patroni*. Given that Herod's first ten years as king coincided with the final – and bloodiest – period of the Roman civil war, and that Herod's patron, Antony, eventually lost, this entailed much desperate tap-dancing on his part. Even in the peaceful period that followed, it was not a simple matter to maintain the goodwill of Augustus and his powerful son-in-law Marcus Agrippa. None of this palliates Herod's impressive moral inadequacies; but we should first of all recognize that Herod was not necessarily worse than his famous violent predecessors and contemporaries, but suffered from worse press for reasons presently to be explored; and, second, if we wish to understand his impact, we had best leave the moral issues to one side. I am advocating not rehabilitating Herod, but evaluating the surprisingly complex influence of his actions on his subjects, neighbours and masters.

Herod and the Roman legionary commander Gaius Sosius spent nearly three years reconquering Palestine, a process which relied heavily on Herod's ability to mobilize local manpower (*Ant.* 14.394–8; cf. 410). The campaign concluded with a siege of Jerusalem in 37 BCE at the successful conclusion of which Herod could barely restrain his troops, who were mostly Idumaeans and Galilaeans, from massacring the inhabitants of the town (14.479). All the parties involved regarded themselves as Jews, yet the episode reveals the tensions just under the surface between the Judaeans and their newly Jewish neighbours, and anticipates the difficult relationship Herod had throughout his reign with Judaea and with its institutional establishment.

Josephus' accounts of Herod's reign concentrate on his disastrous family life. Herod had a total of ten wives, many of them concurrently, making him the only Jew in the Hellenistic and Roman periods known to have practised polygamy (in itself odd, since both biblical and rabbinic texts take the legitimacy and diffusion of the practice for granted; Katzoff 1995). Josephus claims that Herod married his wives for their beauty, not their connections (*Jewish War* 1.477). Though this is conceivably true of some about whom nothing else is known, several of them manifestly constituted links to constituencies Herod needed to pacify or reward. His most important wife was Mariamme (Miriam), granddaughter of both Hyrcanus II and Aristobulus II, and so a full-blooded Hasmonean who brought with her a complex of alliances and friendships which Herod can only have viewed as an asset;[3] her mother Alexandra, for example, was an intimate of Cleopatra's. Still more importantly, she could, and did, provide Herod with Hasmonean heirs, and so offered him the hope of legitimacy among that segment of the Judaean elite which had eventually made its peace with the earlier dynasty. The same Mariamme and her surviving relatives were also Herod's most dangerous enemies (Josephus tells a story of love tragically doomed by the mischief of resentful relatives; the aforementioned rabbinic story – written many centuries after the fact – of Herod's love of Mariamme's preserved corpse is an uncanny, perhaps parodic, echo of this: Feintuch 2011). He may not have been wrong to think that Mariamme and her mother were plotting against him, especially after he had had her younger brother Aristobulus 'III' murdered (no one can have believed the claim that it was a swimming mishap: *Ant.* 15.50–6)[4] for serving as high priest to unnerving popular acclaim. And so Herod executed them too (*Ant.* 15.232–52), and also the aged Hyrcanus II, recalled from exile and suspected, implausibly, of hatching plots with his friend King Malikos of Nabataea (*Ant.* 15.165–78). Herod and Mariamme had two sons, given the significant dynastic names of Alexander and Aristobulus, and he eventually suspected them of plotting as well, goaded by his son from his first marriage, Antipater, who resented the dynastic primacy of his younger half-brothers (his

---

[3] She was allegedly betrothed to Herod before the Parthian invasion (*Ant.* 14.300).

[4] Subject of still another magnificent poem of Cavafy, "Aristoboulos", quoted as epigraph of Kokkinos 1998.

mother was a 'commoner'); and so they were executed later in Herod's reign (*Ant.* 16.392–4), as was eventually Antipater (*Ant.* 17.187). But they all had surviving children, and the sons of Mariamme sired enduring dynasties of Roman client kings, some of whom were absorbed into the Roman senatorial elite. The descendants of Aristobulus retained their Jewish connections, while those of Alexander let them lapse. The last known Hasmoneans are some early to mid-second-century Roman senators from Asia Minor who served in the college of *quindecimviri sacris faciundis*; so the descendants of the men who had fought to purify Jerusalem of idolatry supervised the municipal temples and priesthoods of the city of Rome (Kokkinos 1998: 254–8).

Josephus' source, the Herodian lackey Nicolaus of Damascus, had transformed Herod's family story into tragedy or rather melodrama in the hope of softening its brutality. Josephus mobilized it to dramatize his conviction that Herod ultimately failed. New states must be built on the foundation of friendships and alliances, and Herod's home life exemplified his deficiencies in the skills necessary for this. He never won over the essential constituencies at home and though he had more success in maintaining the goodwill of his shifting corps of *patroni*, these too eventually all tired of him. But we can easily see that the story was more complex. Herod was an imperfect husband and father (Augustus is said to have joked that Herod's pigs were safer than his sons),[5] but he was a consummately skilful client. Josephus provides an excellent illustration of this in the remarkable story of Herod's behaviour during and after the Battle of Actium, the final battle of the Roman Civil War, in 31 BCE. Herod had long been a fixture of the Antonian faction, largely because Antony had been more powerful in the east than Octavian, but he still refrained from sending troops and ships to support his patron in his final battle. At its conclusion, he presented himself as a supplicant to the victor Octavian, apologizing to the future *princeps* for failing to provide adequate support to Antony (*Ant.* 15.187–93)! (The story has been dismissed as implausible by many scholars, but it is entirely plausible; whether it is also true, there is no way of knowing.) Both Herod and Octavian understood the thrust of the apology. Herod had done nothing to harm Octavian, but the latter could nevertheless count on the king's full loyalty. And so Octavian pardoned Herod and welcomed him into his *amicitia*. Likewise, Herod brought great skill to bear on the far more complex project of winning over his constituents, and was surprisingly successful. Herod never truly succeeded

⁵ In a very late source: Macrobius *Saturnalia* 2.4.11.

in transforming his alliances into an institutional state, but their range was impressive nonetheless (S. Schwartz 2000).

Like his new friend Octavian, Herod proceeded on all fronts simultaneously. He provided his Roman friends not only with tribute[6] but with honours and memorials, founding cities and fortresses in their names (Caesarea, Sebaste, Agrippeion, Antonia, Julias – Schürer-Vermes 1.287–329), thereby breaking with Hasmonean practice. At Jerusalem he introduced Roman-style euergetism – building a theatre and an amphitheatre, and establishing 'isactian' games of the traditional Greco-Roman type, featuring footraces, dramatic competitions and wild beast hunts – with mixed success (Spielman 2010). But he also practised on a vast scale traditionally Jewish concern for the weak, the starving, the indigent (S. Schwartz 2010: 96–103). He extravagantly funded the imperial cult in his newly founded cities of Caesarea and Sebaste, and the Olympic games and other symbols of Hellenism, but also rebuilt the Jerusalem temple and tirelessly used his connections at Rome to defend the interests of vulnerable Jewish communities in Asia Minor and elsewhere (extrapolating from *Ant.* 16.27–65; Richardson 1996: 174–214). In fact it is possible to discern a broad tendency, if not a policy, in Herod's actions. Among the Jews, Herod worked to bring about integration, within his kingdom, in the Jewish world as a whole, and between the Jews and the Roman Empire (Baltrusch 2009). Among his subjects, though, his actions tended to sharpen divisions, between Jews (including Judaeans, Idumaeans and Galilaeans), Samaritans, who now re-emerge as a body separate from the Jews, Greeks and Syrians. The only thing integrating the Jewish and non-Jewish components of Herod's kingdom was loyalty to his person.

Crucial features of his attempt to integrate the Jews were his reconstruction of the Jerusalem temple (the temple of 'Zerubbabel' was demolished, not refurbished), and his reformation of the high priesthood. The new temple was one of the largest structures in the Roman world (Jacobson 2007); and Herod transformed the high priesthood from a hereditary to an appointed office (Rocca 2008: 281–7; he lacked the proper ancestry to assume the position himself, and strongly disfavoured in his appointments traditional Jerusalem aristocrats, after the failed appointment of his young Hasmonean brother-in-law). These, along with construction of a large harbour in the new city of Caesarea Maritima and Herod's defence of diaspora Jewish communities, were part of a probably conscious effort to transform what had previously been small-scale, specifically local Judaean

---

[6] A controversial point (Labbé 2012: 49–54; Gabba 1999); at any rate, gifts and bribes.

institutions, into generally Jewish ones, there to serve the interests of a greatly expanded Jewish population both inside (due to the Hasmonean conquests) and outside (due to growth of the diaspora) of Palestine (S. Schwartz 2001: 42–8; Raban and Holum 1996; S. Schwartz 2009a).

But the character of the great port city of Caesarea reveals some of the ways in which Herod tried to promote integration into the Roman world. Though the city's population was probably divided roughly evenly between Jews and 'Greeks', the city was emphatically Roman in character (Levine 1975: 15–33). A sea-side temple of Roma and Augustus stood on a platform constructed to be the first thing Jewish pilgrims, among others, saw as they entered the harbour (Holum 2004; Raban 2009). Likewise at Jerusalem itself Herod established quinquennial games perhaps modelled on the Actian games, complete with gladiatorial competitions and wild beast hunts – among the very earliest appearance of such entertainments in the eastern Empire – and built an amphitheatre to house them (*Ant.* 15.267–79; Patrich 2009). Though Herod was strongly Jewish-identified, he also lavished benefactions on the non-Jewish regions of his kingdom, but the standard practices of Roman euergetism were far less fraught there (Richardson 1996: 198–201).

CONSEQUENCES OF HEROD'S REIGN

The authors of the Gospels were, by and large, imperfectly informed about conditions in Palestine in the early first century CE; certainly they all lived a few generations later, and probably not in Palestine. Yet they conveyed effectively something of the scene, especially when it shifts to Jerusalem towards the conclusion of the story. Theirs is the Jerusalem of the great pilgrimage festivals, packed with Jews from all over the world, always poised on the brink, ready to spiral into disorder and violence, with Jewish authorities and Roman soldiers struggling to maintain the peace; yet also a scene of intense, if factionalized, solidarities, and powerful pious yearning and devotion (Philo, *Spec. Leg.* 1.68).

Such scenes, replicated in the writings of Josephus and in later rabbinic story-telling, never occurred before Herod's reign. Most basically, they were enabled by Herod's reconstruction of the Jerusalem temple – its tremendous size presumably intended not only to demonstrate Herod's piety, but also to accommodate expanded traffic – and by his improvements of the harbour at Caesarea, and of security on the roads and paths through the reduction of brigandage. They were also enabled by the relatively peaceful and secure conditions that prevailed in the Mediterranean basin and the Near East with the establishment of the Principate (27 BCE), which eased long-distance travel, even from beyond the borders of the Empire, where a large Jewish settlement remained in Mesopotamia, now part of the Parthian kingdom. All these factors allowed a Jewish population greatly expanded by the growth of the diaspora and the Hasmonean conquests to flood into Jerusalem on a regular basis.

But many of the details of the scene reflect less direct consequences of Herod's actions. As a result of pilgrimage, but also of Herod's cultivation of friendship with the main diaspora Jewish communities, scattered Jewish communities probably never shared more, or were in closer contact with each other and with their religious centre, until modern times (cf. J. Feldman 2006). Contact and devotion went hand in hand; from an oration of Cicero we learn that even before Herod Jews in Asia Minor collected gold and silver to send to Jerusalem (*Pro Flacco* 28.66–9), but this now became even more common, and pilgrims themselves brought money to spend on food, sacrifices and lodging, not to mention pious generosity to the priests, the poor and the temple itself. Jerusalem was awash in money to an unprecedented extent (Ben-Ami and Tchekhanovets 2011), and the money funded not only the temple staff and the poor, but provisioners, construction and maintenance workers (Josephus tells us that, when construction was completed in 64 CE, 18,000 labourers were left unemployed: *Ant.* 20.219–22; we should not take the number literally), people who had rooms or outdoor space for visitors to rent, plus pedlars, hawkers, frauds religious and secular, among many others (Sanders 1992: 125–45; Goodman 2006: 59–67). Manufactured goods – ceramic lamps and stone vessels – flowed out of Jerusalem, as we now know, but there seems little doubt about which way the balance of trade tilted.[7] The economy of Judaea necessarily became highly inflationary, and real-estate prices rose in a way that rendered traditional Mediterranean-style subsistence dry agriculture impractical, which in turn swelled the ranks of the urban poor.[8] Josephus also tells us about gangs of toughs for hire in mid-first-century Jerusalem, who went to work for the local aristocrats who

---

[7] See the suggestive Adan-Bayewitz 2008: a large percentage of 'Herodian' lamps used in Galilee and nearby areas can be shown to have been imported from potteries at Horvat Ha-Motza and Binyenei Ha-Umah, near Jerusalem, but coins and common pottery in and near Galilee followed more predictable patterns, distributed locally within a small radius from the point of production. At 'Jewish sites' (Sepphoris, Jotapata and Gamala) the percentage of imported lamps is higher than at pagan ones (Dor and Scythopolis), though it is substantial even in the latter. In an oral presentation, Adan-Bayewitz has suggested that limestone vessels found in Galilee were also Judaean imports.

[8] On the economy of Herod's kingdom, see the detailed, though rather positivistic and optimistic, discussion of Ariel and Fontanille 2012: 11–20.

were in increasingly violent competition with one another (*Ant.* 20.180–1; 206–7; 213–14).

THE SECTS

Many were enriched by the flood of silver, though to be sure much of it went up in smoke on the temple's altars; even so, victims had to be purchased and wood cut and hauled from ever greater distances, and people got paid for this. Sectarianism, a self-conscious pietistic self-differentiation among Jewish elites and sub-elites, which was characteristic of the Jews especially in Judaea in the first century, was a paradoxical effect of this process.[9] It required the existence of large numbers of relatively well-to-do underemployed young men whose intense dedication to the ideological core of Judaism reflected the fact that Judaism's success had made them rich, freeing them from the need to worry about anything else (Baumgarten 1997).

Sectarianism was one of the key features of predestruction Palestinian Judaism, one which has been eccentrically interpreted in the past (Sanders 1992: 315–491). All discussion must begin with the fact that we know very little about the phenomenon – just enough to have the impression that it was important. Josephus names three sects: Pharisees, Sadducees, and Essenes (*Life* 1.10; *Jewish War* 2.119–61; *Ant.* 18.18–22); and in one polemical passage, he lists without naming a fourth one, apparently a group of anti-Roman revolutionaries, who certainly did not belong on the list (*Ant.* 18.23). The New Testament and rabbinic literature likewise mention Pharisees and Sadducees, though apparently not Essenes, but some rabbinic texts and many early Christian accounts of 'heresies' add many more groups to the list, some of which may have even existed. One sect which certainly existed but is not mentioned by Josephus is the earliest Christians. One senses that Josephus' three had enhanced status; they were more 'official' than the various little splinter groups. That certainly is how Josephus characterizes them, and this may mean that they were more acceptable in the sorts of 'middle-' and upper-class Judaean and Jerusalemite circles to which Josephus himself had belonged, whereas other groups were smaller, associated with individual charismatics and little-institutionalized (like the pre-crucifixion followers of Christ, or those of John the Baptist), with the non-Judaean districts of the country (the Christians again), or non-elites (summarizing S. Schwartz 2001: 91–8).

---

[9] Definitional issues: Chalcraft 2007.

The 'main' sects in the first century shared not only a social profile (Jerusalemite or Judaean, elite and sub-elite, male, especially attractive to youthful dabblers), but also a history: all seem to have arisen around the time of, and in reaction to, the Maccabean Revolt and the rise of the Hasmonean dynasty – perhaps in opposition to the latter. They all eventually made their peace with the usurpers to a greater or lesser degree. Even the Dead Sea sect, which was probably an offshoot of the Essenes, the most extreme and countercultural of the three, had largely peaceful relations with the authorities after some episodes of apparently very mild persecution early in the group's history. Indeed, in light of what we now know from archaeology about the immediate vicinity of Qumran, the site's sectarian splinter group lived in an area which was inhabited, farmed, fortified and relatively well travelled, especially in periods of tension with the nearby Nabataeans – a magnificently forbidding site nearer to civilization than we might have expected.[10] Pharisees and Sadducees, for their part, were quickly co-opted by the new dynasty, and came to form components of the kingdom's legal and judicial establishments; indeed, in the second and early first centuries BCE there is no reason to think of Pharisees and Sadducees as sects. Rather, they were primarily opposing schools of legal interpretation among the bureaucracy. We cannot be sure whether any of Josephus' comments about the differences between the groups applies to their early history or only to the first century CE, but a document preserving a precious bit of legal polemic found among the Dead Sea scrolls and dating perhaps to the earlier first century BCE does suggest to us that the Sadducees, along with the Essenes, may have preserved some distinctive traditions of pre-Hasmonean legal practice – their very name suggests an association with the Zadokite high priests – whereas the Pharisees introduced innovations. Behind this fact may be the theoretical distinction Josephus ascribes to the later groups: the Sadducees accepted the legal authority of the text of the Torah alone. Contrary to a view once popular, this does not mean that the Sadducees were biblical 'literalists'; no living

---

[10] The traditional consensus about Qumran – that the site was for some of its history a monastic settlement of an extremist branch of the Essene sect described by Philo, Josephus and the Elder Pliny, that the community was responsible for collecting if not composing or copying the scrolls found in the adjacent caves, that monastic Essenes were celibate males, but another branch conducted their sectarian lives dedicated to holiness and purity while living in normative domestic arrangements, that all Essenes had complex and somewhat fraught relations with the political authorities and the Jerusalem temple – is battered and bowed but still standing with some modification: most important is that the beginning of the monastic settlement at Qumran has been pushed down to the first century BCE from the second, throwing the origin of the movement in the Maccabean period into question. For full discussion see Collins 2010; on the geographical context, Magness 2002: 210–25; Hirschfeld and Ariel 2005.

law-code can be applied to the letter, but must necessarily be subjected to interpretation. Josephus means only to contrast the Sadducees with their competitors; the Pharisees had a source of law in addition to the text of the Torah, but somehow related to it, called in Greek the 'tradition of the fathers' (*paradosis tôn paterôn*), preserved orally (Cf. Regev 2005: 203–46).

Beyond this, little is known about the groups. Josephus tells us that the Sadducees believed in free will, the Essenes only in fate, and the Pharisees in some mixture; the latter two believed in the survival of the soul after death and/or bodily resurrection of the dead, and eternal reward and punishment, whereas the Sadducees rejected these beliefs. From the Gospels we learn that the Pharisees were careful about tithing and ritual purity (Matt. 23.23–6), though these concerns were probably shared by all groups with priestly associations, including the Sadducees and Essenes (Regev 2005, exhaustively). Probably a significant proportion of the early rabbinic law preserved in the Mishnah and the Tosefta (see below) was inherited from the Pharisees, but no one has yet produced a convincing method for isolating the various sources of rabbinic law, so we cannot advance far beyond such unsatisfactory generalizations. Furthermore, we know of only one Pharisee whose writings survive, but the apostle Paul was not a typical Pharisee. Many scholars regard Josephus himself as a Pharisee, but if we read his comment on the matter closely, we can see that he is careful to identify himself not as a member of the sect, but only as a 'fellow traveller' (*Life* 10–12; Mason 1989). Josephus describes the Essenes as living lives of monastic seclusion in desert settlements but also as living amidst urban communities; even in the latter, they were devoted to utter simplicity of lifestyle, sharing of property and extreme legal rigour. If the Dead Sea sect was a subgroup of Essenes, then we also know that their internal organization was rigidly hierarchical, their cosmology was dualistic, and they lived in permanent expectation of the imminence of the final apocalyptic battle between the forces of good and evil, which would result in the restoration of God's kingdom on earth (Collins 2010).

To return to politics, different Hasmonean rulers patronized different factions: John Hyrcanus first the Pharisees then the Sadducees (*Ant.* 13.288–98), Alexander Jannaeus only the Sadducees (*Ant.* 13.398–404); Salome Alexandra restored the Pharisees (*Ant.* 13.408–15).[11] Scholars' attempts to continue the story beyond the point where Josephus leaves it off – into the civil war and the reign of Herod – are misguided. Hyrcanus

---

[11] Collins 2010: 116 sets the Dead Sea Scrolls' memories of persecution in the reign of Alexandra, two generations later than prior convention. See in detail Regev 2005: 247–92.

and Aristobulus – who is said to have opposed the Pharisees in his mother's lifetime but not after (*Ant.* 13.423) – needed military manpower, not legal scholars, in their entourages, so Josephus is surely right to focus on the role of Antipater and his kind. The civil war marginalized the religious/legal organizations, and Herod kept them marginal by patronizing none of them; they were Judaean organizations and Herod tried to promote non-Judaeans in his kingdom. It was under Herod that Pharisees and Sadducees were finally transformed from bureaucratic organizations into proper sects – that is, organizations characterized by some type of pietistic religious extremism, by extraordinary devotion to the Torah, *vel sim.*, which is how Josephus presents them both in summary accounts and in historical narratives. Josephus also reports numbers for the Pharisees (6,000: *Ant.* 17.42) and for the Essenes (4,000; *Ant.* 18.21; same number in Philo, *Quod Omnis Probus* 75), and the numbers are amazingly high if correctly interpreted by remembering that the sects consisted of adult Judaean males (Pharisees and Sadducees married, Essenes usually did not). Thus, 6,000 Pharisees reflects a general population of close to 20,000, out of a general Judaean population of perhaps at most around 100,000. If Josephus' and Philo's numbers are correct within an order of magnitude, they suggest that the main sects were not peripheral organizations, certainly not within Judaea. This in turn confirms the view that the economy and society of Judaea were radically abnormal; that 20–25 per cent or more of adult males in Judaea belonged to a pietistic religious organization gives us a strong sense of the impact of Herod's projects in Palestine.

But it also suggests that there was the potential for things to go radically wrong. The competition between Roman and Jewish institutions was a zero-sum game, notwithstanding Herod's zealous romanization. The pilgrims to Jerusalem arriving at Caesarea could not pay their respects at the temple of Augustus and Roma that they saw as they sailed into the harbour. The more devotion to the Jerusalem temple and the Torah Herod's investments generated, the more the Jews would experience political marginalization and maladjustment in the Roman system, however much Herod was prepared to invest in the Jews' integration in that system.[12] It should be noted, too, that, though Herod's temple flourished, his theatre, amphitheatre, and 'isactian' games are never heard of again. The Roman version of politics, which relied heavily on thematized and valourized ideas of honour, reciprocity, monumentality, does seem – exactly as Josephus claimed – to have had less appeal to the Jews than Herod had

---

[12] The Jews' marginality is compellingly but somewhat differently explored in Avidov 2009.

hoped (S. Schwartz 2010). Many Jews to be sure were content to follow the advice the Gospels attribute to Jesus and, as we would say, compartmentalize – render unto Caesar what was his and unto God what was His. But as a national group the Jews could not easily be absorbed in the Roman system, especially because of the paradoxical impact of Herod's policies. In broad terms Herod may be compared to the rulers of some Arab oil states, who owe their positions to their congeniality to the western powers and do all they can to maintain their standing, but at the same time invest heavily in fundamentalist anti-western versions of Islam – because they always have to be concerned about shoring up their legitimacy at home, among other things. At any rate, it seems nearly certain that a large segment of the population of Jewish Palestine, especially the Jerusalemite elites and sub-elites who played a disproportionate role in the first Jewish revolt, experienced a process of radicalization in the course of the first century (see below), and one paradoxical cause of this was the policies of the integrationist Herod.

ARCHELAUS TO THE REVOLT (4 BCE–66 CE)

Much of the plotting and murderous violence that beset Herod's household in his final years focused on the question of succession, but in the event it was Augustus, not the king, who seized the right to dispose of Herod's property (Labbé 2012: 67–87). By 4 BCE the leading heirs were all dead, and the Hasmonean grandchildren were very young, which may be one reason Augustus split Herod's kingdom in three. The core, consisting of Samaria, Judaea and Idumaea, proved the most contentious; Galilee, given to Antipas (reigned 4 BCE–39 CE), and the mainly non-Jewish north-eastern portions of the kingdom, given to Philip (4 BCE–34 CE), appear to have been ruled calmly and peacefully for many decades. But Archelaus was generally unpopular, prone to violence, ineffective, and exiled by the emperor in 6 CE in response to a joint petition from the leading men among both Judaeans and Samaritans, some of whom had opposed Archelaus' appointment from the start. From this point on, the central regions of Palestine were ruled by a direct representative of the emperor of equestrian rank called first a praefect and after 44 CE a procurator (Gabba 1999: 134), who governed in conjunction with the senior Herodian, initially Antipas – to whom the emperor had granted administrative control over the Jerusalem temple and its huge treasury – and also with the Roman governor of Syria. Roman rule in the east had not yet settled into a standard pattern and still involved much improvisation and uncertainty.[13] Given the enduring connection between the Julio-Claudians and the Herodian family, probably Palestine was being held for a suitable heir (Gabba 1999: 141–2).

Yet the leading Hasmonean Herodian, Marcus Julius Agrippa, reached middle age before receiving the throne and he did so only as a personal favour from his friend Gaius (Caligula). In fact, Agrippa had grown up with Gaius' uncle Claudius – they were precise contemporaries and had both lived in Augustus' house, Claudius because Livia was his grandmother and Augustus his great-uncle, and Agrippa because the children of client kings were held in the imperial palace as privileged hostages whose position did not preclude the forming of friendships with the imperial children. Agrippa's reign began with the accession of Gaius in 38 and his grant of Philip's territory, and the expansion of his kingdom the following year when Agrippa secured the banishment of his uncle Antipas, and culminated with Claudius' grant of all his grandfather's territory plus some additional land farther north in Syria at his accession in 41. Josephus' account of the reign is sharply different from his account of Agrippa's prior career. Agrippa starts as an unscrupulous adventurer figure, Caligula's co-conspirator-in-chief (*Ant.* 18.143–256), magically transformed, like Shakespeare's Prince Hal, into a sober and pious king (*Ant.* 236–359; transition at 18.289–301). In fact his piety as king was so renowned that memory of it survived among the rabbis centuries later (Schürer-Vermes I: 442–54; Wilker 2007: 131–92).

This was so despite one of the last episodes of his life (44 CE), when he allowed himself to be acclaimed a god in the theatre of Caesarea Maritima (*Ant.* 19.343–50), and God's retribution was immediate and final. This episode makes it likely that, like his grandfather Herod, Agrippa was blessed with a talent for cultural flexibility, trying to appeal to whatever constituency happened to be present at the moment. Agrippa did so more convincingly among the Jews, including Judaeans, than his grandfather had done. Herod's generosity to the central Judaean institutions had been unparalleled, but this never convinced the Judaeans of his piety as opposed to his desire for honour and acclamation, while Agrippa's was far more limited, but somehow worked better; despite a youth spent at Rome Agrippa had mastered the code more effectively than Herod (S. Schwartz 2010). By the same token, he was less convincing than his grandfather had been in a Greek (as opposed to Roman) or Syrian setting – Josephus

---

[13] Note Labbé's (2012) massive – probably self-refuting – effort to provide clarity. Cf. Wilker 2007: 68–130; Schürer-Vermes I: 350–98.

describes celebrations at Caesarea and Sebaste at his death, and notes that the townspeople abused statues of Agrippa's daughters (*Ant.* 19.356–9); it is noteworthy that these existed in the first place, given what should have been Agrippa's attitude to images, though they appear on his coins.

Despite this, it seems likely that Agrippa's cultural chameleon act held things together while he was alive. Like his grandfather, he never transformed his diverse kingdom into a state, but elements of all sectors of the population were personally loyal to him – some Caesareans rejoiced at his death, but others had declared him a god. Herod's death had been followed by an explosive release of intercommunal and other tensions – some uprisings were led by Herodian troops who had not been paid in a long time; the reaction to Agrippa's death was less explosive, but the pace of development of intercommunal frictions accelerated. The interests of Jews, Greeks and Syrians in Palestine seemed increasingly irreconcilable, and the compromises involved in submission to Roman rule for a community whose native institutions were at the height of their power and prosperity seemed unacceptable to growing numbers.

After Agrippa's death, Judaea, Idumaea and Samaria returned to the control of the equestrian administrator now called 'procurator' in association with the Herodian overseer of the Jerusalem temple – initially Agrippa's brother Herod, whom Claudius had named king of the principality of Chalkis in the Beq'a valley of Lebanon, and later Agrippa's son Agrippa II, who inherited the northern half of his father's realm but never its core – and the governor of Syria (Wilker 2007: 192–205). Josephus' account of these last twenty years before the outbreak of the Great Revolt stresses the spiralling disorder and violence, but there is reason to be cautious in accepting this, at least until the very end of the period when violence was undoubtedly on the rise. Josephus sought to produce a narrative that would neatly and symmetrically account for the outbreak of the revolt, and he also happened to know more about the 40s, 50s and 60s than about any other period, having lived through those decades.[14] In truth, a rather high level of disorder and violence was simply normal in an empire where soldiers were thin on the ground outside the Rhine–Danube frontier regions, there were no police, and subjects were normally armed and reliant on 'self-help' (Nippel 1995: 100–12). What appeared intolerable to participants and victims might seem routine to people at the imperial centre – a hypothesis neatly proved by comparing Josephus' and Tacitus' accounts of the prefectship of Pontius Pilate. For Josephus

---

[14] Full discussion of scholarship: McLaren 1998; Goodman (1987 and 2007) is discussed below.

it constituted the pre-Agrippan low-point: Pilate engaged in constant provocation and the Jews responded, usually but not always, with violence and rioting (*Ant.* 18.55–89). No citizen of an orderly first-world state would ever choose to live in such an environment. This at any rate is the perspective from the provinces. By contrast, Tacitus, the Roman consular, devoted three words to Pilate's administration in Judaea: *sub Tiberio quies!* (Tacitus, *Hist.* 5.9.2).

We may speculate though that the nature of the disorder shifted. There was a resurgence of brigandage – like street crime in our world both a problem in itself and a symptom of other problems, some of them economic, perhaps in this case a symptom of inflationary land prices in Judaea. Josephus has ever more to report about intercommunal violence, including what amounted to a small war between Galileans and Judaeans, on one side, and Samaritans, on the other, in 52 CE, which was quelled with difficulty and led to the deposition of the procurator and the arrest and execution of many leading figures on both sides. Furthermore, there was a rise in tensions between Jews and 'Greeks', culminating in some very violent rioting and reported massacres in the early and middle 60s. In most places the Greeks are said to have massacred the Jews, but in Tiberias the opposite occurred and in Caesarea the sides were evenly matched, with disastrous results all around. Finally, Josephus reports factional rivalry among the Judaean high priests which occasionally turned violent as the factions hired armed thugs to attack each other (Schürer-Vermes 1.455–70). These factions consisted of the families, by now wealthy and powerful landowners but not necessarily famous for their piety, of the high priests appointed by Herod to replace the massacred Hasmoneans, among some others (Goodman 1987; not every post-Herodian high priest can be proved a descendant of a Herodian high priest, though many can be).

Josephus blamed the impotence and venality of the last procurators for the rising tide of disorder, and there is probably some truth to this, since they were struggling to cope without real access to troops, and so had little choice but to cut deals. They were in fact in an unsustainable situation; constitutionally, Palestine was uniquely complicated. We do not actually know for certain how power and authority were distributed among the procurator, the commander of the small military garrisons, the various high priestly factions, King Agrippa II and his entourage, and the Roman governor of Syria. The distribution of power is likely to have been poorly understood and much contested even by the participants themselves. For example, the little documentary evidence that survives suggests that in

Judaea, though it was ostensibly under direct Roman rule, the Jews lived under Jewish, not Roman provincial, law (Cotton 2002: 16), and so for some purposes – but which, exactly? – they must have regarded the high priest and his retainers as authoritative. Even for routine matters, then, there were several competing centres of authority in the district (Gabba 1999; Labbé 2012).

CHAPTER 4

The Jewish revolts, 66–135 CE

BIRDS

Tacitus noted that 'the Jews' patience endured until the procuratorship of Gessius Florus' (*Hist.* 5.10). The chain of events which sparked the revolt certainly confirms the historian's view, which our main source, Josephus, shared, that Florus was a scoundrel (*Ant.* 20.252–6/*Jewish War* 2.277–9), but the initial episode in Josephus' narrative chain has always defied interpretation (*Jewish War* 2.285–92): a 'Greek' of Caesarea Maritima owned a plot of land next to the synagogue and as an act of provocation built workshops on the land in a way which partly blocked access to the synagogue. The Jews offered Florus (whose palace was in the city) a bribe of eight silver talents, presumably to permit demolition of the workshops, but Florus took the money and decamped to Sebaste, leaving Caesarea in a state of high tension. One Sabbath the Jews arrived at the synagogue to find a Greek youth sacrificing birds on an upturned pot in the disputed passageway, an intolerable provocation. Violence erupted despite the intervention of the commander of the local equestrian *ala*, in the course of which the Jews seized 'their laws' and fled to the nearby Jewish town of Narbata. The leading Jewish citizen of Caesarea, John the Publican (*telōnēs*, perhaps a port official), marched off to Sebaste to remind Florus of the Jews' generosity, but, instead of expressing gratitude, Florus put John and his entourage in chains on the charge of having removed 'the laws' from the city. News of this episode brought Jerusalem to the brink, and an ill-timed visit by the procurator himself to seize seventeen talents from the temple treasury nudged the city into open revolt (*Jewish War* 2.293–6).

In the background of this episode was a history of Jews' and Greeks' competing claims over Caesarea, culminating in Nero's decision favouring the Greeks, issued several years before the incident of the birds (Levine 1974; Kasher 1990: 245–68). Josephus observes that the Jews had the advantage in numbers and wealth (or physical strength), but the Greeks had the sympathy of the governors and the garrison (*Jewish War* 2.268), which consisted of troops who, like the Caesarean Greeks, were of Syrian background. 'Syrians' were notorious, Josephus and Tacitus once again agree (*Hist.* 5.1, referring to the troops of Sohaemus of Emesa as *Arabes*), for their hatred of the Jews. The nature of the provocation itself is opaque; if provocation was intended, there were surely more obvious ways of achieving it than by slaughtering birds on a pot. The explanation repeated in the commentary tradition since the eighteenth century, that, according to the Pentateuch, birds were the appropriate sacrifice for recovered 'lepers' (sufferers from an unidentified skin ailment, not Hansen's disease), alluded to the Alexandrian Greek anti-Jewish historiographical tradition that the Jews had started as Egyptian lepers expelled from their native country to wander in the desert.[1] That Caesarean Jews and Greeks should have shared so much scholarly lore is obviously incredible; anyway, for what it's worth, Leviticus 14.5 seems to require that the purificatory bird be slaughtered *into* a pot, not on an inverted pot. Josephus does indeed describe the youth's act as sacrifice (the verb is *epithuein*) but perhaps the simplest explanation is that the Greek was preparing his lunch, and tensions in the city were so severe that any act could have served as provocation. Equally difficult is Josephus' statement that John the Publican and friends were imprisoned for removing what were apparently Torah scrolls from the Caesarean synagogue. Why this was a crime is not explained.

WHAT CAUSED THE REVOLT? EXPLANATIONS STRUCTURAL AND POLYBIAN

There are different ways of thinking about the events set into motion by the Caesarean bird episode.[2] For one broad historiographical tendency, such episodes explain everything; modern scholars recapitulate the theory advanced by Josephus in the *Jewish War*, a work which in theoretical terms is more Polybian than Thucydidean: *tykhē* – fortune or chance – not economic, religious, or political developments, generates historical change. The Jewish Revolt was caused by a series of misfortunes: the ineptitude of the last Roman procurators, the folly of a small group of Jewish brigands-turned-rebels, and an aggregation of unfortunate episodes culminating in the decision of the incompetent governor of Syria, Cestius Gallus, to

---

[1] The Loeb Classical Library comment *ad loc.* traces the suggestion back to Adrian Reland, in the early eighteenth century.
[2] For a brief, lucid introduction see Goodman 2002.

withdraw his troops from the tumult of Jerusalem just at the moment when firm intervention might have forestalled disaster. Gallus hesitated, his legion was almost entirely destroyed by the Jerusalemites, who possessed as weapons only rocks and familiarity with the steep topography, and Roman rule in Palestine evaporated. There is no systematic or structural explanation for the string of disasters which began in May 66 and came to an end with the failure of the third Jewish revolt sometime in 135; things simply went wrong for a while before they improved, just a long series of accidents. Such episodes as the one just recounted explain everything, a view both ancient and postmodern (Goodman 2007; Gambash forthcoming; critique in S. Schwartz 2009b).

Others adopt a more systematic approach to causation. One of the more plausible versions of this eschews any type of structuralist explanation but instead speculates about mid-range causes. According to Martin Goodman's first major treatment of the subject (1987), for example, behind the rebellion was a crisis of legitimacy faced by the Jewish leadership. This consisted primarily of friends and relatives promoted by King Herod to replace the destroyed Hasmonean aristocracy, who had had legitimacy problems of their own. The Herodians and their descendants were not an entrenched class of landowners, priests, and administrators, but 'new men' who lacked local bases of support and so could not be profitably manipulated by the Roman state. In the first century the Jews were literally ungovernable, not because they were Jews but because of a set of political problems specific to the first century. There is indubitably some truth to this, but one wonders why it led to repeated disasters of the scale which came to characterize Roman–Jewish relations in the first and second centuries. There were furthermore plenty of eastern districts (and some western ones as well) where the local leadership consisted more or less of Roman creatures originally without local clout. Few Roman-appointed client kings in Asia and Syria had strong local connections; if anything Herod had a better than average supply of them. To be sure there were plenty of disturbances in such places, as there were elsewhere in the Roman world. But no one rebelled as often and as disastrously as the Jews; there must have been more to it than the legitimacy problems of the Herodian family and their high priestly retainers (cf. Goodman 2002).

At one time one of the most popular forms of structural interpretation among historians in general was naïve marxizing, but this has only rarely been used to explain the catastrophe of Roman–Jewish relations (but see Kreissig 1970; Brunt 1977), perhaps because so many Marxists and marxizers have striven to distance themselves from the 'parochialism' of specifically Jewish concerns, both in life and in scholarship.[3] It has been far more common for historians to argue, or assert or assume, that religious or cultural factors hardwired into Judaism made the Jews ungovernable (traceable to Gibbon 1776 [1983]: 382–7). Frequently the reasoning has been circular, and echoed the ideas of such Roman critics of the Jews as Tacitus: the Jews rebelled because they were rebellious, ignoring the fact that they had not been especially rebellious before the first century, nor were they after 135. A similar argument maintains that their monotheism and religious scruples in general led them inexorably to political extremism – much the same 'universalist'-style argument as used against Muslims since 2001. Some writers have presented the same general argument in positive terms, since one man's fanaticism is another's heroic resistance (Hengel 1989: 313–79).

It is better to eschew moral judgement, bland truism, dismissive or ignorant reductionism and nationalist preaching. We should acknowledge that some subtle and complex structural approach is necessitated by the scale of the events, which ended up producing a structural change in Jewish life and in Judaism itself. This is not to say that any of the three Jewish rebellions and their aftermaths were inevitable, or that there weren't contingent or mid-range factors that shaped them. In chapter 3 I constructed the outlines of a case for the systemic unassimilability of the Jews as a corporate and localized entity in the Roman imperial state as it was emerging in its first century of existence. Here I would like to add some detail by analysing parts of Josephus' story.

Josephus' individual set pieces do not tell us everything we need to know about the factors behind the revolt, but I would argue that they remain important as nuggets of culture and politics. We can still learn a lot from them. From the bird episode we learn that the leader of the Caesarean Jews was no revolutionary but an imperial official. That he had lost the ability to influence the governor perhaps reflects a more general unwillingness on the part of the later Julio-Claudians to support Jews' aspirations to citizenship and prestige in Greek cities; the uprisings at Alexandria in 38 and 115, and in Palestine in 66 and 132, may all have deep in their backgrounds the Roman state's declining sympathy for whatever integrationist interests some Jews had, not just its *aporia* in coping with

---

[3] This is true for Jewish Marxists and *marxisants* (like Finley, but cf. Vidal-Naquet, e.g., 1980; on Finley's strange essay on the Jewish Revolt see S. Schwartz, forthcoming), but not for De Ste Croix 1981, who devotes a few sentences to the Great Revolt (pp. 192 and 442), and not a word to the later revolts. There is a *marxisant* quality, mediated through liberation theology, to some New-Testament-based scholars who have written about the Revolt, e.g., Horsley and Hanson 1999.

Jewish separatism. At least for Caesarea Goodman may have got it backwards; John the Publican, whoever he was, ironically *had* a Jewish constituency – it was his relation to the state which was in tatters. We can understand the plight of John, a prominent Jewish leader and an imperial official – the perfect local mediator figure – as symptomatic. Lacking effective access to a hostile and peremptory government, and living in a turbulent and dangerous environment, some Jews may have felt they were in an intolerable bind.

The story provides some suggestive information about Caesarea itself. Josephus tried in *Jewish War* to produce a strongly pro-Roman account but never hid his hatred of Palestinian gentiles. His conflation of the Caesarean Greeks with 'Syrians' (*Jewish War* 2.266) certainly constitutes an attempt to discredit them; it reflects in a quite direct way a Jewish insider's view of the struggle. It is impossible to say much, beyond generalizations about concerns over citizenship, about why the Jews and Greeks of the city had been feuding and what Nero's decision meant to it, but the fact that the removal of Torah scrolls could be thought a crime at least suggests that the Jews' holy things remained part of the fabric of the city's official religious life, and perhaps that the Jews' God was one of the tutelary deities of the city.[4]

Caesarea Maritima can be seen as still another Herodian experiment in integrating the king's subjects into a Roman system itself still in the throes of political experimentation and improvisation. Both Jews and Greeks had separatist and exclusivist cultural norms. For their part, the Romans, like many successful imperialists, tended to cultural voracity and 'universalism' (Dench 2005). But like all universalists they took some quite specific cultural practices for granted as components simply of *humanitas*, and the gods help anyone beyond the cultural boundaries. In other words, even before they fully imposed the provincial system and Roman law on the East, the Romans' tendency to statism and to interventionism made life complicated for people who had competing loyalties (Shaw 1993, in the service of a different argument). The Jews had come into existence and largely flourished under the very different political conditions of Achaemenid and Macedonian rule. These were empires which were indeed interventionist compared to their predecessors, but still based their politics on general recognition of the validity of at least some of the native institutions and practices of their subjects. To be sure

---

[4] That the city and the harbour constituted distinct municipalities, the former Greek, the latter Jewish, and that competition between these entities is behind the story, as argued by Raban 2009: 49–62, is unsupported by Josephus' narrative.

they manipulated and pressed, though also rewarded and empowered, local rulers, and the Macedonians always expected their native intermediaries to be 'civilized' (that is, to speak and act Greek), but intermediaries were useful precisely inasmuch as they appealed to the sentiments and preferences of their dependents. This political system fostered the development and rise of the Jews' specific corporate institutions and culture. It even functioned to preserve their traditional, pre-Achaemenid language, Hebrew (S. Schwartz 2005).

Even early on, by contrast, the Romans expected broader conformity to their own cultural preferences and political practices, and the Jews were certainly not the only ones to pay the price for this. But they did pay a higher price than anyone else. This was partly to be sure because their God, religion, and laws were exclusivist. Some scattered Jews might be happy enough to conflate their god with Zeus, for example, to keep their fingers crossed while participating in municipal religious life in Greek cities, or while witnessing the pagan rituals that accompanied most elements of public life in the Roman world. But these practices were inconsistent with the Judaism institutionalized in Jerusalem and normative for anyone loyal to those institutions. By a familiar irony it was the conditions of Roman rule itself which enabled material and human resources to pour into the Jews' central institutions, and which therefore promoted greater and more widespread loyalty to these institutions' countercultural values than had ever previously existed. There was no reason for the Jews not to speak Greek, or Latin; they could certainly adopt elements of Greek culture and political practice. But there were sharp limits, some of them surprising, such as the Jews' resistance to standard types of euergetism, discussed above, and systemic state pressure to overstep them.

Group politics was another reason the Jews lost out. When push came to shove, the Romans in the East would always favour the Greeks over all others; Greeks might have a sense of being defeated and reduced, but they were never actually crushed. Indeed, they became the very foundation of Roman rule (Woolf 1994). The only powerful non-Greek or Greek-controlled entity in the east, apart from the Jews' temple-based quasi-state whose influence was felt throughout the eastern Roman and the western Parthian empires, was the Nabataean kingdom, not as yet subjected to Roman rule (Millar 1993). No immediate upheavals seem to have accompanied the kingdom's reduction to provincial status in 106 CE, but so little is known about such crucial questions as whether there ever was a powerful Nabataean self-consciousness in the kingdom (demonstrably there was some), and how life was organized both before and after 106, not to mention the most basic facts of Arabia's political history, that we cannot be sure that the transition to Roman rule did not create significant upheavals (Millar 1993: 387–426; Cotton 2003).

REVOLT AND AFTERMATH

'The Great Revolt' is a misleading name. When Cestius Gallus retreated from Jerusalem in autumn 66 – the result of a small-scale local guerrilla action whose outcome was a fluke – no revolt, great or otherwise, still less a revolution, ensued (*Jewish War* 2.499–555). To be sure only a very small number even of aristocrats was openly pro-Roman, but then again Roman rule had collapsed and there was little advantage for the time being in loyalty to the empire. Indeed, a group of young Jerusalem priestly aristocrats quickly tried to seize control of the revolt and establish something like a state throughout Jewish Palestine (*Jewish War* 2.563–8), but with very little success, especially outside the district of Judaea (Price 1992: 51–80). A critical reading of Josephus' *Autobiography* tells us something of the chaos that prevailed in the second most important Jewish district of the country, Galilee. Josephus claims that he was dispatched by the Jerusalem authorities to oversee affairs in Galilee.[5] If we regard this claim with cautious scepticism, then we should probably see Josephus himself as a symptom of disorder, since it is more likely that he was an unauthorized adventurer/entrepreneur, like the other big-men he was in competition with in Galilee. Indeed, Josephus was the least successful of them. Of the two cities in Galilee, Sepphoris remained loyal to Rome – it assumed the name Eirenopolis – and Tiberias rebelled but rejected Josephus and had its own leadership, and the countryside was dominated by a wealthy and well-connected magnate, named John, from the Upper Galilean village of Gischala (Gush-Halav; modern Jish; Rappaport 1982). Josephus was only able to raise a few hundred troops for hire, brigands and mercenaries, and controlled only a place called Tarichaeae, possibly identical with the Magdala of New Testament fame. Josephus called this settlement a *polis*, but it was apparently only a small village – indeed, archaeologists have not yet identified its site with certainty. Readers of the *Jewish War*, where Josephus describes himself as a largely successful general in command of tens of thousands of troops, may find this account surprising, but the *Autobiography*, though it contains evasions and – though it is unfashionable to say so about ancient writers – lies of its own, is certainly

---

[5] The essential analysis of the relation between these accounts remains S. Cohen 1979.

more reliable when it comes to the small scale and general shabbiness of Josephus' wartime exploits. Part of Galilee had belonged to King Agrippa II, whose main city was outside Jewish territory, at Paneas, but the king made little effort to assert control.

Galilee reverted to the Romans almost as soon as Vespasian arrived at the head of a massive force of 60,000 troops (three legions, plus additional legionary detachments, auxiliary units, and armies of the local client kings), in the spring and summer of 67. Josephus had only a handful of followers left to commit suicide in a cave near the Galilean village of Jotapata (Yodefat), and his surrender to Vespasian is famous because he himself wrote it up so dramatically in the *Jewish War* (3.340–408).[6] Josephus says that before he left his cave God inspired him to surrender (350–4), and then to prophesy that the Roman general would become emperor – this well before Nero's suicide in 68 (399–408). Scholars are sceptical, but Josephus' prophecy was the only thing his Roman contemporaries knew about him; it was on Vespasian's official list of *omina imperii*, and an argument can be made that the story is true. The future historian did what he could, including invent a treasonous prophecy in which the commander – not immune to the attractions of the Roman version of orientalism – would be thought complicit, to avoid execution. Josephus admits that Vespasian was initially suspicious of him but was reminded of the other 'signs' predicting his accession to the throne.

Much more significant for our understanding of the revolt is the fact that John of Gischala and his followers, who surely numbered in the thousands, chose to flee to Jerusalem rather than fight in Galilee, a pattern that was repeated wherever Vespasian went in the Palestinian countryside.[7] The result was that Roman control was quickly restored throughout the country apart from the district of Judaea, and almost everyone who wished to resist or even just avoid the Romans converged on Jerusalem – a catastrophe in the making. This once again testifies to the city's and its institutions' tremendous growth in authority and attractive power in the wake of Herod's building and propagandistic projects.

---

[6] On Jotapata see Adan-Bayewitz and Aviam 1997: archaeology confirms the historicity of the siege, but notwithstanding Josephus' baroque and surely mainly invented detail, it also shows that the siege of Gamala, a much larger fortified town across the lake, was much more significant: *Jewish War* 4.1–83.

[7] Rappaport 1982 argues convincingly that John had shown no clear signs of opposition to Rome before his flight, which is why Titus brought only a small force to John's heavily fortified town (*Jewish War* 4.84–120): he assumed it would surrender. Only at Jerusalem did John finally join the rebellion.

It also demonstrates the military and political weakness of the rebels in their places of origin. To be sure thousands of refugees eventually assembled in Jerusalem, but the general fight against the Romans was over almost before it began.

The reduction of the country was variously delayed. Though news of the loss of the province reached Nero quickly, the assembly of a large army to deal with it – larger than was usual for a provincial revolt (Gambash forthcoming) – took many months. Then the war halted after the emperor's death and resumed only in 69 (*Jewish War* 4.550–5), shortly before Vespasian seized the imperial throne with the help of troops raised in Alexandria (*Jewish War* 4.592–620; Tacitus, *Hist.* 2.79–81; Suetonius, *Div. Vesp.* 6). He then left the Palestinian legions to his son Titus (*Jewish War* 4.658–63). His father having previously reduced Judaea, in the spring of 70 Titus began to besiege Jerusalem. The siege lasted from around Passover (14 Nisan, March/April) until the eighth or ninth of Av (July/August), and the temple was burnt on the tenth of the month. It took an additional month to subdue the city entirely, and capture the two competing Jewish generals, John of Gischala and Simon Bar-Giora (*Jewish War* 6.274–407). Though Josephus always overdramatized, there is no doubt that for the first time since the defeat of Cestius Gallus, the fighting was intense, passionate and bloody on both sides (*Jewish War* books 5–6; Price 1992). Josephus stated that 1.1 million Jews eventually died in the siege and its aftermath, but this is impossible (*Jewish War* 6.420–1). That a total of 97,000 Jews were taken captive throughout the war, as Josephus also says (*Jewish War* 6.420), is not impossible, however; captives were commodities and the Romans surely kept track of how many they took and sold to slave dealers, or put to work in the fleets and the silver mines. Even Josephus acknowledged the implausibility of his casualty figure, but it may still give some sense of just how crowded Jerusalem, whose peacetime population is unlikely to have exceeded 50,000, was during the siege.[8]

The siege ended in utter destruction: the city was razed to the ground, and it seems unlikely that many Jews were left alive in Jerusalem or its immediate vicinity. Josephus describes several waves of desertion from the city both before and during the siege (Price 1992: 255–63), and a much later rabbinic tradition describes one of the founders of the rabbinic

[8] Josephus compounds the implausibility by claiming that a rough count that Cestius Gallus had conducted at Passover, 65 – based on multiplying the number of paschal lambs by ten – found over 2.5 million people in the city, inhabitants and pilgrims (6.423–7). A nearly identical story (with different numbers) appears at T. Pesahim 4.15.

movement, Yohanan ben Zakkai, as such a deserter.[9] However, it is likely that the rabbinic story of Yohanan's escape and prophecy to Vespasian (*sic*; he was already emperor at the time of the siege) is an adaptation both of Josephus' story of his own desertion at Jotapata, and of his stories of Jerusalem in its final year (Price 1992: 264–70). Josephus says that Titus settled one group of deserters in the northern Judaean village of Gophna (*Jewish War* 6.115), and the Talmud places Yohanan at Iamneia/Yavneh, a tiny city on the coast owned personally by the emperor (*Ant.* 18.31; 158). That refugees or deserters from the city might be lodged in purpose-built villages may now be implied by the discovery at Shu'afat, about 5 km north of Jerusalem, of remains of a settlement built around 70 and abandoned around 130, built on a grid plan, like a Roman town. But the identification of this prosperous site as a Jewish village or (quite luxurious) 'refugee camp' – it is near the site of a modern Palestinian refugee camp – is based on the use there of limestone vessels, in addition to ceramic. Though some archaeologists regard these as reliable tracers for Jewish, or more precisely priestly or pietistic Jewish, identity (since, unlike ceramic, stone vessels can never become ritually impure), there are no convincing grounds for doing so in every case. The vessels were introduced in Judaea as a by-product of Herodian building projects, which opened extensive limestone quarries around Jerusalem, and their mass production was enabled by a new lathe technology. Furthermore, limestone, unlike clay, is ubiquitous in Judaea, so transportation costs for limestone vessels were low, and ceramics required firing, in an environment where appropriate fuel was increasingly hard to come by (see discussion in Miller 2010; S. Schwartz 2013). Residents of Judaea probably used such vessels not because they were Jewish priests or exceptionally pious, but because worked limestone had become cheap. Still, they were distinctively Judaean products, and such vessels when exported to places like Galilee might actually have been attractive to Jewish customers looking for evocations of their Judaean metropolis. But the village near Shu'afat was more likely to have been inhabited by Roman military and administrative personnel than by Jewish refugees.[10] Indeed, the usual fates of Jews caught in Jerusalem and its

---

[9] Avot de-Rabbi Natan version A, chapter 4; version B, chapter 6; Midrash Lamentations Rabbah 1.31; B. Gittin 56a–b; Midrash Proverbs, chapter 15. None of these texts pre-dates the fifth century: Lapin 2012: 43–4.

[10] See the preliminary publication: Sklar-Parnes, Rapuano and Bar-Nathan 2004. The paper itself, as opposed to its title, offers no ethnic identification of the site. By contrast, two studies published in 2007 are more insistent, largely because installations identified as *miqva'ot* –ritual baths – were found after the initial season of salvage excavation. But this identification is even more doubtful than usual because some of the alleged *miqva'ot* are tiny, and another was found in an insula which

vicinity were death, enslavement, and property confiscation, not resettle-
ment in garden suburbs, though many stretches of territory elsewhere
escaped destruction or quickly recovered.

The destruction of Jerusalem in the summer of 70 constituted as sharp
a turning-point as any in Jewish history. This bears emphasis, because
a revisionist trend in Judaic scholarship argues otherwise (D. Schwartz
2012; Klawans 2012). For some scholars, revisionism has been enabled by
the ideology-driven conviction of the unity and stability of the Jewish
people through the ages: the destruction was a catastrophe but it made
no real difference to the Jewish people in existential terms (Herr 2009).
For other scholars, revisionism starts from the reception of the events of
that year in both Jewish and Christian traditions. Jewish tradition would
domesticate and ritualize the memory of the destruction, in the form of
a three-week mourning period culminating in the fast of the Ninth of
Av (July–August), by focusing on the Temple and the cult. Christians
engaged in a comparable act of reductionism, but rather than mourning for the Temple adduced its fate as further evidence for the Church's
supersession of the Jews. Theologically inclined scholars have responded
to these traditional narratives by questioning whether all Jews in the
first century – most of whom lived far from Jerusalem – were really so
totally dedicated to the Temple and the sacrificial cult that they experienced the destruction as a trauma. These scholars have noted that various Jewish groups even in Palestine had reservations about the Temple's
legitimacy, or had found compelling substitutes for it even before its
destruction, even if they did not question its sanctity, simply because it
was too distant (Fraade 2009; even to some extent S. Cohen 1984: 27).
In any case, before the refoundation of Jerusalem as a pagan city under
Hadrian, around 130 CE, it was possible to believe that the ruination of
the Temple and cessation of the cult were temporary, that, just as it had
been rebuilt after its destruction by the Babylonians in 586 BCE, so it
would be rebuilt again.

seemed to contain workshops and so was probably a small pool used in manufacture. In one residential insula the identification of one of the small pools as a *miqvah* seems at least possible, and
this would suggest that a resident of the village was concerned about purity which in turn would
imply that he was of priestly or sectarian background: he could have been a slave. Anyway there
is little justification for the by-now standard identification of the site as a Jewish village. See Bar
Nathan and Sklar-Parnes 2007; Cotton 2007a.

Even this view is debatable, though, since it generalizes from a handful of texts – by definition unrepresentative of a society which was largely illiterate – and ignores the Temple's well-attested popularity, and religious and political importance. Very few Jews presumably rejected the legitimacy of the Temple, though indubitably Jews living in distant communities could ignore it if they wished, though surprisingly many of them demonstrably did not.

WHY 70 CE WAS A TURNING-POINT

The destruction of the Jerusalem temple was an important but small part of the story, and it is a serious historical error to allow traditional narrative (or nationalist ideology) to constrain our understanding of the aftermath of the Great Revolt. The year 70 CE marked transformations in demography, politics, Jewish civic status, Palestinian and more general Jewish economic and social structures, Jewish religious life beyond the sacrificial cult, and even Roman politics and the topography of the city of Rome itself. In the pages that follow I will briefly address each of these issues.

The Revolt's failure had, to begin with, a demographic impact on the Jews of Palestine; many died in battle and as a result of siege conditions, not only in Jerusalem. No numbers are available, and there seems little point in speculating, since we do not know the size of the Jewish population of Palestine before 66 CE (we can guess, but only guess, at a figure like 300,000–500,000). As indicated above (p. 000), the figures for captives are *conceivably* more reliable. If 97,000 is roughly correct as a total for the war, it would mean that a huge percentage of the population was removed from the country, or at the very least displaced from their homes. Nevertheless, only sixty years later, there was a large enough population in the Judaean countryside to stage a massively disruptive second rebellion (see below); this one appears to have ended, in 135, with devastation and depopulation of the district. In between (115–16), the Jews in Egypt, Cyrenaica, Crete and Cyprus rebelled, also with devastating results. Whatever the precise figures may have been, we may suppose that the world's Jewish population reached a pre-eighteenth-century peak in the year 66, and contracted severely by 135.

In addition, the destruction was part of a transformation of Palestinian Jewish politics. I have described above the complicated political arrangements which obtained before 66: the country was ruled by a Roman procurator, the high priest of the Jerusalem temple, and the senior member of the Herodian family, with the governor of Syria somewhere in the background. In the summer of 70 these arrangements were officially swept away; there was still a Herodian king in northern Palestine, Agrippa II, and conceivably some members of the high priestly class survived and remained on the scene, but they were now stripped of authority (Wilker 2007: 449–64). Palestine west of the Jordan was made into a standard Roman province, called Judaea, complete with an ex-praetorian governor and a legion, the Tenth Fretensis, stationed initially near Jerusalem (*Jewish War* 7.17; 163). About forty years later a second legion, possibly the Sixth Ferrata or the Second Traiana, joined the provincial garrison, stationed at Kefar Otnai in the Jezreel valley (later named Legio-Capercotna, later still, Maximianopolis), and the rank of the governor was correspondingly raised to consular (Isaac 1990: 427–35).

The full annexation of Provincia Judaea almost certainly meant that the Jewish nation, as an entity whose partial autonomy was recognized by the state, as it had been for five centuries or more, ceased to exist; there was no room for an autonomous nation in a standard Roman province.[11] It is not clear whether this was true only in Palestine or in the Roman Empire in general. The only evidence that Jews outside Palestine continued to have separate legal 'personality' is the imposition on them of a special tax (see below). All the Jewish nation's central institutions lost their official standing. The Torah ceased to be the law of the land for the Jews of Palestine, and the priests, judges and other officials who derived their authority from it ceased to perform any official functions, though survivors were not necessarily deprived of their prestige.

The failure of the Great Revolt transformed the economy and social organization of Palestine and in a more limited way of the Jewish world in general, since pilgrims and silver had come into the country from all over the Roman and Parthian Empires. As suggested above, the temple establishment had come by the first century to sustain a vast and unstable economy which concentrated tremendous wealth in Jerusalem and transformed Judaea into a most unusual district socially and culturally as well. This all came sharply to an end. Furthermore, Vespasian confiscated and sold off either all Jewish land (*Jewish War* 7.216–17), according to Josephus, or all land belonging to Jews who had participated in the rebellion, according to modern scholars (Isaac 1984). Josephus may have been closer to the truth, because, once Gallus was defeated in 66, all Jews in Palestine

---

[11] This was the view of Mommsen, later widely rejected (Isaac 1984), mainly out of apologetic squeamishness. If the Flavians did indeed regard the *Bellum Iudaicum* as a foreign conquest rather than a provincial uprising, then Mommsen was technically correct that the Jews were now *peregrini dediticii*: Gambash forthcoming: chapter 7; contrast Ziosi 2012: 95.

could be regarded as having participated in the rebellion (except the citizens of Sepphoris; cf. Gambash forthcoming: chapter 7). The government would presumably have imposed on any Jews attempting to reclaim land the practically impossible burden of proving otherwise. However, not all repurchasers of the land were necessarily gentiles (Ziosi 2012: 96–7).

Even beyond the very significant fact that at least for the time being cult and pilgrimage – the central features of pre-70 Judaism – were impossible; the destruction transformed the religious life of the Jews. Later rabbinic stories provide pat-seeming solutions to the religious problems created by the fact that sacrifices could no longer be offered. Israel could now secure God's goodwill and atonement for its sins by acts of mercy, or by prayer; study of the laws of sacrifice was tantamount to the act itself. But it is important to remember that the earliest rabbinic text, the Mishnah, was compiled 150 years after the destruction, and other rabbinic texts are much later. To be sure, the ancient rabbis were not practitioners of modern liberal religion; they presumably took very seriously the idea that animal sacrifice expiated sins and regarded its cessation very gravely. But after a few centuries the issue had lost some of its urgency, and anyway the rabbis' solutions to their theological crises may have seemed more radical to them than they do to us seventeen centuries later. Jews living in the immediate aftermath of the destruction might have been still less sanguine. But this was not the only problem; the God of Israel had been defeated, his house razed. In the *Jewish War* Josephus stated that God had gone over to the Roman side, but what did this mean for his relationship with the Jews? Was it permanently over, or had the Jews sinned and God awaited their repentance? But even if they had sinned, why, the author of 4 Ezra, writing shortly after 70, asked, was God showering benefits on the Romans who were manifestly so much worse than the Jews?

Finally, the defeat of the Jews played an important role in Flavian propaganda because Vespasian was a usurper; he needed to parade a victory to enhance his and his family's legitimacy. This need probably made the final year of the rebellion, which featured the most concentrated fighting, and the war's aftermath even bloodier than they would have been otherwise, and may also account for the utter devastation inflicted on Jerusalem. The victory was immediately celebrated with a flood of coinage bearing the inscription IUDAEA CAPTA ('Judaea taken captive'), and a triumph celebrated by the emperor and his elder son, featuring a display of items plundered from the Jerusalem temple, and the most prominent and handsome rebels, who were being led to their death (*Jewish War* 7.123–57). Technically of course there were no grounds for any of this. The Flavians had defeated scattered bands of Roman subjects in Roman territory, not a foreign enemy. But the advertisement of the war did not stop there. The Roman Forum itself was reshaped by the Flavians to reflect their victory, with the Templum Pacis built in 75 (*Jewish War* 7.158–62), and the Arch of Titus and the Amphitheatrum Flavianum (the Colosseum), located on the site of Nero's notorious Golden House, built around 80; the signs over the entrances to the amphitheatre indicated that it had been built *ex manubiis belli*, 'from the spoils of the war' (Millar 2005).

Even the main temple of the Roman municipal cult, dedicated to Jupiter Optimus Maximus, on the Capitoline hill at the opposite end of the Via Sacra, had a connection to the Jewish War. After the destruction of Jerusalem Vespasian decreed that the two-denarius (= half-shekel, or didrachmon) per annum tax Jews throughout the empire had previously been permitted to remit to the temple there be paid into a fund called the *fiscus iudaicus*. This fund was used to rebuild the Temple of Jupiter on the Capitol, which had been accidentally damaged in 69 (*Jewish War* 7.218; Cassius Dio, *Hist. Rom.* 66.7.2). It is hard to imagine that this was not meant as a symbolic mark of Capitoline Jupiter's victory over the God of Israel. The Jews continued to pay this tax at least into the third century (Goodman 2007: 449–54; it would presumably have lapsed in any case when the emperor Constantine converted to Christianity). Though presumably the humiliation implicit in it eventually faded into routine, it does not take a huge feat of empathetic imagination to guess how most surviving Jews might have occasionally felt, especially in the immediate aftermath of the revolt, at the official celebration of their ruin.

THE END OF EGYPTIAN JEWRY? THE DIASPORA REVOLT, 116–17 CE

Meanwhile the Jews in the region of Cyrene had put a certain Andreas at their head, and were destroying both the Romans and the Greeks. They would eat the flesh of their victims, make belts for themselves of their entrails, anoint themselves with their blood and wear their skins for clothing; many they sawed in two, from the head downwards; others they gave to wild beasts, and still others they forced to fight as gladiators. In all two hundred and twenty thousand persons perished. In Egypt, too, they perpetrated many similar outrages and in Cyprus under the leadership of a certain Artemion. There, also, two hundred and forty thousand perished, and for this reason no Jew may set foot on this island, but if one of them is driven upon its shores by a storm he is put to death.

Cassius Dio, *Historia Romana* 68.32.1–3 (in the epitome of Xiphilinus)

Aside from some bits of information about his own later life at Rome, Josephus' account comes to an end with the reduction of the last rebel stronghold, Masada, near the shore of the Dead Sea, in 73 or 74 CE. His works are the last extant general Jewish narrative history for many, many centuries to come, arguably until late in the Italian Renaissance. This means that even the most basic facts about how the Jews organized themselves and conducted their lives in the wake of the destruction have to be laboriously reconstructed from poor and scattered sources, often from material whose very relevance to the questions it is called on to answer is uncertain. I will address this issue below. For our present purposes, the absence of a narrative history means that we know very little about the two catastrophic events which followed the destruction in 70, the Diaspora Revolt of 116–17, and the Bar Kokhba Revolt, centred again in Judaea, 132–5. At least there seem excellent grounds for supposing that these events were catastrophic; all evidence for Jewish presence in Egypt fails for almost two centuries after 117, and archaeological surveys and excavations appear to confirm the claim of Cassius Dio that the district of Judaea was largely depopulated by 135; it recovered only in the fourth century, and then as a Christian district.[12]

It is curious that the slender literary evidence for the rebellion gives short shrift to Egypt, not even reporting the name of the revolt's leader, despite the fact that Egypt's Jewish settlement was the most populous and ancient in the Roman diaspora (not, as usual, that we can provide numbers). To be sure, Appian of Alexandria notes in passing that 'in my time', while the emperor Trajan was in the process of 'exterminating the race of the Jews' in Egypt, the Jews destroyed the shrine of Nemesis (built by Caesar to house the head of Pompey) near Alexandria, and also reports the Jews' military activity near Pelusium (*GLAJJ* 350 and 348). But otherwise the fragmentary Greco-Roman historiographical and Christian chronographic traditions say less about Egypt than about Cyrene, Cyprus and recently conquered Roman territories in Mesopotamia. Papyrology, too, provides only scattered hints about the causes, location and progress of the fighting in rural Egypt, and no information at all about Alexandria. But land registration documents, in some cases from decades later, make it clear that land in rural Egypt which had once belonged to Jews was routinely confiscated (attested for the Oxyrhynchite, Athribite and Arsinoite nomes); as late as 200, Oxyrhynchites still celebrated an annual festival

---

[12] Barring new discoveries, there will be little to add to Pucci Ben Zeev 2005 on the subject of the Diaspora Revolt.

commemorating the defeat of the Jews. It is surprising that we hear so little about upheavals in Alexandria beyond Appian's incongruously light-hearted notices, but then again the riots of 38 and 41, amply described by Philo and Josephus, are scarcely mentioned by non-Jewish writers, either (though they are in the background of the 'Acta Alexandrinorum': Harker 2008: 9–47).

The reasons for the rebellion are wholly unknown. It is hard to avoid connecting it to what we can infer about the impact of Roman policies in former Ptolemaic lands (in Mesopotamia the Jews appear to have rebelled against the Romans side by side with their neighbours). The Macedonians had apparently recognized all non-Egyptian immigrants to Egypt as in effect 'Hellenes', authorized to use the laws of their *poleis* of origin (*politikoi nomoi*; in the Jews' case this meant the laws of the Torah). This made Judaean settlers in rural Egypt the civic and political equivalent of Greek settlers there, as opposed to native Egyptians (Modrzejewski 1997). The classification of Jews as Hellenes presumably did not constitute a grant of citizenship to those who settled in Alexandria, but it did give them a sense, and maybe even in some limited way, the legal reality, of equality of status to Greeks who enjoyed technical Alexandrian citizenship (Kasher 1985; Harker 2008: 212–20). Some individual Jews in any case probably attained it. As far as we can tell, rural Jews, while in some cases still making use of their native *politikoi nomoi* (this is attested for Herakleopolis but curiously not for any other place), quickly came to identify linguistically and to some extent culturally with Greeks, and not Egyptians (Cowey and Maresch 2001; *CPJ* I). Alexandria probably absorbed a constant trickle of immigration from Palestine and elsewhere, and its Jewish community was large and necessarily culturally, religiously, and socio-economically highly complex. Some Jews were indubitably regarded as among the aristocracy of the city. Philo of Alexandria's family was wealthy, well connected at Rome, and benefited from extensive Greek educations, identifying quite thoroughly with Greeks' cultural aspirations, but most of them also had close connections in Judaea, and were without ambiguities Jewish, though 'hellenized' and aristocratic. Philo certainly followed the Jewish *politikoi nomoi*, which he regarded as being in complete harmony with Platonic philosophy – indeed, he was one of their most profound expositors.

But the Romans gradually blocked the Jews' integration with the Greeks of Egypt, in a way which disastrously revived competition between the two groups especially at Alexandria (Harker 2008: 212–20; Barclay 1996). As in Palestine, here too the Romans tended to favour the Greeks (though later Alexandrian Greeks produced a bizarrely paranoid set of writings which modern scholars call *Acts of the Alexandrian Martyrs*, which accuse Trajan, among other emperors, of favouring the Jews over the Greeks. To be sure many Alexandrian Greeks felt mistreated by Rome, but it is worth remembering Appian's casual remark). When, in the wake of the disturbances of 38 CE the Alexandrian Jews petitioned the emperor for 'isopolity' (the meaning is uncertain: possibly the recognition of something like a 'Jewish' citizenship in the city in some sense equal to that enjoyed by the Greeks; possibly a grant of Alexandrian citizenship: Kasher 1985), Claudius eventually responded that the Jews may as always follow their own laws but they must make no claims for any civic status in Alexandria, 'a city which does not belong to them' (*CPJ* II.153 ll. 94–5; Harker 2008: 9–24; Gambetti 2009, promoting a darker view of the outcome). It is tempting to say that these episodes discredited the Jews' integrationist upper class and tended to radicalize them. Indeed, there were renewed disturbances at the time of the Great Revolt, and Josephus claims that some Judaean rebels fleeing after 70 found plenty of Jewish followers in Egypt. But we can do no more than offer these obviously unsatisfactory generalizations, which are complicated by the possibility that the rebellion started not in Alexandria or elsewhere in Egypt, but in neighbouring Cyrene. Indeed, we do not even know whether the disturbances in Cyrene, Egypt, Cyprus, Mesopotamia and elsewhere were connected and, if so, how. Dio's account of the atrocities the Jews committed is a set of *topoi* of barbarity. The interesting exception is the claim that the Jews forced their enemies to endure such sanguinary arena entertainments as wild beast hunts and gladiatorial combats – these are *topoi* of Romanness, though inverted. Be this as it may, the limited evidence seems to support the maximalist view that these rebellions effectively brought Jewish life in Egypt, Libya and Cyprus to an end for about two centuries.[13] In Egypt there was a late antique revival, and it went on to contain a major Jewish community in the Middle Ages.

BAR KOKHBA

From Shimon bar Kosiba to the men of Eingeddi, to Mesabala and to Jonathan bar Ba'ayan, greetings. You are luxuriating, eating and drinking from the property of House of Israel, showing no concern for your brothers whatsoever. As to the boats that they've inspected in your place, you've done nothing at all. Know that

---

[13] Harker 2008: 7 claims that the Jews of Alexandria sustained heavy casualties but were not wiped out in 117, unlike those in the *chora*; but there is no evidence for Jews in Alexandria for a long time after 117.

I am on to you; as far as the crops are concerned, take care with them and unload them from the boat in your harbour at once ... Farewell.

P. Yadin 49, undated, Hebrew/Aramaic on papyrus

In the year 129 the emperor Hadrian, who had acceded to the throne in 117, advertised his love of all things Greek by touring the eastern part of his empire and lavishing benefits wherever he went. If Cassius Dio can be believed (*Historia Romana* 49.11–12) one of his stops was the ruined Jerusalem, now the camp of the Tenth Legion Fretensis. This site the emperor refounded as a city – possibly planned from the start as a Roman colony – to be called Aelia Capitolina and on the site of the temple of the God of Israel he built a temple of the city's new tutelary deity, Jupiter Optimus Maximus (Capitolinus; Hadrian's *nomen* was Aelius, which explains the first part of the name). There was thus nothing Greek about either the city which had previously occupied the site, or that which was now founded; it is difficult to understand Hadrian's act in Judaea as an aspect of the theatrical philhellenism he displayed elsewhere. If there is any truth to Dio's account – and there is mounting numismatic and archaeological evidence confirming that the city was founded in 129/130, with construction having begun even earlier, and not in 135/136 (Wexler-Bdolah 2009; R. Baker 2012) – Hadrian was not so much being generous to the Greeks (hardly to be found in Judaea in 130) as dancing on the Jews' collective grave. He cannot have been unaware of the history of the site. Moreover, he could have easily learned, if he did not already know, that the Jews' gifts to the God of Israel had been diverted to the very same Jupiter Optimus Maximus. Perhaps Hadrian was playing to some segments of upper-class Greek sentiment in the East in founding Aelia, but Judaea had by no means yet been emptied of its Jewish inhabitants. The events which followed show that, on the contrary, it retained a large rural Jewish population guaranteed to be outraged by Hadrian's act. Perhaps some had even expected Hadrian to refound Jewish Jerusalem and rebuild the temple.

Once again our information about this revolt is defective, though a bit richer than that about the Diaspora Revolt; the Bar Kokhba Revolt is also more easily susceptible to inferences based on archaeology because geographically, so it seems, it was highly concentrated. It was evidently restricted to the district of Judaea – indeed, the findspots of the coinage of the revolt correspond almost precisely to the historic borders of the district, from Lydda–Ramallah–Wadi Daliyeh (north of Jericho) in the north to the northern Negev in the south (Mildenberg 1984; Zissu 2000–2). Practically none of the coinage has been discovered in northern Samaria, Galilee, or the northern coastal plain, though strays have turned up as far away as the Rhine–Danube frontier – souvenirs brought by legionaries (Eshel, Zissu and Barkay 2010). Another archaeological tracer for the geographical extent of the revolt – singled out as a distinctive feature by Cassius Dio – are 'hiding complexes', tunnels dug under houses, though these are difficult to date, and it seems a priori unlikely that every such tunnel was dug in connection with this rebellion. Nevertheless, these too are concentrated in Judaea (Kloner and Zissu 2003; Shahar 2003). Archaeologists have discovered around twenty similar structures in what appear to have been Jewish areas of Galilee, but hardly anyone has ever seriously suggested that there was more than sporadic military activity there (contrast Eck 1999). We do know, however, that Galilaeans joined the rebellion in Judaea (P. Murab. 43). There is fragmentary and not unproblematic evidence for Nabataean participation, too (Cotton 2003; Bowersock 2003).

The two main historiographical traditions (something of a misnomer, since one 'tradition' consists of a few paragraphs and the other is not really historiographical but folkloristic or legendary) about the revolt present it very differently (Isaac 1998: 211–9). It owes its common modern name to the chronographic tradition of the church fathers, who identified the leader as a certain Bar Cochebas – Son of the Star, a manifest allusion to Numbers 24.17–18, a prophecy of a 'star' which would rise from Israel and defeat all its neighbours. Rabbinic tradition gave the same man an insulting deformation of the name, Bar Koziba – son of deception – and called him a false messiah, but still recorded tales of his heroic feats. Presumably some Jews remembered him as a great man but a failure, or an attractive fraud. The same sources recount his blood-soaked last stand near the Judaean village Beitar.[14]

Cassius Dio, by contrast, never mentions the name of the leader of the revolt. Indeed he describes it somewhat inconsistently. On one hand, it was a very widespread guerrilla operation which Julius Severus, called in for the purpose from Britannia, gradually quelled through a war of attrition which involved few (Roman) losses; on the other, it was a massive uprising crushed with tremendous loss of life of both sides. It is worth remembering that Dio's *Historia Romana* is actually lost at this point and we rely on a medieval summary. Xiphilinos, its author, may be responsible for the mild confusion of the account, not Dio, but in any case it presents a very different picture than the Jewish and Christian sources.

---

[14] Much older historiography relied heavily on rabbinic sources. Schäfer 1981 effectively dismantled this approach; cf. Schäfer 2003: 1–22.

Archaeological discoveries have confirmed elements of both 'traditions'. The revolt did have a leader, whose name was neither Bar Kokhba nor Bar Koziba, but Shim'on Bar (or, in Hebrew, Ben) Kosibah, a name of unknown derivation. He was the authority behind the rebel coinage mentioned previously, but all the silver coins were crudely produced overstrikes, unlike the magnificent coinage of the first revolt. The coins inform us that he assumed the title *nesi' Yisrael*, 'chief' or 'prince of Israel', and they commemorate the liberation or redemption of Jerusalem or of Zion, one of the hills of Jerusalem. But he probably never conquered the city, which may explain the modesty of his assumed title (S. Schwartz 2006: 35); he could not be king without possessing Jerusalem. The archaeologist Yigael Yadin discovered in 1960 in the Judaean desert a cache of about a dozen letters, written on papyrus, in Hebrew, Aramaic or Greek, sent from Ben Kosibah mainly to two subordinates, named Mesabala and Jonathan, apparently his representatives in the important desert oasis town of Eingeddi. These letters, and others previously published, reveal something about the ideology of the rebellion (P. Yadin 49–63; P. Murab. 43–8). The rebels were 'brothers', and constituted the 'House of Israel'. Ben Kosibah preferred to employ Hebrew in his correspondence – a language with much symbolic weight – but his secretaries could not write it very successfully. It is hard to know whether to characterize the language of the letter quoted above as hebraized Aramaic or as aramaicized Hebrew. On one occasion, the scribe wrote in Greek but felt constrained to apologize that he 'was unable to write in Hebrew' (P. Yadin 52). Several of the letters express pious concern for Jewish laws and rituals, including specifically such temple- and priesthood-associated practices as the separation of tithes from all agricultural products to serve as a tax-in-kind for priests. This practice could no longer have been enforceable in the absence of a temple and a high priest. The Sabbath is acknowledged, as is the vintage-related Feast of Tabernacles (Sukkot). Ben Kosibah and his supporters clearly presented themselves as fighters for the Torah, the temple, and the nation of Israel (full discussion in Schäfer 2003: 8–15).

However, the letters themselves are without exception querulous in tone and trivial in content, with threats against the recipients usually more explicit than in the letter quoted above. The ensemble makes the strong impression that Ben Kosibah's leadership was more aspirational than real, and this may explain Dio's failure to name him, and the poor quality of the coinage, though it is noteworthy that it was issued over so long a period and in such apparent abundance. The Bar Kokhba Revolt may in fact have been a localized but very intense guerrilla uprising. Who exactly Shim'on

ben Kosibah was, where he came from, what sort of military experience he
had and where he got it (there is a single possible answer to this, in effect:
the Roman army), why he would have thought that anyone would regard
him as the messianic saviour predicted – according to the type of reading
common in the first and second centuries – in the Hebrew Bible, indeed,
whether he did so (see Schäfer 1981; 2003), we will probably never know.
His attempt to control and organize the Jewish rebellion was not a complete failure, especially in the desert-fringe towns and villages named in
his correspondence,[15] but it seems to have started without him, proceeded
mainly on its own, and ended without him, too. The Talmudic tales of
his – and the people of Israel's – heroically catastrophic last stand at Beitar
are only ambiguously confirmed by archaeology.[16]

The outcome of this final rebellion was catastrophic nonetheless.
Cassius Dio provides figures which are, as usual, manifestly unlikely, but
still evocative:

Fifty of their most noteworthy fortresses and nine hundred and eighty-five of the
most famous villages were demolished, five hundred and eighty thousand men
were slaughtered in raids and battles – the number of those who perished from
hunger and disease and fire could not be determined ... practically all of Judaea
was made desolate.

(*Historia Romana* 69.14.1–2)

That the district – not the province – of Judaea was largely devastated is
confirmed by archaeology, and the ironic effect of this fact was to ensure
that the Hadrianic foundation which had sparked the rebellion was never
more than a tiny, insignificant place – the price of the city was the complete destruction of its hinterland.

In honour of its dejudaization, so it seems, the province of Judaea was
now renamed Syria Palaestina (Eck 2003: 168–9). Later rabbinic traditions
recalled a period of persecution after the revolt – featuring the prohibition
of practising or even teaching Jewish law on pain of death. The rabbinic
storytellers associated the persecution only with the name of Hadrian, so
they probably assumed it ended with the emperor's death in 138. Whether
there was such a persecution is less certain. Paradoxically, the later the
source, the more detailed the information, suggesting that the stories
about the persecution took on a life of their own in rabbinic tradition

---

[15] See P. Yadin 42–7; XHever/Seiyal 8–8a, legal documents dated by an era of Simon, prince of Israel,
and/or "the freedom of Israel".

[16] There is chronologically appropriate evidence of fortification and fighting at the likely site of
Beitar, but the site is small. Rabbinic sources necessarily vastly exaggerate the scale of activities
there (Ussishkin 2008).

(Schäfer 1981). There is only one piece of information in non-rabbinic sources which resonates with rabbinic traditions: Hadrian prohibited circumcision, an extension of traditional Roman taboos about male genital mutilation. The Jews were not the only practitioners: Egyptian priests and various Arab groups also practised circumcision, and the prohibition applied to all. The law against circumcision may have been a coincidence, or it may have been intended specifically to punish the Jews (*GLAJJ* II: 619–21). Is this the factual basis of the rabbinic traditions? In any case, Antoninus (reigned 138–161) subsequently permitted Jews to circumcise their own sons, but no one else, for example, male converts to Judaism and slaves (*Digest* 48.8.11; Linder 1987: 99–102). Whether or not there was a period of formal persecution, though, there is no question that the Jews were for the time being decisively crushed – their deconstitution as a nation strongly confirmed, their numbers sharply reduced, their presence in their own land of Judaea diminished nearly to nothing.

CHAPTER 5

Jews in the High Roman Empire

INTRODUCTION

This chapter focuses on the rabbis. The rabbis (*rabbi* in Hebrew/Aramaic is an honorific title meaning 'my master'; the term was already used as a substantive noun in antiquity, but rabbinic literature usually calls its protagonists sages – *hakhamim* – or elders – *zeqenim*) were a group centred in northern Palestine, the remaining centre of Jewish population after the devastation of Judaea in 135. The origins and role of the rabbis are obscure and controversial despite the survival of a large quantity of rabbinic literature. The rabbis were unusual or even unique as a provincial group, since they were elite or sub-elite preservers, rationalizers and elaborators of a recalcitrantly unromanized but very much altered local tradition transmitted in its original Semitic languages. As such they have much to teach about the possibilities and limits of cultural resistance in the Roman Empire. The following pages are dedicated to the tasks of explaining the controversy about them, piecing together what we can know about their origins, coalescence as a group, and role. In my view, little can be known, but that little points mainly to the rabbis' limitations as authorities and cultural role models. What we know about Jews in Palestine outside rabbinic circles points to their imbrication, at long last, in the political, social and cultural environment of the eastern Empire. Things began to change by the later third century; most of the evidence for this change concerns the rise of a dynasty designated in rabbinic sources *nesi'im* (singular, *nasi*; 'prince', see above on Bar Kokhba's use of the title) and in Roman law-codes, patriarchs. Like the rabbis, the patriarchs are largely without close parallel in the Roman Empire but there is no doubt that in the fourth century they were transformed from a venerable rabbinic family into important imperial officials of senatorial rank; this tells us something about larger changes in the eastern Empire on the eve of christianization.

THE TRIUMPH OF RABBINIC JUDAISM?

The period of the revolts ending in 135 initiates the most controversial era in Jewish history. The controversy concerns the role and function of a newly emerging group, the rabbis – men who had attained expertise in the Torah and in Jewish law (both civil and ritual) and were authorized to teach and judge. Maximalists argue that almost immediately after 70 the rabbis replaced priests and their kind as the Jews' religious authorities.[1] A recent refinement of this view claims that the rabbis constituted the embodiment of the Jews' collective cultural identity, and so had tremendous influence and prestige whether or not they possessed any formal authority (Miller 2006; 2010; Schremer 2010). Minimalists respond that the only evidence for this view, rabbinic literature, is inevitably biased (Neusner 1970), and that archaeological evidence, which demonstrates the cultural 'normality' of High Imperial urban Palestine – home of the rabbis – makes the maximalist view unlikely (S. Schwartz 2001; cf. Goodman 1983; S. Cohen 1984, 1999a; Hezser 1997; Lapin 2012). The rabbis did not emerge as a component of a Jewish leadership until the end of antiquity at earliest. This controversy is fuelled by the paucity of firmly datable and contextualizable evidence, especially historiography.

Indeed, our ability to produce any sort of narrative history at this point fails, in particular if we are unwilling to construct such a narrative by assembling and sifting Talmudic stories about the rabbinic past, stories which in generic terms are homilies, fables, legal cases or *chriae* rather than historiography. Furthermore, for reasons to be explored in detail in this chapter, even if these stories do have historical 'kernels', it takes a particular type of strong misreading to read them as evidence for the history of the Jews in general, rather than for the history of a small aggregation of scribes and legal experts in the conflict-ridden process of institutionalization. Such misreading begins from the assumption that, starting in 70 CE, 'the rabbis' enjoyed unfraught legitimacy not merely as quasi-judicial arbitrators but as political leaders of the Jews. Reasonable people may debate the question of whether the rabbis enjoyed legal authority and if they did what form it took. But I think even the most conservative scholars would feel self-conscious about arguing that the rabbis constituted a provincial political leadership (but see Safrai 1995; Oppenheimer 2007; Herr 2009).

---

[1] Before 1970 this was the consensus. Neusner 1970 inaugurated its systematic dismantling. For a survey of the historiography on this subject see S. Schwartz 2002a.

EVENTS

Before exploring the controversy, it is worth briefly running through the very few things known about the *histoire événementielle* of the Jews between 135 and Constantine's conquest of the eastern Roman Empire in 324.[2] A stray comment of Ammianus (*Res Gestae* 22.5.5 = *GLAJJ* II.605–7) vaguely suggests that (some?) Palestinian Jews supported Avidius Cassius against Aurelius in the civil war of 175 (Smallwood 1981: 482–4; Isaac 1990: 88). The evidence that Palestinian Jews supported Severus against Pescennius Niger in 193 is likewise fragmentary and vague. Nothing is known of the ethnic background of the brigand Claudius, said to have been overrunning Syria and 'Judaea' in the 190s (Cassius Dio, *Historia Romana* 75.2.4 = *GLAJJ* II.406–7); nor do we know whether the Jews supported or opposed him (*pace* Smallwood 1981: 488–90). More reliably attested are the Severan grants of municipal status to Beth-Gubrin-Eleutheropolis and Lydda-Diospolis, central Palestinian towns with mixed populations, but the reasons for these grants are unknown (S. Schwartz 2006: 46; Millar 1993: 118–25; 374–6). Nevertheless there is no doubt that during the century following the Bar Kokhba Revolt the emperors founded cities and built new roads in Palaestina (Isaac 1990: 108–13; Lapin 2012: 26–33). The surviving Jews presumably benefited economically from these processes along with the other inhabitants of the province, but the common notion of a Jewish 'golden age' under the Severans is open to doubt. It is based entirely on scraps, supplemented by rabbinic stories of meetings between the patriarch Rabbi Judah I (see below) and an emperor named Antoninos, identified by scholarly consensus as Caracalla. But the tales are fictional, and reflect, if anything, the patronage of Judah's descendants – the patriarchs of Tiberias – by the Theodosian family in the later fourth century (S. Cohen 1998; Lapin 2012: 23–4). The existence of an 'alliance' between the Roman Senate and the city of Sepphoris-Diocaesarea, brokered by the same Judah, asserted in many handbooks, is an imaginative inference from a misread coin legend (Kraay 1980). It has long been assumed that the Jews were included in Caracalla's universal grant of Roman citizenship of 212 (*Constitutio Antoniniana*). There is no compelling reason to doubt this for parts of the diaspora but in the wake of two failed revolts in Palestine we cannot be certain that the Jews there were not counted among the *dediticii*, and so excluded from the grant (Gambash forthcoming: chapter 7). There is no secure evidence for general Jewish possession of the Roman citizenship before 398 (*Cod. Theod.* 2.1.10; S. Schwartz 2010).

[2] For surveys see Lapin 1995: 8–12; S. Schwartz 2006: 45–8.

WHEN DID THE JEWS BECOME RABBINIC?

We begin by jumping ahead several centuries to the period when everyone agrees rabbis played an important role in most Jewish communal life. This will help set the parameters of the discussion, and allow us to know what we should be looking for. However, it is hard to specify when this period begins, because, poor as our information is for the five centuries beginning in 70, thereafter it fails almost completely, and not only for the Jews. It is no longer common to speak of 'dark ages',[3] but the fact remains that around 600 the Mediterranean world and the Near East entered an informational shadow from which the region exited only three hundred years later, with the emergence of a full-blown Islamic, largely Arabophone, urban civilization replacing the Greek one. By around 900, the Jews were an important, well-attested and literarily productive component of this civilization; by contrast there were only small and scattered Jewish communities in early medieval Christendom, chiefly in Italy and in the Rhine valley (M. Cohen 1994). The successors to the Jews of the eastern Roman and western Sasanian Empires had several distinctive characteristics, but for our purposes the most important are the following: (1) Greek was completely lost as a language of speech, as a liturgical/sacred language, and as a literary language; Jews ceased copying Greek texts which as a result were lost to them; those that survived were preserved exclusively by Christians. The same is true of non-biblical books composed in Hebrew or Aramaic between 300 BCE and 100 CE: the Jews lost them (except for the *Wisdom of Ben Sira*), but the Christians preserved a small number of such texts in translation. (2) Hebrew was revived, in both the Islamic and Christian worlds, as a liturgical, literary and learned language (Simonsohn 1975). Nevertheless, the linguistic situation in Jewish communities was interestingly varied, with Judeo-Arabic enjoying a literary and religious prestige among Jews in the Islamic world that Latin and its descendants and German lacked among Jews in the Christian world (Brody 1998: xxi; 138–40). (3) Jews were organized in local communities whose very limited autonomy was recognized or conceded de facto by local political authorities.[4] The Torah was back in business as the constitution of the Jews, but in most places it was now refracted through the interpretation of rabbis – experts who drew their authority from their mastery not only of the Bible

---

[3] But see Ward-Perkins 2005, and, with tremendous nuance and much detail, Wickham 2006.
[4] Not to overstate the point, since even where Jews had a recognized right to use Jewish civil law, administered by rabbis, they frequently resorted to non-Jewish courts despite rabbinic, and sometimes, ecclesiastical, objections.

but, much more importantly, of the Talmud. Indeed, of all literature written by Jews in post-biblical antiquity, medieval and later Jews (until they rediscovered Jewish Greek literature and other non-biblical ancient Jewish texts in the context of Renaissance humanism and nineteenth-century romanticism) preserved almost but not quite exclusively texts written by ancient and late antique rabbis.[5] The increasing cultural and religious importance of rabbis and their texts as the Middle Ages progressed is demonstrated by the coalescence of an opposition, especially in the Muslim world, called Qaraites (literally, followers of Scripture [alone]), though in practice the boundaries between Qaraites and 'Rabbanites' was often fuzzier than the groups' leaders wished (Rustow 2008).

The controversy about the period after the revolts concerns the timing of these changes; those whom I called above 'maximalists' posit a swift transition from temple to synagogue/community and from priest to rabbi. The speed of the change was enabled by the alleged fact that the later model existed *in nuce* by the later Second Temple period, at a time when the legitimacy of the older institutions had largely crumbled. The group thought to have embodied and led popular non-Temple-centred Judaism were the Pharisees; the rabbis have traditionally been regarded as their post-70 remnant. Thus, the 'genuine' Jewish national leadership survived the revolts. It was, to be sure, much reduced, but it had also shed its traditional competitors, the priests and the Herodians.[6] The second, 'minimalist', view, to which I adhere, prefers to date the transition closer to the time it is fully attested, sometime at any rate in late antiquity or the earlier Middle Ages.

---

[5] Surveys of rabbinic literature: Strack and Stemberger 1996; Fonrobert and Jaffee 2007; Millar, Ben-Eliyahu and Cohn 2013. The primary rabbinic legal texts (which are not codes but compendious textbooks, recording variant opinions and legal argumentation – not to mention varying amounts of non-legal material – which have no meaningful place in a law-code *stricto sensu*) are the Mishnah (*c.* 200 CE), Tosefta (*c.* 250–300), Palestinian Talmud (also called Yerushalmi or Jerusalem Talmud, edited *c.* 380–400), Babylonian Talmud (Bavli, 600–700). The first three were produced in or near Tiberias, Galilee, the last in the vicinity of Baghdad, possibly before the foundation of that city. All the post-Mishnah corpora include commentary on the Mishnah, and replicate its thematic organization into six orders, subdivided into tractates. The Mishnah and Tosefta are written in an aramaicized Hebrew not unlike the language of the Bar Kokhba letters, while the Talmuds have portions in Hebrew and portions in Aramaic; the language of the Palestinian Talmud contains a lot of Greek, that of the Babylonian Talmud little Greek but some Persian though not much. In addition, there are collections of *midrash*, that is biblical exegesis and commentary: some attempt to derive rabbinic law from pentateuchal law through a distinctive type of 'close reading'. Other collections seem more like academic commentary (Genesis Rabbah), while still others are collections of homilies on biblical texts, probably meant to provide raw material to preachers. Some of these texts will be discussed in more detail in Chapter 6.

[6] Alon 1977 (articles originally published in the 1930s and 1940s) provides the classic formulation of this view.

If the former view were correct, its effect would be to domesticate the high and later Roman imperial Jews; they would be recognizably like medieval and early modern Jews, organized in local religious communities, partially separated from their non-Jewish environment, practising a familiar type of rabbinic piety. Lurking not far in the background is an implicit claim or assumption about the transhistorical authenticity of the communal/rabbinic model of Jewish life, which is imagined to have been normatively Jewish even before the destruction in 70. The distinguished Jewish historian Salo Baron (1895–1989) had gone so far as to backdate the emergence of the local Jewish religious community to the Early Iron Age, arguing that it was a necessary response to weak central political control (Baron 1942). The argument is assuredly valid in so far as local forms of political and social organization assume enhanced importance in the absence of a strong political centre, but it is revealingly unclear why Baron thought that those Iron Age Palestinian local organizations were anything like traditional Jewish communities. The argument is circular, or essentialist: the ancient organizations must have been like Jewish communities, because that is how Jews naturally organize themselves unless some disaster, or a strong state, intervenes – as in the second century BCE, say, or the nineteenth century CE.[7]

The specific problems with supposing that semi- or quasi-rabbinic-style local Jewish communal organization was the norm in the High and Later Roman Empire have been adumbrated earlier in this book: though the village community and, in the diaspora, some type of local Jewish community were necessarily important types of organization, there is no evidence that they were anything like the medieval and early modern model. We know next to nothing about what went on in Palestinian Jewish villages or indeed in most diaspora communities pre-70, but the little we do know puts the Jerusalem Temple at the centre of their piety (Sanders 1992). The view that local Jewish religious life was controlled by the Pharisees is not supported by any evidence beyond a single dubious and hard-to-parse statement by Josephus (*Ant.* 18.15). By the first century, Jewish settlements in the diaspora might often have synagogues, or prayer houses, as well, but even here there is no evidence for the sort of self-conception that all medieval local Jewish communities shared, as constituting a holy assembly, a miniaturized version of biblical Israel. There is also no evidence that ancient communities performed the sorts of social and redistributive functions – caring for the sick, the elderly,

---

[7] A version of this critique appears already in Baer 1950.

widows, and orphans, burying the dead, providing dowries for needy brides, redeeming captives, and so on – that medieval and early modern ones ideally did (S. Schwartz 2001: 275–89). Nor is there any evidence for the existence of a distinct class of religious experts/judges/liturgical professionals, in other words, rabbis. There is plenty of evidence that diaspora communities, especially in the third century and following, were led for almost all purposes by their wealthier members (Rajak and Noy 1993).

The failed rebellions had a devastating impact on all forms of Jewish corporate organization. The obvious reason for this is that they ended in death, enslavement and dislocation, all on a very large scale. The two largest concentrations of Jews in the Roman world, in the district of Judaea and in Alexandria and Egypt, had simply been destroyed. The focal point of Jewish piety, the temple of Jerusalem, by 130 was irrevocably gone. The maximalists tend to suppose that ancient rabbis had some sort of recognized authority – recognized primarily by the Jews themselves, but also at least by default by the Roman state. In this view, the authority of the Torah survived 70 largely unscathed, in fact conceivably enhanced, since the rabbis who interpreted the Torah no longer had to compete with the priests who ran the temple, or the romanizing Herodians who controlled secular politics. Indeed, the rabbinic organization which quickly emerged after 70 constituted in what was left of Jewish settlement in Palestine after Bar Kokhba (Galilee, eventually – perhaps starting in the fourth century – western Golan, parts of the Carmel region and the Beth Shean valley, and the southern and north-western fringes of Judaea, plus scattered Jewish settlement in coastal and desert-fringe cities: Lapin 2012: 25–37) a kind of state within a state, whose authority was more or less recognized in what was left of the diaspora, too.

This view is untenable. Until Roman authority began to crumble in the later third century, and then drastically shifted focus in the fourth in the wake of Constantine's conversion to Christianity, the Jews simply could not constitute anything like a state within a state in northern Palestine. The Jews had had partial autonomy within the Roman system before 66. One of the points of fully annexing the province in 70 was to prevent a recurrence of the chaos that that unworkable situation had produced; the Jews had no vestiges of autonomy, and no leadership, rabbinic or otherwise. By 135, they not only were tremendously reduced in number but also largely lacked meaningful legal personality. As far as the Roman state was concerned, Jewishness was a voluntary status which was regarded at best with indifference but in reality, at least in the second century, more often with suspicion and hostility. What mattered about the Jews now was that they were Roman subjects, politically ruled by the governor of Judaea/Palaestina in conjunction with the city councils of the *poleis* of the province, expected to conduct their lives in accordance with some type of Roman law.[8] If they were not among the *dediticii*, then in 212 they became Roman citizens (Lapin 2012: 25–37). By then, the distinction may not have mattered much in day-to-day practice: before and after 212, whether subjects or citizens, they probably preferred the prestige of Roman law and Roman courts but often resorted to local arbitrators (Cotton 2007b).

Presumably despite this there were villages in Palestine, and, especially, Jewish communities outside it, where life went on to some extent as previously – some elements, at least, of an earlier lifestyle could be preserved. We know amazingly little about what this may have entailed. The Torah was not just a ritual code but a civil and criminal code as well. The Torah's criminal law could not be observed any longer; at most it could be adduced as justification for judicial 'self-help'. There is only one dubious story, told by Origen, about an influential Jew after 70 constituting a court and trying and executing a criminal (*Ad Africanum* 20 (14)). As a ritual code, the Torah focused heavily on instructions concerning sacrifice and ritual purity but there were other rules as well not dependent on the temple. Rural Palestinian Jews could easily enough avoid work on the Sabbath, but this was a much bigger challenge for Jews living in Roman cities, though it was possible even there provided there was a bit of outside help to ensure that Jews were not summoned to court or pressed into public service on their holy day. In fact, there is now excellent evidence that in the absence of such help Jews did routinely violate basic Jewish laws in diasporic environments.[9] They could also observe the laws prohibiting consumption of certain animals. What other marked Jewish practices they engaged in

---

[8] This summarizes the argument of S. Schwartz 2001: 103–76; for discussion of its reception, see S. Schwartz forthcoming.

[9] Clarysse, Remijsen and Depauw 2010: an incisive and unchallengeable demonstration that at Apollinopolis Magna (Edfu) in Egypt, between 69 and 117 CE, the Jews made their tax payments on Sabbaths as commonly as on other days of the week; at least as significantly, they almost never paid the tax to the *fiscus Iudaicus* on the Sabbath, demonstrating that (1) when offered the opportunity they would not handle money or perform government services on the Sabbath; (2) the tax to the *fiscus Iudaicus* was presumably collected at Edfu by a Jew, who respected Jewish religious sensibilities (contrast the comments in *CPJ* II: 109, 115–16 and on no. 240, an ostrakon mentioning a Jewish collector of the 'bath-tax', not the Jewish tax); (3) the Jews of Edfu were engaged in conscious religious compromise by paying regular taxes on the Sabbath; (4) thus, they compartmentalized, because the Roman state and/or local authorities did not normally acknowledge and respect their wishes and desires.

we cannot know. Nowadays the most familiar Jewish rituals are Sabbath prayers in a synagogue, fasting on Yom Kippur, the *seder* on Passover eve, and lighting Hanukkah candles. But before 400 CE in Palestine there were very few synagogues, and the *seder* is a specifically rabbinic practice first attested in the Mishnah. It is a remote adaptation of the Paschal sacrifice, and there is no way of knowing how common it was outside of rabbinic circles. The Palestinian Talmud itself tells of a Jew living at Rome but in close contact with the Palestinian rabbis who observed Passover not with a *seder* but with the sacrificial slaughter of a lamb, something the rabbis strongly opposed. Though the Day of Atonement was fundamentally a cultic, temple-based observance, there is some evidence for the attractiveness of the fast and rituals of penitence outside the temple, too. Philo knew of Jews at Alexandria whose Jewish practice, in a surprising anticipation of modern behaviour, was limited to fasting and praying on Yom Kippur; evidently some Jews had figured out ways to observe the essentially cultic Jewish festivals outside Jerusalem (Stökl Ben Ezra 2003: 107–14). Hanukkah candles are certainly attested but are a very trivial ritual, important in our world because Jews living in Christian countries want a Christmas-substitute for their children, but peripheral even in the recent past. What *ancient* Jewish popular piety might have consisted of otherwise, beyond some type of Sabbath observance, avoidance of pork and circumcision of males (S. Cohen 2008) – a concatenation of practices mentioned repeatedly in ancient sources, Jewish, pagan and Christian – we can scarcely guess.

Perhaps the most important thing that some Jewish villagers might have done was to eschew Roman courts for some civil legal matters and bring cases to traditional Jewish judges and administrators instead. Now these officials had lost formal governmental authority, and so they would have functioned as arbitrators and advisers. The Roman state would hardly have opposed the use of arbitrators, and such former officials at least had some legal expertise. Some might conceivably have preferred their judicial services to the ministrations of, say, doddering village elders (Cotton 2002; Lapin 2012: 119–23). There is, however, very little evidence that this happened, at least before the later third and fourth centuries, when arbitrators using the laws of the Torah began to acquire a measure of official status (culminating in *Cod. Theod.* 2.1.10, 398 CE). On the other hand, if no Jews used such arbitrators, the arbitrators would have ceased to exist, but demonstrably they did not. Instead, they became the rabbis, exerted a profound impact on Jewish posterity, and so deserve some special attention.

WHERE DID THE RABBIS COME FROM?

In rabbinic literature, the rabbis refer to themselves as *hakhamim* (sages), or as *zeqenim* (elders), or occasionally as *rabbanim* (rabbis). Sage and elder are very different sorts of social roles; in an ancient Near Eastern setting, sages constituted a profession, elders members of a weakly institutionalized leadership class, especially in villages. In the rabbis' actual, Roman, world, neither of these roles was important any longer, and the fact that the rabbis used these terms tells us little – though not nothing – about who they were, beyond their embrace of archaism. It bears repeating that there were no rabbis before 70. Rabbinic literature itself never applies the title 'rabbi' even to pre-70 figures who clearly played an important role in rabbinic prehistory, such as Hillel (often erroneously called Rabbi Hillel by modern writers), a contemporary of Herod. It has often been supposed that the rabbis were simply the post-70 version of the Pharisees – a supposition fundamental to the maximalist view: if the rabbis were Pharisees, and the Pharisees actually did control Jewish life outside the temple before 70, then they could simply continue after 70 to exercise the authority they had achieved earlier. If by contrast they were a new group, they had to struggle for legitimacy and for a role in Jewish life. But were they in fact Pharisees?

The Pharisees and the rabbis constituted very different sorts of organizations. By the first century the former were a relatively closed pietistic group – a sect – while the rabbis emerged in the course of the second and third centuries as a professional class, whose primary role was to serve as judges or legal advisers (Hezser 1997; Lapin 2012). Pharisees presumably had to be initiated into their sect, an act which seems not to have conferred on the initiates anything like judicial authority, whereas rabbis received 'appointments' (in Palestine), or ordination (in Babylonia; Y. Sanhedrin 1.2, 19a). The qualification for appointment or ordination was a long period of study with and in effect apprenticeship to another rabbi (S. Cohen 1999b: 950–6). Josephus said that there were 6,000 Pharisees in his day, but there were never more than a few dozen 'appointed' rabbis in Palestine at any one time; this certainly in part reflects the status of rabbis as a professional group: how many unauthorized judges were needed in Galilee? And there could at some period have been a larger number of 'disciples of the sages' (*talmidei hakhamim*), or 'associates' (*haverim*) – students and scholars who had not received appointment (Beer 1982). But partly there was a shift in scale (Lapin 2012: 83–7).

For the first post-destruction generation – long before the institution-alization of rabbinic training – we know only about thirty names. Even those of the leading rabbinic figures, in terms of the quantity of their pre-served legal opinions and their prominence in later rabbinic narratives, men like Rabban Yohanan ben Zakkai, Rabbi Eliezer ben Hyrcanus, and Rabbi Tarfon, are unattested outside rabbinic literature, except in some later patristic works. They had no known careers before 70, and are never mentioned by Josephus or in the New Testament. Who were they, then? Josephus tends to mention the names of members of two overlapping groups of Jews, political leaders and rebel leaders. We can infer that the earliest rabbis, with one or two exceptions, were neither. It stands to rea-son that they were the remnant of the Judaean clerisy; about half of the first generation of rabbis were identifiably priests, but with one exception not members of the high priestly families (the one exception is someone called Hanina, Captain of the Priests, apparently formerly a high-ranking temple administrator, but peripheral in rabbinic tradition).[10] Presumably the future rabbis had been mostly the sort of people Josephus did not mention: not political leaders, great landowners or leading high priests, but administrators, judges, scribes. The lower priesthood, the main sect-arian groups, and the religious and civil administration of pre-66 Jewish Palestine probably heavily overlapped, and the rabbis were their remnant. That so few names of the first generation were remembered reminds us of how thoroughly the Jews' institutional centre had been crushed in 70.

RABBIS AND PHARISEES

The one post-70 rabbi whose family is mentioned by Josephus and in the New Testament, though he himself is not, is Rabban Gamaliel.[11] His grand-father, also named Gamaliel (who is also mentioned in rabbinic texts) was the teacher and defender of the apostle Paul, in the unlikely event that we can trust the reports in *Acts of the Apostles* (5.34–40; 22.3). Gamaliel II's father Simon is a somewhat less fuzzy historical character, since he fig-ures importantly in Josephus' accounts of the revolt. He was a leader of the *demos*, probably meaning the non-priests, of Jerusalem and an ally of the rebel high priest and Sadducee Ananus son of Ananus, and also a per-sonal opponent of Josephus, instrumental in an attempt to dislodge him

---

[10] Quoted at M. Pesahim 1.6; M. Eduyot 2.1–2; M. Avot 3.2; M. Zevahim 12.4; M. Negaim 1.4; M. Parah 3.1. He was manifestly remembered as an expert on the 'priestly' topics of sacrifice and purity.

[11] Sources are assembled in Kanter 1980.

from his post in Galilee (*Jewish War* 4.159; *V.* 190ff.). Josephus does not report his fate, but it is inconceivable that he survived the revolt, in fact rather surprising that his son did. According to both Acts and Josephus, the family were prominent Pharisees. Since no one was born into sectarian membership, we do not know whether Rabban Gamaliel was himself a Pharisee, but he is certainly the only rabbi known to have come from a Pharisaic background; the rabbis are thus running slightly behind the early Christians, who boasted an actual initiated Pharisee in an influential position: Paul. (Whether the boast is true or not is a different matter.)

There is thus no prosopographical justification for positing a special relationship between Pharisees and rabbis, but the idea may have some basis nonetheless. Some of the views Josephus and the New Testament attribute to the Pharisees strongly resonate with views expressed in rabbinic texts. These range from lofty theological notions to odd details of religious law. Pharisees and rabbis (but also Christians!) believed in bodily resurrection of the dead at some future point (M. Sanhedrin 10.1); both believed that the law of the written Torah was supplemented by a body of legal traditions transmitted orally, though the Pharisees called this 'the tradition of the fathers', and the rabbis, 'the oral Torah',[12] or simply, 'the Torah' (M. Avot 1.1); and both required Jews to tithe even herbs – the most negligible agricultural product – and offer them as gifts to priests and Levites (Matt. 23.23; Luke 11.42; M. Demai 2.1; M. Ma'aserot 4.5). Some scholars have posited that Paul's style of argumentation is indebted to his Pharisaic background, because it seems 'talmudical'. But this view is almost certainly incorrect, since the 'rabbinic' style of argumentation probably owes little or nothing to the Pharisees, having been one of the latest rabbinic characteristics to develop. In fact the resemblances are slight and probably accidental. By contrast, the 'midrashic' elements present in all New Testament books (see note 5 above), though perhaps most common in Matthew and Paul, were the common property of all Jewish groups in the first century, not just Pharisees.

Nevertheless, there is no justification for supposing that even the earliest rabbinic text, the Mishnah (*c.* 200 CE), can be used to reconstruct Pharisaic law. It certainly contains a few such laws, and may even contain many, but our ignorance of Pharisaic law is nearly complete, so we simply

---

[12] Though the term itself never appears in early rabbinic texts – the earliest is probably Lamentations Rabbah, ed. Buber, proem 2, *c.* fifth–sixth centuries – and only twice in the *c.* seventh-century Babylonian Talmud (Yoma 28b; Qiddushin 66a). Nevertheless, all rabbinic texts seem to assume that rabbinic teaching is Torah-like or a component of Torah, and that it is ideally transmitted orally. See Strack and Stemberger 1996: 31–44; Jaffee 2001.

have no way of knowing. There is almost certainly material from non-Pharisaic sources in the Mishnah as well. Indeed, the classic minimalist argument advanced by Jacob Neusner in 1981 maintains that the Mishnah contains not only Pharisaic material (Neusner regarded all demonstrably early anonymous material on purity law, among other topics, as Pharisaic), but also priestly material, and material based on nonsectarian scribal and judicial practice (Neusner 1981). Shaye Cohen pushed the argument further, claiming that there is probably even less Pharisaic material in the Mishnah than Neusner thought (since there is no reason a priori to think that early rabbinic purity law is of Pharisaic origin), and that the crucial feature of the Mishnah, its apparent embrace of legal variety or disagreement, demonstrates that a kind of 'pluralism' was hardwired into rabbinic ideology from the very start, right after 70. The first rabbis were a coalition of sectarians and priests, maybe or maybe not mainly Pharisaic, who made the hard decision to abandon their sectarian divisions and 'agree to disagree', without, that is, the legal disagreements being allowed to generate separate social organization, as before 70. Anyone who refused, who remained wedded to a sectarian identity, was barred from the organization (S. Cohen 1984). This is meant to be contrasted with Church councils in the fourth century and later, which rejected pluralism and relied instead on compromise. (Though on closer examination the models are not very different; the compromises just took different forms.) In this view, to return to the rabbis, the group may have owed more to the Pharisees than they were willing to admit, since their ideology of anti-sectarian legal pluralism led them to conceal such ties as did exist. The Mishnah's single report of Pharisaic law (Yadayim 4.6–7), which the text seems to identify as 'ours', is vestigial, and the much more common rabbinic self-identification with the Pharisees found in the Talmuds, and a similar identification scattered about in patristic literature, are due in one case to rabbinic antiquarianism, and in the other, to Christian anti-Jewish polemic.

Possibly, though, the opposite is true. Rabbinic literature claims *more* connection between rabbis and Pharisees than had existed in reality (Lapin 2012: 46–9). We can never really know. We can however, follow Neusner, Cohen and Lapin, in posing the problem, something maximalists have not done. But we must admit that the answers are circular. We should also (following Lapin and Hezser 1997) be very sceptical about the existence of anything like a rabbinic movement immediately after 70, or indeed after 135. I would suggest, again, that the early figures recalled by rabbinic literature were the scattered and crushed remnant of the old clerical class. This implies that, whatever divided them, they also shared a great deal, but the first real evidence that they began to form a distinctive and self-conscious organization – one which did not resemble the pre-70 Pharisaic organization – is the Mishnah itself. This text, by constantly naming 'rabbis', setting them in dialogue with one another and attributing to them legal opinions presented as more or less authoritative, in effect *constructs* a rabbinic organisation. It testifies to the emergence of a sense of corporate self-consciousness among Torah-based arbitrators and teachers (Lapin 2012: 56–9; contrast S. Cohen 1999b). How long before 200 this self-consciousness is likely to have emerged we have no way of knowing; there is no reason to accept Cohen's view that the rabbinic 'agreement to disagree' was a feature of the earliest post-70 figures. Sectarian and priestly self-consciousness may have survived among proto-rabbis longer than Cohen thought.

NEW VALUES

Two centuries or more passed between the annexation of Provincia Judaea and the institutional consolidation of the rabbis and their leader, the patriarch, to be discussed below. It was only then, in the course of the third century, that they emerged as meaningful competitors for influence and prestige among the Jews of Palestine and its neighbours. They were in competition not with a group of alternative Torah scholars, or others who claimed to represent, interpret and mediate the traditional institutions and practices of the Jews. Rather, they were in competition with what we can designate Roman urban localism, that is, with Palestinian Roman provincial culture. This culture had its human representatives, too, city councillors and other wealthy citizens in places like Tiberias, Sepphoris, Caesarea Maritima, Joppa, Lydda-Diospolis, and a few other cities.

Archaeology, epigraphy, numismatics and even rabbinic texts indicate that the public life of the province of Judaea/Palaestina in the second and third centuries in both the largely Jewish region of Galilee, and the mixed areas near Galilee and along the coast, had little or nothing about it that was specifically Jewish. The small, hilly region of upper Galilee was enduringly unurbanized, but otherwise the province had an abundance of cities (Jones 1931). Most, aside from the provincial capital Caesarea, were quite small, but to all appearances they played the same role, as political, social, economic and cultural centres, as cities did in other urbanized areas of the Roman East. If we relied on archaeology alone, we would have no reason to think that High Imperial Palestine, even in heavily Jewish areas like Galilee, was in any way unusual.

Let us focus briefly on the two Galilean cities which are the most likely to have been overwhelmingly Jewish in population, Tiberias and Sepphoris. Both cities were founded by Antipas son of Herod early in the first century CE. Tiberias lay on the site of a tiny fishing village near the centre of the western shore of the Sea of Galilee (Josephus *Ant.* 18.36–8). Sepphoris was already a large village, 25 km west-south-west of Tiberias, in the low hills of south-western Galilee when Antipas declared it a city and named it Autokratoris (Emperorville; Josephus *Ant.* 18.27) – like Tiberias, it advertised the ruler's friendship with the emperor, though it was still usually called by its old name. Sepphoris seems to have had an entirely Jewish population in the early first century, but Tiberias had a 'Greek' minority, massacred by the Jews around the time of the outbreak of the Great Revolt (Josephus *V.* 67). Josephus regarded the Tiberians, who had been assembled from elsewhere, unlike the Sepphorites, as a rabble, but this reflects in part his own bad experiences in the city in 66 (detailed in *V.*).

Very little is known about the public life of the cities. They appear to have been constitutionally Greek, in the sense that they had notional autonomy – citizenship, attached rural territories and city councils. Tiberias may have had a hippodrome or stadium, Sepphoris eventually had an impressive theatre, as did Tiberias, but probably not before the second century. Before 70, neither town seems to have had pagan temples (unless Tiberias had some discreet shrines kept by its Greeks), or much in the way of public statuary. In one residential district of Sepphoris, probably built in the first century, many of the houses were equipped with bathing installations identified by most archaeologists as *miqva'ot* (Rutgers 1998). If the consensus is correct, then a segment of the Sepphorite population was careful to observe Jewish rules of ritual purity. Josephus says that, when Tiberias rebelled in 66, the rebels destroyed the animal friezes decorating the Herodian palace (*V.* 65). They did this out of a sense of pious outrage at the use of images; if there had been statuary to destroy, Josephus is likely to have mentioned it. Tiberias did, however, have a synagogue (*V.* 277). In some aspects of their public life, then, the cities were quite unlike standard Greek cities.

Both cities experienced a rather mysterious change in the early second century. Perhaps behind it was the arrival of a second Roman legion probably around 120 CE, encamped near though not in Galilee; or heightened anxiety on the part of northern Palestinian Jews over the rebellion sweeping through north Africa; or whatever unknown episodes lay in the background of the Bar Kokhba Revolt. Or perhaps the Jews were simply participating in an empire-wide political and cultural shift, the consolidation and standardization of the provincial system. Whatever the explanation, the facts are straightforward: all the Palestinian cities became more 'Roman', and less 'Jewish'. This is unlikely to have been commanded from above, as used to be thought, because the shift occurred at different times in different cities, though generally between 100 and 140 CE.[13] In practice this meant that Tiberias and Sepphoris for the first time acquired such crucial municipal institutions as theatres. The Sepphorites now built a Roman temple, very recently excavated, and also gave their city a revealing new name, Diocaesarea (Zeus-and-Caesartown). Both cities jettisoned their traditional Jewish coinages – never completely Jewish, anyway, because they used images of the emperor – and adopted more emphatically pagan coinages, featuring images of gods and temples. If we can trust the Palestinian Talmud, Tiberias, which had been largely image-free before 70, was now as image-filled as any other eastern Roman city. Other cities, like Neapolis, which was Israelite (or Samaritan) rather than Jewish, and eventually Lydda (raised to city status in 192 and renamed Diospolis – Zeusville: Smallwood 1981: 491), and Ioppa, behaved similarly. By 140, not only had Palestine been urbanized, but its cities had been thoroughly romanized, in terms of the sort of public institutions and social behaviour that leave monumental archaeological traces; in this new model of municipal culture and politics there was no room for more than trace elements of Jewishness. However, one peculiarity should be noted: until the adlection of the Tiberian patriarchs sometime in the fourth century, no Jew residing in any province, no Palestinian of whatever ethnic-religious background, and no resident of the province of Arabia, was admitted to the Roman Senate. The exclusion seems intentional but there is no obvious explanation for it (Bowersock 1994 [1984]).

Rather surprisingly, there is no evidence for any shift in the demographic balance of these cities after 100, nor any reason to think the composition of their city councils changed (since the same changes are attested in all-Jewish, part-Jewish, and not-very-Jewish cities in the same general period). Furthermore, there is more evidence in Palestine than elsewhere for the survival and even the promulgation of a version – in fact a highly rationalized, intellectually substantial, 'high-culture' version – of the local pre-Roman culture. In other words, what we learn from the earliest

[13] Detailed discussion: S. Schwartz 2001: 129–61; on the coinage of Neapolis, Tiberias and Sepphoris: Kushnir-Stein 2008; 2009; Dionysiac mosaic at Sepphoris: Talgam and Weiss 2004; pagan temple at Sepphoris: Weiss 2010; citadel of Sepphoris: Strange, Longstaff and Groh 2006; Tiberias: Hirschfeld 2004; 2007.

rabbinic literature is that, unusually for a Roman provincial setting, the local culture – Judaism in this case – survived not as a folk culture, partially preserved by a not yet fully deracinated peasantry, though perhaps it did so. It survived precisely as the high culture of a kind of elite.

But that elite was marginalized by romanization.[14] 'Romanization' is a misleadingly bland term; it makes one think of a process that happened on its own, due to some internal dynamic. The political realities the term conceals were in this case especially gruesome. Whatever else was going through the minds of the city councillors of Tiberias and Sepphoris among other places when they transformed their towns into proper small Roman cities, we can be pretty sure that existential dread was not far under the surface; they knew the price of resistance and understood that the time had finally come to yield. And even so, a reduced element of the former clerisy continued to do its work out of view, continued to make claims on aspects of what was left of Jewish life in Palestine. It continued to promote the Torah, not Roman provincial law, as the code by which Jews should lead their lives.

It seems very unlikely that these scattered proto-rabbinic survivors at first had much of an audience. The Jews had been crushed, and the Romans had won. Some, at least, of the survivors must have thought that, even in theological terms, this justified the celebration, as on the coinage of Diocaesarea-Sepphoris, if not even the worship, of Jupiter Optimus Maximus and friends. It is also hard to see how the rabbis could have competed with the cultural prestige of the Roman city at its second-century high water mark, and how, as judges or advocates, they could have competed with the governors' courts or the city councils (S. Cohen 1999b: 961–71). In fact, there is a set of texts which suggests that they could not (Cotton 1998). These are the papyri known as the Babatha archive (P. Yadin) and the Salome Komaise archive (XHever/Seiyal).

The papyri – among which were the Bar Kokhba letters, discussed above – were the personal papers of a moderately well-to-do Jewish woman named Babatha daughter of Simon, from the town of Mahoza or Mahoz Eglatain at the southern tip of the Dead Sea. Mahoza was not in Judaea/Palaestina, but before 106 in the kingdom of Nabataea, and from 106 in Provincia Arabia. Babatha's papers indicate that the population of her town was divided into two roughly separate but thoroughly intertwined groups, Jews and Arabs/Nabataeans, which can be distinguished,

---

[14] A term I retain in full consciousness of recent critiques: Le Roux 2004; Wallace-Hadrill 2008; Mattingly 2011.

like Serbs and Croats in modern times, by the slightly different versions of the same language, in our case Aramaic, they sometimes used (when they weren't using Greek; Jewish and Nabataean Aramaic were written differently but may have sounded the same), and by the types of names they chose to give their children, when they weren't giving them neutrally Greek or Latin names. In brief, people with biblical Hebrew names did not give their children Arabic names, and people with Arabic names did not give their children biblical Hebrew names. Documents concerning interactions between people with Arabic names are written in either Greek or Nabataean Aramaic, but not Jewish Aramaic; those concerning people with Jewish names are written in either Greek or Jewish Aramaic, but not Nabataean (Cotton 1999). There is only one exceptional man in the documents with a Hebrew name and an Arabic patronym (P. Yadin 6). Otherwise there is no clear evidence of marriage between the groups though there almost inescapably was; they were in any case neighbours, friends, business partners, and socially close to the extent of serving as guardians for one another's children (Cotton 1993).

Babatha's papers reached their final resting-place in the Judaean desert around the time of the Bar Kokhba revolt. Presumably she fled there, but we do not know why. Previously, Babatha had been a moderately successful landowner and businesswoman – despite her illiteracy (P. Yadin 15) – and was also widowed and had remarried, and had a son by her first husband. Some of Babatha's papers pre-date the Roman annexation of Arabia in 106, but most of them are later. Roman historians have learned much from the documents about the impact of romanization on provincial legal practice, but for our purposes the pre-annexation documents are disappointing, since none of them concerns legal transactions between Jews alone and so do not inform us whether Jews in Nabataean Mahoza followed Jewish law or Nabataean law or some other code.[15]

Strikingly, there is no hint in the entire collection, although many of the documents concern transactions between Jews, that Jews ever used the services of Jewish legal experts. Some of the documents show some Jewish legal influence, and one, the contract which formed Babatha's second marriage, is a *ketubbah*, written in Jewish Aramaic (P. Yadin 10). *Ketubbah* (Hebrew; literally, written contract) is the traditional Jewish name for such a document, and it is traditional because it is the term the rabbis used, and their version of the *ketubbah* is still used by Jews who adhere to tradition. Like the rabbinic marriage contract, Babatha's contract is

---

[15] Cotton 1998; 1999; 2002; 2007b; Wolff 1978; Galsterer 1986.

also designated *ketubta* (the Aramaic equivalent of the Hebrew term); but its contents are not identical to those of the rabbinic document. It does, however, bear a definite family resemblance. Babatha's *ketubbah* was written not by a rabbi or even by a Jewish scribe, but by the groom himself. Germanos bar Yehudah, the town scribe of Mahoza, was Jewish, to judge by his patronym, but his work provides no evidence that this fact was professionally relevant; he was a scribe who was Jewish – and could write in Jewish Aramaic, Nabataean, and Greek – not a Jewish scribe.

Most of Babatha's transactions followed some version of Roman provincial law; when Babatha went to court, she did not use a Jewish arbitrator but the city council of Petra, then capital of Arabia, a very long walk from Mahoza (P. Yadin 12–15). If we were to extrapolate from Babatha's case, then we would have to conclude that even quite strongly identified Jews, who cultivated a sense of separation from their neighbours, and also a sense of connection to a distinctive pre-Roman past (as implied by the continuing use of biblical names), might prefer Roman to Jewish civil law, and Roman courts to Jewish arbitrators. The exception among Babatha's activities was marriage; at least some Jews might prefer to be married *ke-din Moshe vi-Yehuda'ei* (P. Yadin 10), according to the law of Moses and the Jews; the rabbinic formulation is similar but not identical, *ke-dat Moshe ve-Yisrael*, according to the rule of Moses and Israel; this refers to the details of the legal and financial relationship between the couple. But Babatha also preserved the marriage contract of her stepdaughter Selampsione, married to Ioudas Kimber in the consulship of Publius Metilius Nepos and Marcus Annius Libo (128 CE), a marriage contracted *hellenikôi nomôi* (by Hellenic law; P. Yadin 18, cf. P. Yadin 37). Jews who married in Babatha's world apparently had options; there was a recognized type of marriage *à la juive*, as well as marriage *à la grecque*; we could speculate about marriages *à l'arabe* and *à la romaine*, too.[16] It is of great importance for our understanding of rabbinic history that the rabbis apparently adopted and adapted the traditional type of Jewish marriage and made it *de rigueur* – for the rabbis; Greek marriage was not a legitimate option for Jews (Lapin 2012: 133–5). If we could extrapolate from this case, we could learn an important lesson about the nature of the rabbis' engagement with Jewish legal traditions: they not only absorbed them, but also tried to regulate, reshape and limit them. But it remains the case that even marriage, the only known Jewish civil legal institution in Babatha's

---

[16] Marriage *ethei rhomaikoi* is mentioned in P. Nessana 18 and 20, both from the mid-sixth century, but *ethos rhomaikon* here may be equivalent to *nomos hellenikos* in the earlier texts. See on this point and on the possibility of 'Nabataean' marriage Cotton 2008.

world, was not always practised as such by the Jews themselves, and when it was, it did not require the intervention of an expert. Yehudah bar Elazar Khthushion, Babatha's second husband, knew on his own what needed to be written, though *how* he knew we do not know.

Babatha and friends largely ignored Jewish civil law, and had no room in their legal lives for rabbis or rabbi-types. The papyri do not tell us whether or how they observed Jewish ritual laws. Did they observe the Sabbath and holidays?[17] Keep kosher? There is no evidence of a synagogue at Mahoza, but the Jews could have assembled to pray outdoors – it almost never rains or gets very cold there – but we do not know if they did so. Did they possess a Torah scroll? Did they hire a teacher to teach their children to read it? The papyri tell us hardly anything about their piety, but we would perhaps not expect them to. So the Babatha papyri provide limited though suggestive information about the attractiveness of Roman legal norms and institutions among Jews, and the virtual failure of Jewish legal institutions, but next to nothing about the survival of a somewhat shrunken Jewish 'little tradition'.

Given what we know from archaeology, epigraphy and papyrology, we can say with certainty that Judaism ceased to function not only as an authorized set of religious and legal norms, but also as an informal component of public life even in the most heavily Jewish areas of High Imperial Palestine. Without any known shift in demography, the formerly Jewish cities of Palestine were now standard Greco-Roman cities in every way, including in their religious life, and larger villages in their territories emulated them. The main component of the elites of Palestine, whatever their background, mediated to their clients and dependents not Jewish culture or some other local culture, but the normative Greek culture of the Roman East. Greco-Roman social institutions, most importantly euergetism and patronage, had had surprisingly limited traction in pre-70 Jewish Palestine, but they now became the standard cultural form of redistributive practice. In Tiberias and Sepphoris, as elsewhere, the aristocracy advertised and celebrated its munificence by providing theatres, bathhouses and other monumental buildings for their cities, as members of their class did in every other city, by having themselves honoured in public, and by showering their friends and clients with their private liberality as well (S. Schwartz 2001: 136–53). The magnificently decorated *triclinia* of

---

[17] For suggestive discussion about the Sabbath in the Greek Babatha papyri, see Katzoff and Schreiber 1998. At very least the Sabbath was familiar in Mahoza as a time marker (P. Yadin 7), and the Jews may conceivably have avoided legal activity and/or writing, too.

the great houses of third-century Sepphoris are familiar to every visitor to the site, and these tell us much about the typicality of the social organization and cultural interests of the city (Talgam and Weiss 2004).

THE RISE OF THE PATRIARCHATE

The version of traditional pre-Roman Jewish norms promulgated by the rabbis certainly had some adherents. Though the rabbis before 180–200 CE probably remained a largely unintegrated, scattered group of sub-elite informal experts, by the end of the second century they began to gravitate to the very cities which were the epicentre of romanization, Tiberias, Sepphoris, Caesarea and Diospolis-Lydda, and were becoming increasingly aware that they had a set of corporate interests which they began to promote (S. Cohen 1999b; Lapin 2012: 76–82; contra: Hezser 1997). Somehow related – my vagueness is intentional – to the coalescence of the rabbis is the rise of a figure with the evocative title of *nasi*, prince, non-royal leader, borne also by Bar Kokhba. Some late rabbinic traditions date the existence of the position – understood in such stories as the presidency of the High Court, or Sanhedrin, in Jerusalem – far back in the Hellenistic period;[18] while responsible modern scholars reject this view, they do not agree whether the *nesi'ut* – called henceforth following the lead of the Theodosian Code among other late antique texts, 'patriarchate' – began shortly after 70, or around 200 (Jacobs 1995: 1–9 surveys the scholarship). The first definite incumbent in the position was Rabbi Judah I (Ha-nasi), the putative compiler/promulgator of the Mishnah. Later rabbinic tradition regarded him not only as the quintessential rabbi (to the extent that he is normally called simply Rabbi, or *Rabbenu Ha-qadosh* – our holy rabbi/master) but also as a powerful political leader, friend of an emperor (see above), and possessing ultimate judicial authority over the Jews as well. These stories manifestly retroject activities and types of authority

[18] Two of the most common features of rabbinic stories about the post-biblical past are (1) that they retroject rabbinic ideas and practices into the pre-rabbinic past and (2) that they think in institutional terms. The first tendency is more or less self-explanatory; the second, which is not, has received far less attention from scholars in part because many of them simply took this rabbinic construction at face value. It is in fact not hard to demonstrate that not only did no Sanhedrin exist after 70 – few scholars believe in it any longer – but no such institution existed previously either, as opposed to a much less formal and fluid body which combined political and judicial functions, like any Greek city council, but did not simply impose rules in a mechanical way, as in the rabbinic imagination (cf. Goodblatt 1994). I would argue that the rabbis imagined or described not only the past but their own role in the present in institutional terms because it was the strongest possible assertion of their own legitimacy. Institutions are frozen power relations: no one needs to force, threaten or cajole, and there is no playing politics.

possessed by later, mainly fourth-century, patriarchs onto one of the dynasty's revered founder figures. Indeed, these stories have a polemical thrust. By the time the patriarchate reached its peak, in the later fourth century, the patriarchs' ties to the rabbis had become frayed or worse; Palestinian rabbis manifestly told stories about Judah I as a way of reminding their constituents and possibly the patriarch himself of a great ancestor who had enjoyed enormous temporal power while remaining a leading figure in the world of Torah scholarship and piety. The historical Judah was a more modest figure, though some elements of the rabbinic stories about him are not implausible. He was both rabbi and patriarch, and may have been primarily a leader of the emerging rabbinic movement and/or the figure instrumental in its consolidation. He probably was a grandson or great-grandson of Gamaliel II, mentioned above – Gamaliel is regarded by some scholars as the founder of the patriarchal dynasty.[19] We cannot evaluate the claim that he compiled the Mishnah; the text itself provides no evidence one way or another.

Judah probably, and his immediate descendants certainly, ran a sort of religio-political establishment which was in the process of acquiring institutional heft, though rabbinic texts exaggerate this aspect of the patriarchal regime in the third century (Levine 1979; Appelbaum 2012). Certainly Judah was a rich man, though there is no knowing how he acquired his wealth (Stern 2003); his ancestral land was in Judaea, not Galilee (he lived in Bet Shearim and Sepphoris, his descendants moved to Tiberias), and his ancestor was a prominent rebel whose land would have been confiscated. In some respects Judah and his immediate descendants behaved simply like patrons, men who possessed bands of dependants and slaves and knew how to throw their weight around (S. Schwartz 2004; but see Appelbaum 2012), and who also enjoyed the ceremonial aspects of their status, rituals of deference designed to limit and mystify access to their persons, such as the *levée* or *salutatio* (Y. Horayot 3.5, 48c). They are described in Talmudic stories writing letters of reference for their clients, in the manner of Cicero, Pliny or Libanius (Y. Yebamot 12.6, 13a; Y. Hagigah 1.8, 76d; cf. Y. Moed Qatan 3.1, 81c).

In the course of the third century they began to build support outside the rabbinic movement. Some of this support came from the recovering Jewish communities of the diaspora. By the early fourth century

---

[19] S. Schwartz 1990; Goodblatt 1994; Contrast S. Stern 2003, arguing that Judah was the first patriarch, and that claims of his descent from Gamaliel were fictional; he was actually a wealthy Galilaean landowner. Lapin 2012: 22–3 also considers Judah the first patriarch but regards the dynasty's claims of Gamlielide/Hillelide ancestry as unassessable.

there is good evidence that the patriarchs employed people called *apostoloi* (envoys) whose interference in the internal affairs of diaspora Jewish communities was tolerated, if not welcomed, and who also raised funds for an increasingly regal patriarchal establishment (Epiphanius, Panarion 30; S. Schwartz 1999). In Palestine, the patriarchs assembled not only clients and other dependants, but a semblance of a little private army, called 'the Goths', maybe more like a gang of enforcers (Y. Horayot 3.1, 47a). They also assumed the right to appoint 'judges' (Y. Sanhedrin 1.2, 19a; Jacobs 1995: 172–5). The church father Origen wrote in 245 CE to his friend Julius Africanus of episodes in which the Jewish 'ethnarch', probably an alternative title for the patriarch, conducted 'secret trials according to the (Jewish) Law, and some are sentenced to death with no general authorization for it, but not without the knowledge of the emperor' (*Epistula ad Africanum* 20 (14)). Though it is customary to take this statement at face value, it may be worth wondering how Origen had come to learn of these trials, if they were secret.[20] Church fathers frequently claimed to know about the Jews' secret misbehaviour, and, though this particular claim is less incredible than most, it should still be recognized for what it is. Nevertheless, the story does presuppose the existence of a powerful but not yet well-known (Origen clearly does not expect Africanus to have heard of such a person) leader of the Jews, who still lacked official recognition; it could at least be imagined that he presided over a judicial establishment. In this respect, Origen supports the conclusions we can derive from a critical reading of Talmudic information about the patriarchs of the third century, as great men whose claims to supervise aspects of Jewish religious and legal life, in both Palestine and parts of the diaspora, were increasingly accepted.

The rise of the patriarchate probably presupposed two related developments. If rabbinic traditions are to be believed, the patriarchal dynasty began as a rabbinic family, and the rabbis never stopped thinking that the patriarch's chief role was to preside over a court which ran according to rabbinic rules. But by the middle of the third century, the patriarchs' clientele extended beyond the boundaries of the rabbinic movement. Patriarchal judicial appointees all employed the title 'rabbi' and wore a distinctive judicial robe, but the rabbis of the Talmud regarded some of these appointees as unacceptable, and spoke insultingly of 'those appointed for money', that is, either because of their wealth, or because they bribed the patriarch (Y. Bikkurim 3.3, 65c; Alon 1977: 375–435). We should try to resist the rabbis' judgement and adopt a 'value-neutral' approach to their

---

[20] A point surprisingly rarely noted in the scholarship on this text; but see Berkowitz 2006: 221 n. 44.

report. What they manifestly meant is that the patriarchs began attracting and offering emoluments to prominent non-rabbinic followers. Such men were not necessarily devoid of Jewish learning even if they lacked the rabbis' dedication and expertise. One of the burial caves at the late antique (probably third through fifth centuries) Jewish necropolis at Bet Shearim, not far from Sepphoris in south-western Galilee, contains a fair number of epitaphs, written in Hebrew, commemorating men titled 'Rabbi'.[21] None of these is identifiable with a rabbi mentioned in the Talmud, and several have names like Gamaliel which identify them as connected to the patriarchal dynasty, not necessarily by ties of kinship (another cave at Bet Shearim is thought by some scholars, plausibly but not provably, to have been used by one or more of the patriarchs). Hebrew is symbolically loaded, its use constituting a strong claim of identification with the Israelite-Jewish past and with the central institutions of Judaism, the temple and the Torah. All other epitaphs at Bet Shearim are written in Greek or Aramaic (in various dialects). The men buried in catacomb 20 of Bet Shearim were strongly distinct socially, claimed the title rabbi, yet cannot be identified with 'our' rabbis. They were probably just like the people the rabbis denounced as rich patriarchal lackeys.

Why did such men attach themselves to the patriarchal family? This brings us to the second development behind the rise of the patriarchate, the decline of the city in the course of the third century both as economic centre and as cultural model. The second-century construction boom in eastern Roman cities was a fact not just of archaeology and economics, but of politics, social organization and culture as well. Subtending it were a neo-oligarchic ideology of munificence, a politics of loyalty to Rome, and a devotion to some version of Hellenism (Zuiderhoek 2009). The building bust of the third century, whether or not we characterize it as a 'crisis', implies the decline (let's not shrink from the word) in the normative status of Greco-Roman culture generally speaking (*CEHGRW* 758–64). The recession of the curial class and its ideals benefited not just Jewish patriarchs and their clients, but other political entrepreneurs offering alternatives to Roman urbanism as well, maybe most importantly, Christian bishops (Liebeschuetz 2001: 104–36). In the third century Christianity rose decisively through the social ranks and for the first time began to attract, admittedly in very small numbers, genuinely elite adherents. Surely this is to some extent because traditional urbanism was losing its power to satisfy, as it ran out of money. The same fact provided

---

[21] Excavation: Avigad 1973; analysis: Lapin 2011, updating and revising S. Cohen 1981.

a ready-made clientele for the Palestinian patriarchs and fuelled rabbinic institutionalization as well.

To the patriarch: Philippianus is made great both by his girdle [office] and by his character, which strives for virtue, and also by the fact that he who will bestow benefits on your cities loves Philippianus. However, he becomes great also by desiring your friendship and wishing to attain it through my letter. Letting him then derive advantage from me being his sweetheart, let him be inscribed as friend and let him make you rejoice by what he says about future things before he gives proof by doing them.

(Libanius, *Epistulae*, 973, 1–2)

By the middle of the fourth century, the patriarchs were sharing clientele with thoroughly elite figures like Libanius of Antioch. They had become in effect a part of the Roman administration, and as such they were more powerful than the governors of Palestine (Newman 1997). The letter just quoted recommends a young member of the incoming governor's staff, formerly a pupil of Libanius, to the patriarch's clientele. The fact that Libanius characterizes the governor as 'benefactor of your cities' raises interesting questions about what he thought the patriarch's role was, but clearly he took it for granted that a young staffer required the patriarch's patronage in order to function in Palestine (see *GLAJJ* 496–504). The same patriarch or his heir turned against a later governor of Palestine, and, to indulge him, the emperor executed the governor (Jerome, *Epistulae* 57.3 [*CSEL* LIV.506]). In some broad sense the patriarch was now recognized ruler of the Jews, whose authority notionally extended even to the diaspora, but the laws about the patriarchs included in Book 16 of the Theodosian Code suggest that this was more a matter of imperial concession than of active policy (S. Schwartz 2004). That is, the laws never indicate that the Jews are required to pay a quasi-tax called the *apostole* or *aurum coronarium* to the patriarch, only that, if they do, the patriarch may keep the money (*Cod. Theod.* 16.8.15). Likewise, the patriarchs' formal authority over appointments in diaspora communities is assumed, but its character is not delineated (*Cod. Theod.* 16.8.8). All in all, the evidence from both legal and patristic sources suggests that in the fourth century the patriarchs were very powerful and influential indeed (Levine 1996), but their power was still rather slightly institutionalized, the distribution of authority between their establishment and the governors being as confusing (so we may guess) as that between the temple establishment, the Herodians, and the Roman governors had been in the first century. Patriarchs may still have been appointing rabbinic judges, but rabbinic literature is silent about the patriarchs of the fourth century; the rabbis may no longer have regarded them as members of the group.

Whatever the precise role of the patriarchs may have been, their very power, their presence on the imperial political scene, marks a shift in the status and role of the Jewish elites in Palestine. After the disappearance/dejudaization of the Herodian family in the later first century, no Jews are known to have been members of the Roman aristocracy. This changed only because in the course of the fourth century the patriarchs were raised to senatorial status, achieving their highest rank, as *viri inlustres* (*Cod. Theod.* 16.8.8 [392], 16.8.11 [396], 16.8.13 [397]) and possessors of the honorary praetorian prefectship (*Cod. Theod.* 16.8.22, a law of 415 depriving the patriarch Gamaliel of the status), under the Theodosian dynasty. The guess (of Hillel Newman) that they enjoyed a personal friendship with Theodosius I and his successors, at least until 415, seems almost inescapable. In the event, though, the patriarchal ascendancy was of brief duration; having been promoted by Theodosius I and Arcadius, the patriarchate was first curtailed and demoted and then eliminated altogether as Theodosius II grew up. By the time the Theodosian Code was published in 438, the office had been abolished for at least a decade (*Cod. Theod.* 16.8.29). Who if anyone replaced the patriarchs as leaders of the Jews in the Roman Empire is unknown. Only under the Fatimid caliphs in the tenth and eleventh centuries do we hear again of an authorized Jewish communal religious leadership in Palestine (Gil 1992: 490–776).

CHAPTER 6

Jews under Christian rule

EVENTS

Like Chapter 5, this chapter analyses the impact on the Jews of a relatively well-understood historical process. Here as there, the analysis is hindered by our nearly complete inability to reconstruct a narrative history of the Jews. Though late antique Jews, unlike their immediate ancestors, left behind abundant physical and literary remains, there is even less historiography *stricto sensu* than before: in fact there is none, whether Jewish or pagan or Christian, historiography having now been replaced by chronography, saints' lives, apocalypses, homiletics and liturgy (the last three in both Jewish and Christian versions). All of these texts aspired to impart religious messages, not describe events, and frequently the events they do describe are incredible, though they are often repeated as fact by modern historians.[1] Aside from the episodes discussed in the body of this chapter there are perhaps three events which have a relatively strong claim on historicity though even these are poorly attested. The Palestinian Jewish rebellion under Gallus Caesar (*c.* 352) has been alternately magnified and dismissed; indeed, it seems certain that some sort of uprising occurred, centred in Galilee, which may explain the destruction at Sepphoris observed by archaeologists and now conventionally attributed to the effects of the earthquake of 363. Perhaps the same event explains the apparent mid-fourth-century decline in settlement in south-eastern Galilee, as well (see below). But the complete silence about the revolt both in the Palestinian Talmud, for whose editors the reign of Gallus Caesar was probably within living memory, and in the works of Gallus' staffer Ammianus Marcellinus, is admittedly mysterious. The best explanation may be that the rabbis

---

[1] For example the incredible adventures of Barsauma the monk (not to be confused with the slightly later bishop Barsauma of Nisibis): Nau 1927; or the desecration of the image of the Virgin by the Jews in Antioch in 609: Fishman-Duker 2012: 789, who furthermore demonstrates the narrowly stereotypical character of episodes involving Jews in all Byzantine chronography.

opposed the uprising and so kept silent about its perpetrators, and for Ammianus it was simply not important enough to mention.[2] The year 352 was a turbulent one and other episodes had a greater claim on his attention (Stemberger 2000: 161–84).

Another certainly historical episode is the abortive reconstruction of the Jerusalem temple under Julian (361–3). Julian was markedly ambivalent about Judaism: on the one hand it was a proper old-time religion focusing on animal sacrifice and priestly ritual. On the other hand, the Jews rejected the gods and had unleashed Christianity on the world. But it seems certain that Julian did in fact permit the Jews to rebuild the temple, as an expression of support for animal sacrifice and in order to confound the Christians, and that the project was brought to an end by his death, which coincided with the earthquake of 363 – a coincidence which Christian writers regarded as miraculous (Stemberger 2000: 185–215). There are several important lessons to be learned from this episode. The first lesson – to extrapolate from the Jewish–pagan alliance that prevailed under Julian – is that Jews and Christians were *potentially* at odds politically, though before the orthodox dominance of imperial politics and administration was complete there was still plenty of give in the system. Thus, between 363 and *c.* 410, Jewish and pagan aristocrats could pursue their friendships while retaining the support of Christian emperors, as noted at the end of the last chapter. As the fifth century proceeded, the Jews' collective clout diminished, and their political vulnerability grew, though it cannot have done so in every locality and some Jews found ways to cope with new, Christian, realities (see below). The second lesson concerns the role of the rabbis: about Julian, too, the Talmud is silent; we must again suppose that the rabbis either opposed Julian's plan or kept themselves apart from it. Even in the mid-fourth century, then, when the rabbis enjoyed a measure of recognition and influence, they were functionaries, not political leaders, whose corporate support for or opposition to important political/religious movements may have mattered little, if they offered any at all. History flowed around them. Alternatively, they were so canny that they anticipated the restoration of Christianity – something that in 361 was by no means inevitable – and so remained cool to Julian. The final lesson concerns our ignorance. The uprising of 352 and the events under Julian were necessarily highly consequential for the Jews, especially but not only in Palestine. Yet we know nothing at all about the Jews' reception of the events. Thus, a nuanced account of the interplay of

---

[2] Note Bijovsky 2007 on the absence of numismatic evidence for the revolt.

events, subjectivities and macrohistorical trends is on the whole impossible to produce. Nevertheless, quite a lot is known about the impact of christianization on the Jews, some of which is surprising.

RECOVERY

The Jews experienced in late antiquity a partial recovery from the traumas of the first and second centuries, a fact securely established by both archaeological and literary evidence, notwithstanding the Christian chronographers' and theologians' nearly exclusive focus on the Jews' violence-tinged degradation and decline. Behind the recovery was presumably demographic growth, but in the absence of real data this must remain an impressionistic view. Surface surveys in Palestine indicate growth in the number and size of settlements, including in Jewish areas, in the fourth, fifth and early sixth centuries; yet a detailed study of a small area in the Jewish heartland of eastern Galilee found evidence for contraction in those centuries, a finding which cannot be ignored even though it has not yet been convincingly integrated into any larger narrative.[3] Judaea recovered, though as a Christian district filled with monasteries, and Christian Jerusalem, a major beneficiary of Roman elite investment, once again was a large city and a destination for pilgrims, though these were mainly Christian (Hirschfeld 1992; Bar 2005). Tiberias and Sepphoris, which remained overwhelmingly Jewish, with functioning Christian communities not attested in the cities until the fifth century, grew, too, as did Scythopolis–Beth Shean – a largely Christian provincial capital but with many Jewish satellite settlements (Tsafrir and Foerster 1997). Tiberias for its part remained

---

[3] The basic survey is Kochavi 1972, with critique and analysis in Lapin 2001; Foss 1995 especially on the Negev cities; Dan 1984 on other cities. South-eastern Galilee: Leibner 2009. Leibner's study focuses on pottery, but his results are in stark tension with the implications of widespread construction of monumental synagogues and churches in villages, which demonstrates availability of extensive surplus (as does evidence for a sharp increase in imported pottery, observed by Leibner). Using the same techniques Ben-David (2006) came to roughly similar conclusions for the western, 'Jewish', Golan Heights: decrease in number of settlements between 250 and 350, construction of monumental synagogues between 350 and 550. (R. Frankel 2001 arrives at more conventional conclusions for Upper Galilee.) Does this demonstrate a smaller but richer population? A process of urbanization? In the absence of reliable data about settlement size, how valid is the technique of counting settlements? The matter requires more fundamental and detailed analysis than I can provide here. In the well-preserved villages of the Syrian limestone massif, Georges Tate (1992: 87–188) was able to count *rooms*: nothing comparable is possible in Galilee and the Golan. Bar 2004, counting settlements in a larger area, retains the pre-Leibnerian view with minor modifications: sustained growth beginning *c*. 200 (not *c*. 300, and so not necessarily related to christianization), well into the sixth century, with small pockets of stagnation or retreat, as in western Golan and south-eastern Galilee. Magness 2009 questions the ceramic studies which form the foundation of Leibner's work.

an important Jewish centre well into the Muslim period (Hirschfeld 2004; Gil 1992). The Golan Heights is one of the many areas of peripheral settlement in Syria which needs work to be habitable, like the limestone massif to the north, near Apamea, famously surveyed in the seminal work of Georges Tchalenko; the relatively abundant rainfall can be exploited only with difficulty. The proliferation of village settlements in such areas is regarded as a symptom of demographic growth and prosperity. In the fifth and sixth centuries the Golan was home to many villages; those on the western part of the plateau had synagogues rather than churches (Ben-David 2006). The impressive ruined cities of the Negev were built in the same period; these cities, Mampsis, Obodas, Nessana and Elousa, did not necessarily have substantial Jewish populations but villages in their distant hinterland, such as Eshtemoa, Zif, Carmel and Aristoboulias, probably did (J. Schwartz 1986). The period of growth ended in the second half of the sixth century, in the opinion of some scholars because of the arrival in the Mediterranean basin of the bubonic plague, but some cities and rural areas continued to flourish well into the Middle Ages (Avni 2011).

In the same period, evidence of Jewish life in Egypt resumes; indeed, the overwhelming majority of archaeological evidence for Jews in the Roman diaspora, including such major items as the Jewish catacombs in Rome and Catania, Sicily; the synagogue of Sardis; the sarcophagi of Korykos and the 'God-Fearers' inscription from Aphrodisias, much of which at one time was dated in the second or third century, almost certainly comes from the fourth or fifth, or later (Rutgers 1995; 1997; Ameling 2004: 70–112, 224–96, 500–19). The same is true for the archaeological synagogues of Palestine, of which over 120 have been discovered (Levine 2005: 9; compared to over 400 churches). In other words, after a gap of more than two centuries, there is once again evidence for the Jews.

Whether or not archaeology demonstrates a demographic change, it certainly marks a cultural change, as does the literature conventionally assigned to the period. All the evidence shows that in late antiquity Jewish public life re-emerged, but organized differently than it had been in the first century. It was now organized in local communities, which could decide who was in and who was out. Jewish communities conducted at least some aspects of their lives according to the Torah, and had officials – basically donors with official titles – whose job it was to administer religious life. The communities all eventually collected money to build and maintain monumental synagogues, and there were presumably other communal endeavours as well, though we know little about them. There is some evidence for poor relief as one such widespread project, but we do not in fact have any detailed information about how communal funds were collected and allocated. We can say, though, that late antique local Jewish communities, whether in rural Palestine or urban Asia Minor or Italy, came to share a conception of themselves as constituting holy fellowships, or miniaturized versions of the community of Israel. What would become the standard vocabulary of Jewish communal life began to develop in late antiquity (S. Schwartz 2001; Baer 1950).

But there were still marked pre-medieval features to the new modes of Jewish life: (1) Hebrew was not widely used, even liturgically and for the reading and study of the Torah, outside limited circles in Palestine (and maybe Mesopotamia). The chief Jewish religious/liturgical language in the Roman Empire, including the west, remained Greek (Colorni 1964). There are signs of the growing use of Hebrew only in the sixth and seventh centuries (Simonsohn 1975). (2) As suggested, late antique communities seem rather inchoate and in all likelihood made fewer claims on the lives and resources of their constituents than medieval and early modern Jewish communities, and had correspondingly less recognized authority over them. (3) Rabbinic influence grew in Palestine in the later third and fourth centuries, may have receded a bit thereafter and grown again in the sixth century and later, but outside Palestine (and Mesopotamia) there is no evidence for rabbinic presence or influence at all before the sixth or seventh centuries (S. Schwartz 2002b).[4] Even in Palestine, there is no reason to suppose rabbis normally served as communal functionaries. Rabbinic literature expresses much ambivalence about the value of the local religious community, and at least some rabbis may have expected their authority to extend beyond the bounds of a local community. Where rabbis were influential in antiquity, it was not as communal officials (unlike in the Middle Ages), and conversely, the local community owed nothing of its development or spread to rabbinic ideas (S. Schwartz 2001).

THE FIRST CENTURY OF CHRISTIANITY, 312–415

The economic and cultural travails that the High Imperial city endured in the later third century were eventually resolved, but the new city that emerged in the fourth century was increasingly Christian. It took decades, arguably even centuries, for a genuinely Christian Roman Empire

---

[4] To the inscriptions discussed there should be added the *duo rabbites* among the twelve learned Jewish *pseudo-apostoli* (often described inaccurately as twelve rabbis) who debated Pope Silvester, according to the popular legend probably written up in Italy in the sixth century (Canella 2006: 269; 284).

to emerge, and this development was accompanied by what some historians have gone back to characterizing without squeamishness as its decline
(Ward-Perkins 2005; Liebeschuetz 2001). Nevertheless, some changes in
patterns of expenditure and social organization, which began as necessary
responses to the shortage of funds in the late third century, were made
permanent and were provided with ideological heft in the fourth. Classical
euergetism did not die, but it merged with and was reshaped by Christian
charity, and as it did so some of the institutions it used to support fell into
disuse; temples, theatres, amphitheatres crumbled or were pressed into
secondary use as housing, or, though not as frequently as has been imagined, as churches (Kennedy 1985; qualifications: Avni 2011). Poor relief,
which had never been at the top of any pagan municipal grandee's agenda,
became a central aim of both secular and ecclesiastical wealth (Finn 2006:
221–57; Brown 2012). According to the widely affirmed Brownian orthodoxy, the fourth century was, with a few lapses, a period of unusually
explicit religious toleration and even pluralism – a period after the persecutions of Christianity had ended, and before an increasingly aggressive
and rigidified Christian orthodoxy emerged. Whatever the merits of this
evaluation may be, some further discussion is in order if we are to make
sense of the impact of christianization on the Jews.

Peter Garnsey (1984) has characterized the pagan Romans as tolerant
by default, though there actually were limits to what they were willing to
accept religiously/culturally. Starting in 70, Judaism straddled the bound-
ary. The destruction of the Jerusalem temple and deconstitution of the
Jewish nation probably meant that Judaism was reduced, in constitutional
terms, from a national, cult-centred religion, to a set of customary practices – *mores* – on the whole of no interest to the Roman state (Rives
2005). And even so, the Jews paid what some people regarded as a two-
denarius-per-annum fine, the tax to the *fiscus iudaicus*, for the right to
practise them. There was pressure on Jews to opt out of Judaism. In real
life, most Jews engaged in ad hoc compromise, and even after the imme-
diacy of the Jewish rebellions and all their attendant bad publicity for the
Jews faded in the course of the second and third centuries, it stands to reason that Jewish life outside the concentrated area of Galilee and western
Golan was not devoid of a certain freight of anxiety and difficulty. The
still common rosy description of happily integrated Roman imperial Jews,
pursuing their own group interests without hindrance while culturally,
politically and economically participating fully and happily in the lives
of their host cities (Gruen 2002; Fredriksen 2010: 79–102), is overly optimistic. Though ostensibly descriptive, this value-laden account is lifted in

its entirety from the ideological platforms of nineteenth- and twentieth-century western integrationist (non-Zionist) Jewish modernizers. Roman Jewry was meant to serve as the precedent, or even the blueprint, for Jewish life in the modern liberal state – something the Roman Empire most certainly was not.

Whatever the frame of mind of their members, though, some Jewish communities existed continuously for a long time, though almost certainly fewer did so than the characteristic scholarly technique of aggregating very scattered evidence into a single account might lead one to think. That is, the entirety of the surviving evidence for most Jewish communities in the Roman Empire is an item or two; we have no idea whether they were successful at maintaining their numbers and integrity for long periods, or whether they rose and quickly fell, their members scattered, or merged into the urban environment. Those responsible for structures like the Roman Jewish catacombs or the Sardis synagogue necessarily had some durability, but there are few parallels in diasporic Jewish archaeology to such monumental remains.[5] In the Middle Ages and modern period, when we know much more about Jewish communities, we know how evanescent and improvisatory they were in many cases. It would be completely unreasonable, even in the absence of rebellions and other catastrophes, to posit for ancient Jewish communities untrammelled continuity, unless there is compelling evidence for it. Instead, we should imagine a more fluid landscape of communities rising and falling, coalescing and scattering, and we should regard compromise, tension and instability as more typical than calm, prosperous respectability, though some communities may occasionally have attained that happy state. What this means is that those Jews who managed to remain Jewish normally did so by making serious compromises with the cultural, social and political ideals of their cities; those who did not manage to remain Jewish made even more serious compromises. But there was no alternative to compromise, whether its purpose and effects were corporate survival or dissolution. In the wake of 70, and 117, and 135, Jews in Roman cities cannot always have felt free to absent themselves from the rituals of civic religion, even if they wished to. In Palestinian cities, as we have seen, they embraced it. We have almost no evidence of how Jews actually behaved in 249 CE, when imperial authorities belatedly decided to solve their Christian problem by trying to force everyone to offer libations to the genius of the emperor. This was just

---

[5] Catacombs: Rutgers 1995. Magness (2005) has argued that the Sardian synagogue was constructed in the sixth century and so, it existed only briefly, until the Persian invasion of 616; its construction is conventionally dated to *c.* 300.

as offensive to Jewish sensibilities as to Christian, yet there was no blanket exemption for Jews (S. Schwartz 2001: 191). In some places they may have constituted powerful enough pressure groups or been willing to offer large enough bribes to get themselves released, but in other places they could not. In the second and third centuries there were no intermediaries to protect them, comparable to Herod and his descendants, or the patriarchs in their moment of florescence in the late fourth century. What then did they do? Presumably they made the necessary idolatrous offering and hoped the God of Israel would forgive them.

The compromises which had enabled Jewish life in the High Empire after the revolts, both in Palestine and in the diaspora, which among other things involved coming to terms with standard municipal paganism, could not long survive christianization. They no longer served any purpose, and worse than that, a comparable sort of compromise with Christianity was dangerous. To be eclectically Jewish and pagan was to show admirable adaptability; to be eclectically Jewish and Christian was heresy, punishable by death and confiscation of property. The first century after the conversion of Constantine was when both the Roman state and the Jews gradually sorted out what form Jewish life could now take. We begin with the state.

THE CHRISTIAN ROMAN STATE AND THE JEWS

The Roman state's toleration of the Jews is a small mystery with large implications. Before the Byzantine period, however harsh official rhetoric about the Jews may have been,[6] and however much the state may have tolerated local misbehaviour directed against Jews by bishops and monks, the right of the Jews to 'practice their own religion' (a formulation which updated the 'use their own laws' that had been traditional since the early Hellenistic period at latest) was consistently affirmed (Linder 1987: 67–74). Why? Scholars asking the same question about the Jewish policies of medieval western Christian kingdoms adduce the theological influence of St Augustine, who argued that the Jews offer independent confirmation of the truth of Christian teaching because they have always preserved and continue to preserve the Hebrew Scriptures, the most basic Christian text (J. Cohen 1999). Therefore Jews must never be eliminated and must never be prohibited from practising their laws. Needless to say, if they choose to

---

[6] Judaism was commonly characterized as a *secta* or a *superstitio*, usually modified by a hostile adjective, though the neutral/positive *religio* is attested too, before 416 CE: Linder 1987: 55–67.

convert to Christianity, they are welcomed, but they must not be forced; they are to be degraded, but maintained. Whether or not this doctrine explains the behaviour of Merovingian and Carolingian kings, it cannot explain that of Constantine and his successors, because the Augustinian doctrine of witness was formulated only around 400.

A more pragmatic approach starts from a text, *The Life of Porphyry Bishop of Gaza*, by Marcus Diaconus (Grégoire and Kugener 1930). This text describes the initially unsuccessful attempt, around 400 CE, by the bishop to have Arcadius, the eastern emperor, enforce in Gaza, a hotbed of paganism, his own laws against sacrifice; the emperor resisted on the grounds that the still pagan Gazans were good citizens who paid their taxes, so there was no point in alienating them with religious persecution. It is often claimed that the Jews too were, by the fourth century, good citizens who paid their taxes (the reasoning echoes *Cod. Theod.* 16.10.24). But this is a strong misreading of the *Life of Porphyry*. 'Marcus' is thematizing the conflict between political and theological interests, and in his account theological interests prevailed, though not without a lot of effort by Porphyry and some divine intervention. To be sure, the emperors did have a vested interest in maintaining a profitable and stable status quo, but they also strongly supported bishops who were doing everything they could to overthrow it. In the *Life*, Porphyry eventually won. Arcadius sent in the troops, the ancient temple of Marnas was destroyed and on its site was built the Church of St Mary Theotokos, and the Gazans eventually joined the Church.[7] The question is why the emperors were willing to let the bishops have their way with the much more numerous and influential pagans (still perhaps 50 per cent of the Empire in 380), or indeed with non-orthodox Christians (however orthodoxy may have been defined at any given moment) than with the small population of Jews, who could have been outlawed at little cost to the state (Sandwell 2007).

Probably the most popular solution to the problem of the Christian emperors' enduring tolerance of the Jews adduces Roman legal conservatism. The emperors had always tolerated the Jews and continued to do so after their conversion despite pressure by (some) bishops. There are both

---

[7] St Ambrose, writing around 388, claimed that there was a Christian basilica at Gaza – as also at Ascalon, Beirut and Damascus – already in the reign of Julian (361–3), destroyed presumably by the local Jews (*Epistulae* 74 [40].14, *CSEL* LXXXII.3, 63). The veracity of this essentially forensic claim is not above suspicion – McLynn 1994: 301; Irshai 2009: 412–14 – but should perhaps be taken more seriously than the tale of Porphyry. Perhaps in any case Ambrose was referring to Maiumas, the already partly Christian port city adjacent to Gaza (Stemberger 2000: 194). The destruction of the main temple of Gaza, the Marneion, appears to be historical, since it was celebrated by Jerome, who was then living in Palestine (*Epistulae* 107.2).

superficial and deep problems with this explanation. The Roman emperors had always tolerated and supported pagans too; why did they stop doing so in the course of the fourth century? (In fact, being a pagan was never forbidden, but the central ritual of Greco-Roman paganism, animal sacrifice, was repeatedly forbidden in the later fourth century.) The deeper problem with this argument is that it misstates Roman policy and law. Explicit recognition of the right of the Jews to follow their own religion was not at all a traditional position, but a novel one. Traditional Roman law did not openly tolerate foreign religions because it did not conceptualize human behaviour in those terms. Before 70 the Jews had had, as a nation, the right to use their own laws, but this right was then abrogated; it is its restoration – in altered form – which is noteworthy, not the laws' alleged traditionalism.

Christianization problematized religion. Whether or not we think that Christians 'invented' religion (Boyarin 2004; contrast S. Schwartz 2011), it is clear that they introduced it as a new legal and political category, and needed to think about how a Christian state would cope with non-Christians, or with heterodox Christians. The old Roman state had prohibited Christianity, for reasons that are still poorly understood, but otherwise had no specific laws or policies about religious affiliation; but simply by leafing through Book 16 of the *Theodosian Code* we can learn a lot about evolving imperial policy in this new field. We can see the emperors struggling with aspects of pagan cult at a time when the imperial aristocracy was still pagan and the emperors themselves were still routinely deified after death. We can witness the coalescence of a Christian orthodoxy and a hardening of imperial attitudes to those who opted out. The crucial decades for the creation of religious policy were the 380s and 390s. The legal disadvantages of Christian heresy had long been obvious, but now pagans and Jews came under scrutiny as well; sacrifice was repeatedly prohibited and the emperors' legal staff gave sustained attention to the status of the Jews (Linder 1987: 55; Sandwell 2007).

The recognition of the Jews' right to their religion, though often couched in degrading language, implied recognition of a privileged clerical class with limited jurisdiction (*Cod. Theod.* 16.8.2; 16.8.8; 16.8.13; 16.8.15). It also entailed recognition of the limited legal personality, or corporate status, of local Jewish communities. In fact, Roman law was now somewhat clearer on this point than rabbinic law, which never had much to say about the legal theory behind the local community (*Cod. Theod.* 16.8.8; limitation: *Cod. Theod.* 13.5.18). The Jews' clergy was also granted privileges similar to, though not as extensive as, those of the Christian clergy, and it was now

that the patriarch was recognized as in effect the chief bishop of the Jews'
Empire-wide ecclesiastical establishment (S. Schwartz 1999). The problem
with much of this legislation was that it imposed on the Jews categories
which did not quite fit; the Jews did not actually have a clergy. Even the
rabbis were only judges, and to say that they and people like them had jurisdiction over religious law but not civil law (*Cod. Theod.* 2.1.10) was to introduce into Jewish law a category which made little theoretical sense. Issues
like marriage and inheritance were civil law to the Romans but religious law
to the rabbis; or rather it was all religious law to the rabbis, except that the
Jews, generally speaking, had long since submitted to a Roman version of
civil law for most purposes. As to the clergy, who were sporadically released
from the burdens of city-council membership, there is evidence from within
the code itself that some Jewish communities exploited the ambiguity of
the category to claim a blanket exemption for all their members: since any
member of a Jewish community could be an *archon* or a *grammateus*, why
shouldn't they all claim the privileges granted to clergy (*Cod. Theod.* 12.1.158,
398, responding to a situation in Apulia and Calabria)?

While the laws recognized the legality of the Jewish religion, the personality of the local Jewish community and the privilege of the Jews' clergy
(while prohibiting conversion to Judaism), they also increasingly worked
to marginalize the Jews socially. The emperors eventually rescinded the
exemption of Jewish officials from city-council service (Linder 1987:
75–6), at a time when such service was normally regarded as burdensome,
but, starting in 404, they also declared Jews ineligible for other types of
office – especially in the army, in provincial government, and in imperial
bureaus (Linder 1987: 76–7). Similarly, Jews were barred first from owning
Christian slaves and then from owning any non-Jewish slaves (*Cod. Theod.*
16.9). The motivation behind these rules was shared: Jews were increasingly recognized and even supported as a separate body, but they were to
be teased out of the social and political fabric of municipal and provincial life. Certainly they were to be removed from any position where they
could exert control over a non-Jew.

The emperors may not have been precocious Augustinians, but their
constitutions and policies certainly tended in an Augustinian direction.
We should perhaps follow Megan Hale Williams (2008) in recognizing
that Augustine did not develop his theology of witness in a vacuum –
predecessors, both bishops and jurists, had already given inchoate expression to aspects of his ideas.

Real life was messier than legal principle. Roman laws were indubitably
sometimes enforced, but the contents of a constitution should always be

understood primarily as an expression of imperial will. Imperial will was powerful and important, but it was not always followed or even meant to be; at very least there was probably considerable lag-time between the issue of a constitution and the imposition of its contents, or significant resistance or simply apathetic inaction. In 388 the bishop of Callinicum on the Euphrates frontier led his flock in an attack on the town's synagogue. This was unambiguously illegal, and Theodosius I ordered the perpetrators to pay for the reconstruction. But St Ambrose, bishop of Milan, wrote an impassioned letter demanding that the emperor rescind his command, and, though he at first resisted, Theodosius, subsequently confronted in church on a visit to Milan, eventually yielded.[8] Older scholarship regarded this episode as the precedent for removing legal protection from the Jews de facto while it was repeatedly affirmed de iure, but this misreads the late Roman state as an anachronistically strong constitutional system. The emperors meant their repeated affirmations of the Jews' legality to be taken seriously, they just did not always act on it.

A somewhat comparable episode occurred in the West thirty years later, in Magona (now Mahon), a small town in the Balearics, or rather, it apparently occurred, since, though Augustine himself had heard about and disapproved of the incident, our only full source, purporting to be a letter written by the perpetrator, Severus bishop of Minorca, tells a short story so gripping that it is obviously unreliable.[9] The episode narrated by 'Severus' is a kind of *reductio ad absurdum* of the situation of the Jews in the later part of the Theodosian era, and an ominous anticipation of the worst episodes of the Middle Ages (apart from being fictionalized if not plain fiction), but the details of the story tell us much about rising political and religious tensions.

Then as now Minorca had two towns. The larger, Magona (Mahon), had a large number of Jews who enjoyed friendly relations with their Christian neighbours. As at Mahoza in southern Palestine three centuries earlier, careful maintenance of difference on both sides did not preclude business partnerships and relationships of social and political dependency. The Jews were thoroughly integrated into the social and political fabric in the town, and the local grandee, Theodorus, was also head of the Jewish community. The episcopal see was situated in the other town, Iamona (Ciutadella), where, Severus tells us, through divine

[8] Ambrose, *Epistulae* 74 [40], *CSEL* LXXXII.3, 54–73; *Epistulae 'extra Collectionem'* 1 [41], *CSEL* LXXXII.3, 145–61; McLynn 1994: 298–309.
[9] Bradbury 1996; for recent discussion, Kraemer 2009.

dispensation no Jew was ever able to live (the story is sct in 417/18 and no pagans are mentioned). The arrival in 417 of the relics of St Stephen the Protomartyr, which had been discovered near Jerusalem several years earlier, threw the island's Christians into a high state of religious enthusiasm, and Severus seized the moment to perform what he characterized as a miracle; he marched on Magona with some followers and coerced the Jews to convert to Christianity. The divine intervention consisted of the fact that, due to a misunderstanding, the Jews thought that their leader Theodorus had announced his intention to convert in response to pressure from Severus and his people – who were remarkably unconcerned that their actions violated both Roman law and some versions of Christian teaching, according to which conversion was invalid if it was not undertaken with free will. In fact Theodorus had done no such thing (some Christians in the crowd called out, 'Theodorus, believe in Christ!', and some Jews misheard it as 'Theodorus believes in Christ!'), but it was too late; the Jews converted, and Theodorus felt he now had no choice. And the moment he agreed to convert, his social standing in Magona was restored; his Christian clients rushed to embrace him, and welcome themselves back into his clientele.

We may take this tale as illustrating one consequence of christianization for the Jews, and explaining indirectly the thrust of those laws in the Theodosian Code which have as their apparent goal the social and political marginalization of the Jews. As the fifth century progressed there were indubitably other local episodes of persecution and forced conversion besides those at Callinicum and Magona (Stemberger 1993 provides a critical assessment). It would not be accurate, though, to use such episodes as tracers for the Jewish experience under Christian rule in general. Augustine should not be mistaken for a philosemite, but his view for long remained the officially prevalent one: the Jews were not to be disturbed, and at least for a while this was translated into policy as limited support for the Jews' internal communal institutions. Indeed, there was nothing actually preventing Christians and Jews from sharing not just physical space, but social practices and economic activities. Severus characterized the friendly relations between the groups at Magona before 417 as damaging to Christ, but it did not displease either Christians or Jews that the latter were among the political leadership of the town, and were important as communal benefactors and individual patrons. But ecclesiastical pressure, produced by ever tightening bonds of orthodoxy, and in this case, too, an outburst of exogenous religious enthusiasm, eventually made this situation untenable. In other places, the result was the social withdrawal of the Jews, and their corporate reliance on individual Christian protectors (something Augustine would hardly have opposed). At Magona, the Jews, subjected to force and threats, ended by retaining their social positions but not their Judaism. In still other places, the little southern Italian city of Venusia serves as the prime example, the Jews were able to retain both social prominence and their gradually rabbinized Jewish loyalties into the sixth century (*CHJ* IV: 492–518). But generally speaking christianization eventually, in most places, required Jews to choose: they could remain Jewish, but at the price of withdrawal from social networks, or they could retain their positions, but only as Christians. The Jews' High Imperial compromise with their rulers and their cities was dead.

THE NEW JEWISH CULTURE, 400–600 CE

Roman law prescribed, in some sense generated, and also reflected, a specifically late antique mode of Jewishness. Many of the specific features of late antique Judaism were shared with Christians, and there is a long history of scholarly debate over priority. Did Judaism, being the older religion, invent in its synagogues ecclesiastical architecture and decoration and bequeath it to Christianity? Was the characteristic style of liturgical poetry that emerged in the sixth century among both Jews and Christians of Jewish or of Christian origin? The truth is we are not always in a position to answer these questions. The apsidal basilica, for example, was originally associated with High Imperial municipal architecture; it was probably adapted for church architecture before Jews of the Beth Shean–Scythopolis area adapted it for synagogues in the sixth century (Levine 2005: 325). Other elements of ecclesiastical design, though, may be attested in synagogues first, like the use of figurative mosaic pavements; but both synagogues and churches are surely indebted to Roman domestic decoration for this, whether or not Christians got the idea of using mosaic pavements in their churches from Jews (Levine 2005: 593–612). Does it matter that the hellenophone Christian who was the alleged originator of the new liturgical poetry, Romanos the Melode, was, according to one Byzantine source, a baptized Jew (others describe him as a Syrian from Emesa: Grosdidier de Matons 1977: 159–75)? Or that the new style was anticipated by the Syriac-speaking Christian writers Ephrem of Nisibis (fourth century) and Jacob of Serugh (fifth century), who lived before Romanos and his Jewish contemporaries Yannai and Elazar Qiliri?[10] I would argue that, though claims of priority can occasionally be resolved, they rarely matter: cultural borrowing means adaptation and appropriation. 'Competitive historiography', which is concerned to argue that its subjects invented things which they then bequeathed to the world, may make amusing reading, but is short on intellectual respectability. My point in this subchapter is that to a surprising extent both the style and the content of Jewish practice were shaped by their late antique Christian environment, while the Jews and Christians both struggled to maintain their distinctiveness despite all that they shared. The process was complex and the results surprising. Late antique synagogues may often have resembled late antique churches, but no one could have predicted from this fact the Hebrew poetry of Yannai, magnificently Byzantine as it is, or midrash compilations such as Genesis Rabbah, which have no meaningful Christian parallels (see below).

The rise and spread of the local community implied patterns of expenditure, social organization and cultural practice which were shared by Jews and Christians. In the fifth and sixth centuries, the village or small settlement achieved greater importance both as a consumer of resources and as an object of ideological commitment. Christians also developed local religious communities. The Jewish version had a more fully articulated ideology, and the Christian one a more fully articulated legal identity, but Jewish and Christian villages looked strikingly similar (S. Schwartz 2001: 275–89). Both Jews and Christians set monumental, heavily decorated purpose-built religious structures – synagogues or churches – at the centre of their villages. (By the fifth century, few villages in Palestine-Syria had both a church and a synagogue; villages had once had mixed populations, but the separation of Jewish and Christians settlements reflects in a curious way their separation in law: Aviam 2004.) Both were built and maintained by mobilizing scarce local surpluses over long periods, and so both are not simply buildings, but reflect a whole set of practices. They reflect a sense of the religious significance of the small settlement; the spread of modified versions of euergetism from its urban home to the countryside; and a shared mode of religiosity, since the buildings themselves are often similar.

[10] There is an ample bibliography on the connections between Syriac and Greek Christian liturgy, but the exploration of their connections to the *piyyut* is at its earliest stages, though the general similarities are obvious and have long been noticed. Scholars of liturgical poetry on both sides of the religious divide have been intensely, even stridently internalist (in the case of Jewish scholars, who not infrequently have actually read some of the Christian texts), or profoundly ignorant (in the case of Christian scholars). The essential though still preliminary study is Münz-Manor 2010; also Lieber 2010: 205–23; Aslanov 2012; on Jacob and Romanos, Papoutsakis 2007.

But the same evidence shows that differences were carefully maintained as well. Churches were built according to a small number of common plans, while synagogues were architecturally more chaotic, though sometimes there are regional patterns. Urban synagogues tended to be built to fit into available spaces, unlike, obviously, urban churches, which were usually specially provided with a centrally located construction site. That said, there are some systematic tendencies. One of these seems banal, but it is undeniably pervasive and almost certainly meaningful: synagogues tend to be more square, less rectangular, than churches. Even the sixth-century synagogues of the Beth Shean valley, apsidal basilicas obviously modelled on local churches, all have reduced ratios of length to width. What could this mean? Synagogues sometimes had chancel screens, like churches, but it seems that despite this the communities who built the structures were somewhat less committed than their neighbours to thematizing the role of a special clergy strongly marked as separate from the congregation – something implicit in the spatial organization of most churches (Levine 2005). Those attending synagogues thought of themselves as a community at prayer. Synagogue inscriptions are rarely phrased as individual prayers, unlike church inscriptions (Oh Lord, help your servant X), and very often phrased as communal prayer on behalf of the donor (May X be remembered for good). Both of these features probably reflect structural differences – which should not be confused with oppositions – in the different communities' organization and/or self-perception. Jewish communities imagined themselves as little egalitarian Israels, and Christian parishes as flocks endowed with shepherds (S. Schwartz 2001: 275–89). The socio-economic realities we can extract from a critical analysis of the inscriptions conformed imperfectly with these ideals. Both Jewish villages/urban communities and Christian parishes were disproportionately supported and managed by their wealthier members; the culture of euergetism which subtends building inscriptions in general was alive and well in late antique settlements, but somewhat obscured behind scrims of slightly different biblicizing pieties.

Both synagogues and churches were heavily decorated, in many areas with mosaic pavements – which are more likely to survive than wall decorations for obvious reasons. Art historians have tended to focus on the elite versions of such items, because they are usually visually richer than their rural counterparts, but the rural mosaics are often surprisingly urbane; indeed one of the points of having them is to make villages seem more like cities. Be this as it may, there is plenty of evidence that churches and synagogues in Palestine-Syria shared artisans, and both drew on a corpus of shared decorative schemes and depictions of biblical and other material – nature scenes, for example. Jews probably embraced figurative decoration in their synagogues more quickly and fully than Christians in their churches. And churches make no use of some common synagogal themes, such as the zodiac circle inscribed in a square with the seasons represented at its corners, or, more understandably, the even more common images of an ark flanked by menorahs and other Jewish ritual objects; and synagogues do not use specifically Christian themes (Hachlili 2009; Levine 2012).

By the sixth century, there is evidence for the emergence of distinctive artistic styles among Jews and Christians (a possibility not explicitly considered in Talgam 2012; Levine 2012). The characteristic early Byzantine frontal style, the most famous early examples of which come from beneficiaries of imperial largess like the churches at Ravenna, was copied in small town and rural churches and monasteries, but so far there is no evidence that Jews ever used it. Instead, the Jews seemed to be developing a characteristic schematic – we would say almost cartoonish – style, most famously on display at Bet Alfa, near Beth Shean (whose churches feature some fine examples of simplified Byzantine style: Sukenik 1932). It may be suggested that this style implies a growing discomfort with the idea of figurative representation, by the sixth century long since traditional in synagogues; in the Middle Ages the Jews would become largely iconophobic, though not as completely as they had been in the first century, and the handful of Palestinian synagogues which remained in use into the Islamic period had their decorations effaced or built over, not by iconophobic Muslims but by the Jews themselves (Levine 2005: 340–3). The fact that the beginnings of Jewish iconophobia were pre-Islamic helps put Islamic iconophobia itself in a broader late antique eastern Mediterranean context of self-distancing from Greco-Roman cultural practice, shared by Jews and Christians.

LITERATURE

One of the features of the 'trough' in Jewish remains between the time of Bar Kokhba and the later fourth century is that there is very little surviving literature from the period which we can definitely characterize as Jewish. The possibility that accident played a role in this non-survival is undeniable. Nothing from the second through to the fourth/fifth centuries survives from outside the tradition of manuscript transmission, whereas for both earlier and later periods substantial quantities of text were discovered in modern times. For the earlier period, the Dead Sea scrolls turned up in a Bedouin shepherd's treasure-hunting expedition in the Judaean desert; for the later period, an even more successful treasure-hunting expedition, this time in a very old Cairo synagogue, initiated by enterprising Christian twin sisters of Scottish background from Cambridge named Agnes Lewis and Margaret Gibson, and continued by a Romanian rabbi (Solomon Schechter, also one of the greatest Judaic scholars of the late nineteenth century), also resident in Cambridge, turned up hundreds of thousands of texts and documents (Reif 2000b). Some of the material found in the Cairo Geniza (used-book depository) was in fact of ancient origin: several (medieval) manuscripts of the lost Hebrew original of the apocryphal (non-canonical, para-biblical) Wisdom of Ben Sira; the 'Damascus Document', a Hebrew text which must have been completely incomprehensible to its medieval Egyptian copyists and readers, since it had wandered into their possession from the ancient Dead Sea sect (how it reached medieval Egypt is a mystery) – we could think of the awestruck but confused reaction a Gnostic text from Nag Hammadi might have received if it had somehow turned up in a monastery in, say, fourteenth-century Switzerland (Reif 2000a).

More abundant in the Geniza collection is hitherto unknown late antique material: poetic, legal, apocalyptic and magical texts which have changed the way we view late antique and early medieval Judaism. By contrast the Geniza contained *almost* no previously lost material composed between 100 and 400 CE – except fragments of partly known, possibly early midrashic texts (Kahane 2006). But perhaps this is not accidental after all; perhaps it suggests, if admittedly not very strongly, that Jews did indeed write relatively little in that period. Early- and high-medieval Jews in the Near East demonstrably copied and read material from outside the narrow high canon of rabbinic texts, but for the second through to the fourth centuries such texts – the Mishnah plus a few related corpora, *if* their conventional datings to the third century are correct, which is entirely unknown (they cannot be earlier) – were indeed all they had. This does not mean that no more was published than survives. Any texts written in Greek in the period would have been lost; the sectarian 'Damascus Document' notwithstanding, books written in Hebrew or Aramaic reflecting strongly non-rabbinic views are also unlikely to have survived. Nevertheless, we may still take a leap of faith and see late antiquity as a period of enhanced productivity – an epiphenomenon of the Jews' demographic and (for a time) political recovery, and of the cultural impact of Christianization.

Yet the literary revival tells a complex cultural story, and a slightly different one from that of archaeology. First, all preserved texts are written in Hebrew or Aramaic, not Greek, and so in the most basic way possible turn their backs on the classical tradition. Second, the more closely associated the text is with rabbinic circles, the less it resembles formally or substantively Christian or indeed pagan texts, or for that matter earlier Jewish texts either. The earliest rabbinic text, the Mishnah (*c.* 200), is like no predestruction text, but does not resemble Roman legal collections either, whether of pagan or of Christian provenance (Simon-Shoshan 2012). The rabbinic biblical commentary collected in midrashic texts only occasionally resembles Christian commentary, but in formal terms the anthological rabbinic texts are utterly unlike the self-consciously 'authored' Christian texts (Jaffee 2007). However, as already noted, liturgical texts are very similar indeed, as are apocalypses, and magical recipes are probably the most culturally labile of all (Bohak 2008). It pays to explore these issues and their implications in more detail.

The Palestinian Talmud, conventionally dated to around 380 CE and almost certainly composed in Tiberias, is an extended commentary on the Mishnah. While it is possible with some imagination to set the Mishnah in the broad intellectual or cultural context of the Second Sophistic – just as some Greek writers created in their works a Greece without Rome, the Mishnah constructs in effect an Israel without Rome – the Talmud fits less comfortably in its environment of burgeoning patristic commentary, theology, and homiletics. Like the Mishnah, the Talmud is an edited rather than an authored text; despite this, like its predecessor, and unlike the later Babylonian Talmud, it has a weak editorial voice. The editors selected and assembled material, sometimes with great cunning but at other times in ways difficult to understand; presumably they often revised material, but they did not embed it in a coherent layer of editorial comment, unlike the editors of the Babylonian Talmud about three centuries later. There is far more argumentation in the Palestinian Talmud than in the Mishnah, but the units tend to be brief, paragraphs rather than pages. The language of the Talmud also differs from that of the Mishnah. The latter is entirely in Hebrew, though it is a Hebrew strongly influenced by Aramaic morphology, grammar and syntax, and containing many Greek loanwords. The Talmud alternates between and sometimes mixes rabbinic Hebrew and Palestinian Jewish Aramaic, and Greek words are more abundant; indeed, it is rather futile to try to make sense of the Talmud without some grasp of Greek. It is also difficult to understand the Talmud without a strong sense of the realia of High and Late Imperial Roman provincial life, to the understanding of which the Talmud makes an important but still little-tapped contribution.[11] (The Babylonian Talmud is written in a similar mixture of Hebrew and Aramaic, the latter in a different dialect; it has relatively few Greek loanwords, but also relatively few Persian loanwords, despite its Sasanian provenance.) This is because the Talmud expresses more concern than the somewhat utopian Mishnah about adapting its laws to the exigencies of life in Roman Palestine. The rabbinic class that produced it was probably larger and more influential than that responsible for the Mishnah (Lapin 2012); in some ways the rabbis became more involuted as their institutionalization progressed, which partly explains the Talmud's relative isolation from the norms of contemporaneous Christian and pagan cultural production.

Closely related to the Talmud are several *midrash* collections. *Midrash* literally means investigation, and it is the specifically rabbinic Hebrew term for a genre of literature whose distinctive feature is that it consists of commentary on biblical verses. These texts are like the Mishnah and Talmud in that they too have no author or authorial voice; and though some of the content is anonymous, much is attributed to named rabbis, largely the same *dramatis personae* as in the other rabbinic texts. The ostensibly earliest texts, called collectively *midrash halakhah*, or legal *midrash*, thought to have been compiled in the third or fourth century, have as their aim the extraction of rabbinic law from pentateuchal legal texts by means of close attention to the latters' linguistic peculiarities, repetitions, contradictions, and so on. There is no halakhic midrash on Genesis because it contains only narrative and lacks legal content, but the other four pentateuchal books each have at least one collection apiece dedicated to them. It is not known whether these collections provide the exegetical foundations for rabbinic law which the editor(s) of the Mishnah took for granted, or whether they are post- or para-mishnaic attempts to determine the biblical sources of mishnaic law (Kahane 2006). The Palestinian Talmud, which also tries to specify the biblical sources of rabbinic laws, frequently replicates the content of these midrashic texts without explicit citation, leaving open the question of chronological priority.

---

[11] On the formal issues see the helpful summary account by L. Moscovitz in *CHJ* 4: 663–77; the Palestinian Talmud has not been adequately translated (not to minimize the significant problems entailed in the project); the translation by Jacob Neusner is error-filled and frequently incomprehensible. This basic desideratum has hindered its effective exploitation by ancient historians. The classic Lieberman 1942 and Lieberman 1950 are still helpful in evoking the 'real' world of the Talmud.

Still more closely related to the Talmud are the texts collectively called *midrash aggadah*, the second term meaning 'narrative'. The earliest of these texts, Genesis Rabbah (*rabbah* means 'great' in Palestinian Aramaic and here probably denotes something like, 'The Big Book of ...', or 'The Great Anthology of ...'), Leviticus Rabbah, Ecclesiastes Rabbah, and Pesiqta de-Rav Kahana (Collection of Rav Kahana) share a great deal of content. They also all share a great deal of content with the Palestinian Talmud, so much so that once again issues of priority are very difficult to disentangle. It is conventional to date these midrashim somewhat later than the Talmud, to the fifth century, but it has proved surprisingly difficult to find any support for this dating in the texts themselves. Unlike some later midrash collections, these earlier ones seem genuine non-pseudepigraphic collections or anthologies, with most of the material in them formulated in the third and fourth centuries (D. Stern 2004). This may explain in part why the texts, both Talmudic and midrashic, pay so little attention to Christianity. Much of their content may post-date Constantine's conversion, but it pre-dates the christianization of northern Palestine in the late fourth century and following. On the other hand, the editorial process, if the conventional datings are correct, was concurrent with christianization, which has induced some scholars to scrutinize the collections for covert polemics against Christianity, in the absence of explicit concern. But the results have been sparse and unconvincing. It might be more correct to argue that the editors are making their point precisely by ignoring Christianity, but their intentions are unrecoverable. Much basic historicist work remains to be done on these books, though they still have some 'internalist' lessons to teach.

One such important lesson may concern the broadening of the rabbinic curriculum, from legal/mishnaic study alone to biblical exegesis. Another lesson, presumably related to the first, concerns the growing role, in the fifth century and following, of rabbis and/or their students in liturgical settings, since one purpose of the aggadic midrash collections was almost certainly to provide raw material for sermons based on the liturgical Torah-reading lectionary cycle. From the collections we learn that there was at least some concern in late antique Palestine that such sermons should have a rabbinic orientation, even though some of the contents of these collections – the many parables and adaptations of folk-narratives and self-styled popular sayings – is not strongly marked as rabbinic. But that may be significant in itself. If the Mishnah constitutes the definitive formulation of the rabbinic 'great tradition', the Talmud but especially the aggadic midrash collections (though not all of them equally: Genesis

Rabbah for example is strongly 'academic') constitute evidence for the rabbis' growing engagement with the 'little traditions' of non-rabbinic Palestinian Jews.

Some of the extensive late antique and early medieval magical (sometimes designated 'mystical', perhaps misleadingly) material discovered in the Cairo Genizah (some of it was also preserved in the manuscript tradition) provides additional evidence for this development (Bohak 2008; Swartz 1996; Boustan 2005). The history of the composition and consolidation of the so-called Heikhalot texts is still very poorly understood but they seem to have existed in some form in late antiquity. Their purpose is to instruct practitioners in the techniques used for ascending through the seven heavens in order to glimpse the chariot of God described in Ezekiel 1, and for adjuring the angelic inhabitants of the heavens whom the magician encounters on the trip – and who are presumably able to perform very specific favours if asked properly. This combination of cosmological speculation and magical practice has roots in Second Temple-period apocalypticism, and ultimately in Mesopotamian priestly lore; and it also has a contemporary Jewish counterpart in the Sefer Ha-Razim (Book of Mysteries) – a probably late antique Hebrew text which embeds explicit magical recipes and spells in its description of the cosmos. What is distinctive about the Heikhalot texts is that they are written in the style of rabbinic texts, with the various segments attributed pseudepigraphically to familiar Mishnaic rabbinic authorities. This means either that late antique rabbis were trying to annex magical practice, or that late antique magicians were claiming rabbinic origins for their teachings, presumably because such a claim would have enhanced their prestige.

The *piyyut* is somewhat harder to characterize, culturally.[12] This is the term – a backformation of the Greek loanword in Hebrew and Aramaic, *payyetan* or *poyyetan* (= *poiētēs*) – for the distinctively complex style of liturgical poetry probably introduced in Palestinian synagogues in the sixth century. It then spread to areas in the Mediterranean basin under Palestinian influence, but by the high to later Middle Ages had basically disappeared from Jewish liturgy, because Iraqi rabbinic authorities, whose influence was on the rise, rejected *piyyut* in favour of a simplified, fixed liturgy. This is why the great corpora of *piyyut* were rediscovered only when

---

[12] A good recent survey of scholarship, the overwhelming majority of which is in Hebrew, on the *piyyut* is van Bekkum 2010; in much greater detail Lieber 2010: 1–299, the second half of whose book provides the most extensive English translation of the works of a major *payyetan* available.

the Cairo Genizah – situated in a synagogue which in the Middle Ages had followed Palestinian rituals – came to light.

The *piyyut*, like late antique Syriac poetry, is remarkable for discarding over two millennia of uninterrupted North-west Semitic poetic tradition (Münz-Manor 2010). From the epic poetry of Ugarit (second millennium BCE), to biblical psalms and prophecies of the Iron Age, to the thanksgiving hymns of the Dead Sea scrolls (second to first century BCE), the defining feature of west Semitic poetry had been not rhyme – though it inevitably occurs sometimes in inflected languages – or metre – which did not exist in any conventional way – but *parallelismus membrorum*, easier to illustrate than to explain:

> Pharaoh's chariots and army were cast in the sea
> His choice officers drowned in the Sea of Reeds
> The abyss covered them
> They fell in the depths like a stone.
>
> (Ex. 15.4–5)

Here is a more complex example:

> On the high mountain ascend, O Heraldess of Zion
> Lift up your voice powerfully, O Heraldess of Jerusalem
> Lift your voice, fear not
> Say to the towns of Judah, 'Here is your God'
> Here is the Lord Yahweh, He comes in force, and has a ruling forearm.
>
> (Is. 40.9–10)

In sum, each half-verse is roughly similar in length, and restates in different language or is otherwise related (sometimes adversative, sometimes intensifying) in content to the half-verse which precedes it. The diction is 'high'; poets preferred rare or archaic language, not conversational or 'prosaic' language. Biblical Hebrew poets frequently used words not found in Hebrew prose, but common in Phoenician or even Ugaritic. Some word pairs (e.g., abyss/depth) are attested in every stratum of the 'Canaanite' poetic tradition; this was, then, a tradition in the strong sense, markedly continuous from the Bronze Age to the early Roman Empire.

The preference for rare or archaic words was retained in the *piyyut*, but parallelism was abandoned, and rhyme and metre were gradually introduced. The classical *piyyut* is an academic or learned poetry, which delighted in its allusiveness and obscurity. Unlike rabbinic language, with its chaotic-seeming mixtures of Hebrew, Aramaic and Greek, *piyyut* is written in 'pure' though difficult Hebrew, indicating that late antique

Jews were not devoid of linguistic self-consciousness, and further problematizing rabbinic language (Yahalom 1985). Modern readers need not only excellent dictionaries, but a biblical concordance and a comprehensive grasp of rabbinics to make sense of *piyyut*, which resembles some midrashic texts in relying on learned though often convoluted readings of biblical verses to make its point. Some *piyyut* reads basically like versified midrash, but *piyyut* was liturgical; in some late antique synagogues the service consisted primarily of such poetry.[13] In one view, the *payyetan* was a communal employee whose job it was to compose and perform, or indeed to improvise, a new poetic cycle – reflecting the week's pentateuchal lection – for each Sabbath and holiday, much as starting in 1723 the city council of Leipzig employed J. S. Bach to compose and perform a new cantata for each Sunday service at the St Thomas Church (Fleischer 1975). There is no specific evidence to support this attractive hypothesis, but it remains possible, and no one has yet produced a better account of how the *piyyut* came into existence.

Few people even in a partly educated urban audience could have understood a full-blown classical *piyyut* in all its learnedly allusive complexity at first audition; and the congregation had no access to written texts, was probably largely illiterate, and anyway knew relatively little Hebrew, as opposed to Aramaic and Greek. To be sure it was presumably *performed* – sung, conceivably with choral accompaniment; and some components of the weekly *piyyut* cycle are likely to have been linguistically relatively simple, litanies, for example. Some *payyetanim* emphasized sound effects: the late sixth century *payyetan* Elazar Qiliri composed a poem for the Sabbath before the holiday of Purim which began as follows: *Atz qotzetz ben qotzetz / qetzutzai leqatzetz / bedibbur mefotzetz / retzutzai leratzetz*, etc. There can have been few people at the first performance who understood that Qiliri was retelling the story of the book of Esther, but there would have been great delight in the fact that he was saying anything at all with all those *tz* sounds. Indeed, this poem became so popular that it was one of the very few classical *piyyutim* to have been preserved in the later liturgical tradition. People must often have appreciated *piyyut* for the reasons their descendants appreciated opera in the days before supertitles: for the spectacle and the virtuosity. That late antique Jewish congregations tolerated a liturgy which consisted largely of mystification (this is what the Iraqi rabbis later reacted against) is a non-trivial fact about

[13] The only English translation of a major part of the corpus is Lieber 2010; this is also the most substantial piece of scholarship in English on pre-Islamic *piyyut*.

them, and one that emphasizes the similarity of their religiosity to that of early Byzantine Christians. The archaeological synagogues and the *piyyut* are thus of a piece, demonstrating the Jews' participation in a shared late antique culture. The extent to which the *piyyut* provides further evidence for rabbinization in the sixth century requires further study. Yannai's rabbinic orientation is well established (Rabinovitz 1965), but whether the same is true of others is less clear.

THE EVE OF THE MUSLIM CONQUEST

In the course of the sixth century the Jews came to assume a geopolitical role they had not played since 116 CE. This was because they constituted a significant (how significant there is to be sure no way of knowing) component of the population in many regions of the Byzantine–Persian frontier zone – including Palestine, Syria and, across the frontier, Mesopotamia – at a time of growing instability. The details of this development have not yet been worked out sufficiently and, as usual, the sources are spotty and difficult. Some of the most interesting recent work concerns a surprising arena of geopolitical proxy competition, Arabia and the east African coast, where Christian Monophysites, Jews and pagans, Romans and Persians, Lakhmids and Ghassanids were caught up in a shifting complex of alliances and friendships.[14] In some vague way this situation constitutes the background of the rise of Islam, but for our purposes the growing importance of Arabia in the sixth and seventh centuries illustrates a revival in the regional political importance of the Jews. In frontier zones religious affiliations were political currency in very straightforward ways, which does not exclude their status as systems of belief and practice: the rulers of Himyar (Yemen) thus converted to Judaism in the fourth century to compete with their powerful Axumite neighbours, who had converted to Monophysite Christianity. This made the Himyarites natural clients of the Persians, which in turn impelled the Byzantines to adopt the Ethiopians, a relationship complicated by the latters' theological error. In the 520s a Byzantine–Axumite alliance brought the Jewish kingdom to an end, but Yathrib (Madina) now emerged as an Arabian Jewish centre, and ever-intensifying hostility between Jews and Christians (with pagan Arabs presumably caught in the middle), and Byzantine patronage of all Christians, automatically drove Jews into the pro-Sasanid camp.

---

[14] The avalanche of recent work on Himyar is summarized in Bowersock 2012 and 2013.

The Persian invasion of Palestine in 614 brought almost seven centuries of Roman rule to an end.[15] The Byzantine emperor Heraclius succeeded in expelling the Persians only in 629, a few years before the arrival of the Arabs. The largely chronographic sources for the Persian conquest are terse and not completely credible. All describe a great massacre of Christians at Jerusalem (it is unlikely that any Jews were living there in 614: they were legally barred from doing so though the law was not necessarily perfectly enforced; Baras 1982: 306–7), and the destruction of many churches.[16] Archaeology, however, tells a different story – in general archaeologically informed historians have tended to minimize the disruption caused by the Persian invasion (Foss 1997: 261–2). There is no evidence for physical damage to any churches, but there is chronologically appropriate evidence for mass burial in seven locations, each containing the remains of several hundred bodies – hardly the (impossible) 90,000 of the chronographic tradition but still significant. In one case the mass grave, situated in a cave near Mamilla pool, was transformed into a chapel, with a surviving simple mosaic pavement with a Greek inscription that provides no information about the circumstances of the burials. Deaths associated with the invasion provide the most likely explanation – 'Antiochus Strategos' explicitly names Mamilla as the site of the greatest slaughter – but this is not the only possibility: plague is a close runner-up.[17]

All relevant sources except the *Chronicon Paschale* describe the Jews as the Persians' avid collaborators, and not just at Jerusalem. Theophanes and 'Antiochus Strategos' both claim that the Jews bought Christians taken captive by the Persians at Jerusalem and slaughtered them ('Antiochus' names additional villains: the Jerusalem circus factions and the 'rebellious' emperor Phocas' second in command, Bonosus; the most reliable version of this text may imply that the Jews planned to commit this guileful

---

[15] The most detailed account is Baras 1982; Avi-Yonah 1976: 257–75, is somewhat briefer, but it is in English. Both accounts are positivistic but Baras expresses greater awareness of the problems of the evidence. Bowersock 2012: 31–51 provides the most cautious and up-to-date account.

[16] Theophanes, *Chronographia*, ed. C. de Boor, Leipzig, 1893, 1.300.30–301.5; *Chronicon Paschale*, ed. L. Dindorf, Bonn, 1832, 1.704.23–28. The most detailed account is Antiochus Strategos' (called in some manuscripts Strategius the Monk), *Capture of Jerusalem by the Persians*, allegedly an eyewitness account, preserved in two late medieval Georgian codices, and several somewhat earlier Arabic ones, apparently translated from Greek, including a mixture of implausibilities and surprisingly reliable-sounding circumstantial detail. For abridged English translation, Conybeare 1910. Full discussion of the textual issues: Baras 1982: 302–4; critical edition of Georgian texts with Latin translation: Garitte 1960.

[17] The graves are too late for the outbreak of 541, as Avni (2010) notes, but there were repeated subsequent outbreaks.

massacre but did not succeed: Bowersock 2012: 37–8).[18] This episode exemplifies so many of the stock anti-Jewish themes beloved of Byzantine chroniclers that it can hardly be taken at face value. We must also not exclude the possibility that Jewish politics was more complicated – whoever the Jewish leaders were, some of them are likely to have had alliances with the Byzantines which would have at least problematized support for the Persians.[19] Nevertheless, in periods of high tension and instability, when there is little ostensible political grey area, the notion that Jews and Christians were in stark political opposition and that this translated automatically into Jewish support for Persia, is a view which cannot be hastily rejected: relevant parallels are easily found within living memory, for example, in political realignments in north-eastern Europe in the wake of the Molotov–Ribbentrop pact, when nearly all Jews, even the most ardent anti-communists, supported the USSR.

Thus, though the sources are poor, we should take seriously their claim that the Jews' reception of the Sasanids was celebratory, and that Jews joined Persians in plunder and slaughter of Christians; but it is cautious scepticism, not only apologetics, which prevents us from taking the chronographers' accounts at face value (*contra* Horowitz 1998). That the Persians rewarded the Jews for their hospitality is also likely but the chronographic tradition reports little about the details. It has been argued on the basis of a dubiously relevant account in the apocalyptic Hebrew Book of Zerubbabel (Himmelfarb 1990; cf. Gil 2006) and a difficult *piyyut* fragment (Fleischer 1984/5) that the Persians allowed the Jews to restore the traditional sacrificial cult on the Temple Mount, or even, that King Khosrau II simply handed Jerusalem over to the Jews (so Avi-Yonah 1976; contra: Baras 1982: 332). The paucity of evidence for what the Jews should have received as glorious news is striking but the possibility, at least of the restoration of sacrifice, cannot be excluded. Like the restoration under Julian, this one too was abortive, even before the end of Persian rule (Baras 1982: 334–5). In any case, the chance of any further restoration was rendered moot by

---

[18] According to the chronographers Bonosus, *comes orientis* under Phocas, was murdered at Constantinople in 610 by one of his own men; he had been active in Palestine previously. Yet 'Antiochus' *seems* to ascribe to Bonosus a direct role in the Persian invasion but on closer reading the account is ambiguous about his role and that of the circus factions. See *PLRE* IIIA, 239–40. One of the factions, the Blues, is attested epigraphically in Byzantine Jerusalem (Cameron 1976: 316), but 'Antiochus' provides the only narrative of their activity.

[19] E.g., the shadowy, perhaps non-existent, Benjamin of Tiberias, mentioned by Theophanes alone (*Chronographia* 328), who successfully interceded on the Jews' behalf in the early stages of Heraclius' reconquest of Palestine in 628/9.

Muslim construction projects on the site, and so memory of the episode was suppressed. Alternatively, it never happened.

Heraclius' treatment of the Jews when he reconquered Syria and Palestine in 629 was indubitably vengeful and harsh, but Jews retained a significant presence in Palestine deep into the Muslim period, with the effective end arriving only during the Crusades (Gil 1992, in great detail). If Bowersock (2012; 2013) is right, Islam had functioned at its rise to break the traditional Arabian religio-political binary:[20] it was neither Christian nor Jewish and so neither pro-Roman nor pro-Persian. The arrival of Islam thus initiated a new and eventually fertile period of ambiguity for the Jews of the Near East and the Mediterranean basin.

---

[20] The binary excludes the pagans who were surely the largest component of the population of pre-Islamic Arabia, so we can accept Bowersock's view only with hesitation.

CHAPTER 7

Jews in the ancient world

The primary reason to study ancient Jewish history and texts is interest in ancient Jewish history and texts. There is enough material, and it is distinctive and rich enough to sustain plenty of attention. Complicating and enriching such interest for many people is the fact that the history and the texts continue to make claims and demands: they are, even today, not completely 'other'. Indeed, defamiliarizing the material, restoring it to antiquity, and, thereby, subjecting contemporary proprietary claims over it to intense and precise analytic scrutiny, retain a measure of ethical and political urgency.

But there are other reasons to study ancient Jewish history, too, and one of the implicit themes of this book has been that ancient historians in particular can ill-afford to ignore it (cf. Goodman and Alexander 2010). Jewish and Christian literary traditions preserved much material relevant to ancient historians' concerns: parts of the Hebrew Bible and much of the so-called Apocrypha and Pseudepigrapha are primary evidence for Hellenistic culture; Philo and Josephus – not to mention the New Testament – are important samples of Early Imperial Greek writing, however far they may deviate from the literary standards of the classical canon; Palestinian rabbinic literature in all its occasional hermeticism is the largest corpus of writing produced by the inhabitants of a single High and Later Imperial Roman province except for Italy (perhaps Asia produced more, but all of it, pagan and Christian, participates in trans-local cultural patterns). That so few ancient historians have embraced this material testifies to the continuing, albeit sometimes vestigial, conception of the field of ancient history as ancillary to classics.

One role of ancient Jewish history is to upset the narratives that ancient historians have produced either on the basis of an inadequate sampling of sources, or as ways of presenting the grand reductive flowcharts of 'global history', which has in recent years established a foothold in the field. An account of responses to Roman rule, or the impact of imperialism on provincial literary cultures cannot begin and end the story with the Second

Sophistic. For globalists, Jewish history and literature (which are of no interest because their scale is too small) should also constitute a stumbling block: culture may, or may not, affect in profound ways basic things like diet, medical regimes, and patterns of exchange. The Jews provide evidence that groups of provincials might sometimes opt out of alleged patterns and so warn us of our ignorance: we do not always know what was going on beneath the surface even in the relatively well-attested high Roman Empire, and this casts systematic doubt on the validity of at least some types of model-building projects. Historians must at least conduct such projects with appropriate caution.

Indeed, one of the basic lessons of ancient Jewish history is just how peculiar it is. The accidental if partial survival of a non-classical ancient culture reveals it to have been remarkably distinctive, to the extent that we can write an internalist history of the Jews, whether or not it is always intellectually desirable to do so. Indeed, the surviving information largely dictates that the history of Hellenistic and Roman Judaea have an internalist quality. No one could ever read, say, Greg Woolf's *Becoming Roman* (1998) as 'Gallic' history, whatever precisely that would mean. Strikingly, even in the period of the Jews' maximal integration in the Roman system, 135–350, we know just enough to know that some of them preserved, altered and reorganized elements of their pre-Roman culture as a coherent high culture. Were the Jews unique in doing so, or more typical than we might have guessed? If we knew more about the Lydians under Roman rule, and if, by chance, there had persisted a community dedicated to the proprietary preservation of a sense of a special Lydian destiny, would we be able to write a history of Roman Lydia which felt distinctly Lydian – as Glen Bowersock (1983) in fact once tried to do for Roman Arabia, in a project continued by Maurice Sartre (2001)?[1]

There is no simple answer to this question, in part because we simply don't know what we don't know. This is true especially for the Roman imperial period. For the Hellenistic period, when the kings indirectly

---

[1] Although sporadically Roman-ruled borderland cities like Edessa and Hatra are clearly different, as is Palmyra, on the whole I tend more towards Millar's view (1993) that the *public* culture even of inland cities in Syria and Arabia was on the whole normatively Greco-Roman, not 'Arabian' or 'Syrian', which does not preclude the maintenance in some such cities of 'Syrian' cults and the very infrequently attested use of Aramaic or Arabic in inscriptions. Roman cities cultivated local colour, and few of the 'traditional'-seeming non-Greco-Roman cults are actually attested before the Roman period. They may be comparable to rabbinic Judaism in being a nativist or traditionalist response (not necessarily expression of opposition) to Roman rule but unlike the Jewish case there is no evidence that there was any group of elites or would-be elites engaged in the project of scrutinizing, sifting and rationalizing the neo-traditionalism. For discussion see Kaizer 2008.

fostered Hellenism while continuing to support local establishments in Egypt, Mesopotamia, Asia, Syria and elsewhere, which preserved non-Greek 'great traditions', the Jews did not yet seem to stand out from the crowd: there were Jews preserving pre-Greek norms in pre-Greek languages, and Jews adapting Judaean traditions to the emerging world of the Near Eastern Greek city. The same was true for Egyptian and Mesopotamian clerisies as well. The Jews' increasingly monotheistic norms may have been unusual but their cultural negotiations with their rulers were after all rather typical. The late Hellenistic Hasmonean dynasty was typical, too, in its merging of Greek and traditionalist or nativist ideologies – a topic not yet sufficiently investigated. This was why Elias Bickermann and Arnaldo Momigliano were so convincing when they argued that Jewish literature of the Hellenistic period, both hellenizing and traditionalist, has to be taken seriously by historians of Hellenistic culture.

The Early and High Roman Empire is a different story. Evidence for the perpetuation of local great traditions (except of course in culturally Greek areas) fades. Nothing comparable to rabbinic literature survives from the Roman world – until the emergence of Coptic near the end of antiquity; even patristic literature is suffused with classical culture: through the fifth century its profusion precisely marks the entry into the church and rise through its ranks of growing numbers of *pepaideumenoi* (elite recipients of classical education). Even the *haplotes* (simplicity) embraced by Christian writers started as a type of classical ideal, though it eventually marked the recession of the influence of classical Greek education. Similarly, to the extent that provincial cultures or local religious systems generated literary remains which have survived – which few of them did and that only very fragmentarily – they were always refracted through classical norms. Herennius Philo of Byblos, whose partly lost account of Phoenician antiquities preserves some Canaanite lore, does so in palatably hellenized style: anyone looking for substantial evidence that the municipal priesthoods of Tyre, Sidon, and so on, maintained a deep engagement with still vibrant local traditions will not find it in the fragments of Herennius Philo.

One might have expected traditional temple establishments not absorbed into the empire-wide system of municipal cults, like that of Atargatis at Hierapolis Bambyke, or perhaps most importantly those which continued to function in Egypt, to provide some help, but they do not. For Atargatis there is only the pseudo-Herodotean, quasi-ethnographic, possibly ironic, possibly Lucianic *De Dea Syria*, and for Egypt ... nothing.[2] The most

---

[2] See, exhaustively, Lightfoot 2003.

profound account of Isiac piety comes from still another arch *litterateur* of the second century, Apuleius, and is found in the eleventh book of the *Golden Ass*; as with the Lucianic essay on Atargatis, it is impossible to know how seriously to take it. A lot can be said about the survival of Egyptian 'little traditions', but we know disappointingly little about any interactions they may have had with any specifically Egyptian 'great tradition' of the literate and the educated. It seems likely that the great tradition of the High Roman Empire, unlike those of the Hellenistic kingdoms, was in fact overwhelmingly Greco-Roman: in this sense, rabbinic literature was *perhaps* unique.

But rabbinic literature in all its oddity turns out to provide an excellent way of testing the limits of resistance to Roman rule. It may get a low grade for typicality but can serve very well as a diagnostic. In fact we need not start there: If we recognize that Jewish history in all its remarkable 'internal' density is nevertheless constituted by constant negotiation with ever-stable and ever-changing sets environmental imperatives (and I mean physical, political, and cultural environments), then Jewish stuff is not just part of that environmental history but may help understand the larger picture, too. What condition does rabbinic literature diagnose? Unlike most pagan writers, and unlike, even, most canonical church fathers (but like the evangelists, Paul and the apostolic fathers), the rabbis were not aristocrats or retainers of aristocrats. Except for the patriarchal family, they were members of the 'middle class' of what, before the later fourth century, was one of the poorest and least distinguished Roman provinces. Most rabbis did not grow up immersed in classical high culture though they were surrounded by the small-town version of it. Rabbinic literature among many other things gives us direct insight into the interests and mentalities of a class which otherwise left few literary traces. Rabbinic literature shows not only how distinctive some Jews could remain after centuries of not-precisely-gentle Roman rule; it also gives us a sense of the unexpectedly strange cultural and political options available to non-elites. If you dig long and hard enough in rabbinic literature, you can find plenty of evidence for the romanization even of the most resistant Jews. What is surprising and important, though, is just how resistant they were able to remain.

Bibliographical essay

There is no reliable one-volume history of the Jews from Cyrus to Muhammad. This is mainly due to the controversies concerning the character of Jewish life after the destruction of Jerusalem in 70 CE. While the first two volumes of the magisterial classic Baron (1952–93) are simply out of date, the popular textbook edited by Ben-Sasson (1976), while quite usable for the biblical and Second Temple periods, is marred for the following period by its lack of methodological caution and wild speculativeness. Smallwood (1981) to be sure covers the Roman side of the story competently (likewise Avi-Yonah 1976) but the discussion of post-70 Jewish sources and the historical narratives based on them are derivative and badly in need of updating. Nevertheless a good starting point at least for part of the period (roughly 200 BCE to 135 CE) is Schürer-Vermes. In fact the second and third volumes provide surveys of topics in ancient Judaism and primary sources that far exceed the chronological limits of the book and, though by now showing signs of age, are still excellent. S. Cohen (2006) is a brief survey intended for university courses, crystalline but over-simple. Still, this book provides one of the best (of the vast number of such books that have been published) and most factually meticulous basic brief orientations in ancient Judaism – but not Jewish history – in the period from 200 BCE to 200 CE. S. Schwartz (2001) argues for the integration of political, social and cultural or religious history, and brings his account through late antiquity.

PRIMARY SOURCES

Some important material, both literary and archaeological, has appeared since the publication of Schürer-Vermes volume III. Though there is no one publication which summarizes Palestinian and diaspora Jewish archaeology (the latter mainly excavations of graves and synagogues), Stern 1993 offers ample guidance for the first, and Levine 2005 and Hachlili 1998 for the second. The website of the Israel Antiquities Authority (www.antiquities.org.il) is also a useful resource; it provides access to the annual round-up *Excavations and Surveys in Israel*. The classic *Corpus Papyrorum Judaicarum* will soon, one prays, receive its long overdue updating, but in the meantime Cowey and Maresch (2001) have provided crucial and previously unknown evidence for Jewish judicial autonomy in mid-Hellenistic Egypt. Palestinian papyrology has been hugely enriched by the long delayed publication of the two volumes of P. Yadin, and of XHever/Seiyal. There has been much progress, as well, towards replacing the inadequate corpora of ancient Jewish inscriptions: Horbury and Noy (1992) and Noy (1993–95), whatever their faults, still constitute vast improvements over the archaic *Corpus Inscriptionum Judaicarum* of J.-B. Frey. Of the *Inscriptiones Iudaicae Orientis* series published by Mohr Siebeck, the most important volume is Ameling (2004), on Asia Minor, the richest find-spot of Jewish-related epigraphical material outside Palestine and Rome. The project of re-editing and publishing all the inscriptions, in whatever language, of Palestine, from Alexander to Muhammad, led by Hannah Cotton and Werner Eck, has been completed. Three fascicles of a projected nine volumes have been published as of June, 2013, as the *Corpus Inscriptionum Iudaeae/Palaestinae* (Berlin, 2010–). Garcia Martinez and Tigchelaar (1997–8) provide texts, translations and bibliographies for all non-biblical scrolls from Qumran.

In the 1990s and 2000s there was a great burst of scholarship on the most important ancient Jewish historian, Josephus (born Jerusalem, 37/8 CE, died Rome, after *c*. 95). Much of this is summed up in the (overblown) Brill commentary series edited by Steve Mason. The Loeb Classical Library Josephus remains more accessible, and is reliable as both text and translation. Rabbinic literature constitutes a special problem (for an excellent guide, see Strack and Stemberger 1996). Few rabbinic texts have been properly edited and so existing translations, made from traditional printed editions, can be relied on only with great caution. The Mishnah is exceptional in that Danby (1933) is reliable. The Soncino (Babylonian) Talmud (26 vols., ed. I. Epstein, London, 1935–59) and the Soncino Midrash Rabbah (10 vols., ed. H. Freedman, London, 1939) provide competent translations of the traditional texts of these works. The Palestinian Talmud survives in a single full manuscript, which has now been published by Yaakov Sussmann (Jerusalem, 2001), as have the fragmentary manuscripts from the Cairo Genizah (Jerusalem, 2012). The one full English translation, by Jacob Neusner (Chicago, 1982) unfortunately cannot be recommended to anyone who cannot read the original text. Somewhat preferable is the as yet incomplete *Übersetzung des Talmud Yerushalmi* (ed. M. Hengel, Tübingen, 1975–). Of non-rabbinic literature of late antiquity, a substantial selection of the corpus of 'classical' (pre-Islamic) *piyyut* is now available in the reliable English translation of Lieber (2010), and Swartz (1996) and Boustan (2005) provide excellent guidance to the world of Heikhalot (magical/mystical) speculation and practice.

CHAPTER I

The debate between scholars who are sceptical about the historicity of the Hebrew Bible (a position classically associated with Julius Wellhausen [1878], though easily traced back to Enlightenment figures like Spinoza) and those who tend to accept it (Kaufmann 1937; Albright 1957) has experienced many permutations in its long history, and at present is radically polarized, with 'minimalists' (e.g., Lemche 1988; Davies 2007) discarding the very notion of a 'biblical Israel' and regarding the entire Hebrew Bible as a product of the Jerusalem priesthood of the Hellenistic period (a view which seems to give far too much credit to the [tiny] Jerusalem priesthood of the Hellenistic period). On the other side, especially in the United States, are growing ranks of the biblical-studies counterparts to 'creation scientists', who use the language of scholarship to promote fundamentalist Protestantism or, very infrequently, Orthodox Judaism (see discussion in Grabbe 2011). Fortunately, there are some alternatives to intellectual anarchy and religious extremism: Van Seters 1983; Clements 1989; Brettler 1995. There remains much of value in Morton Smith 1971: of particular importance is the argument that monolatry (worship of one god) was a minority position in monarchic Judah, and it, or even the more extreme monotheism (belief in one universal god, first securely attested in Isaiah chapters 40–9), became mainstream only under the Persians, as a result of a series of political struggles.

The impact of Macedonian rule on the Jews was subject of a lively debate but in this case the opponents have lately grown less extreme. It was once thought that the Jews became radically hellenized very soon after Alexander the Great (the basic position of Bickermann 1979/1937 was greatly exaggerated by Hengel 1974), with only some traditionalists offering strong opposition (L. Feldman 1993). The re-evaluation of the cultural implications especially of Seleucid rule (Sherwin-White and Kuhrt 1993) has softened the edges of the debate. It is no longer possible to imagine a Jewish nation thoroughly 'hellenized' by 200 BCE. So far, however, few Jewish historians have absorbed the implications of John Ma's (2000a) more activist portrayal of the Seleucids.

CHAPTER 2

That some elements of the Judaean population *aspired* to join the Greek world seems certain. The crucial episodes are the events that preceded the Maccabean Revolt and the revolt itself. On the whole there been little progress in understanding these events since the classic expositions of Bickermann (1979/1937) – who ascribed the reforms and persecutions to the initiatives of Jewish hellenizers and regarded the resisters as a minority – and Tcherikover (1959) – who blamed the king and regarded resistance as the majority option. Habicht's (1976) meticulous study of the documents quoted in 2 Maccabees tended to support Bickermann's views, while the Tyriaion inscription has been taken to support Tcherikover's (Ameling 2003) but probably does not (as I argue). The most novel and convincing interpretation of the revolt and its precipitants since the days of Bickermann and Tcherikover is just now being published by Ma (forthcoming).

The formative discussion of the Hasmonean conquests and conversions is J. Cohen 1999, but in the following decade the individual episodes were exhaustively re-examined by Shatzman (2005) and Leibner (2012), writing in Hebrew, and Shatzman (2007) and Eckhardt (2012), in English. Furthermore Dąbrowa (2010) and Regev (2011, 2012) have been promoting comprehensive re-examinations of the history of the Hasmonean dynasty, with mixed success.

CHAPTER 3

The explosion of publication about the ever-fascinating figure of Herod the Great is not easy to explain, though the successful promotion by the late Ehud Netzer of his archaeological work at major Herodian sites (Netzer 2006; note also the major 2013 exhibition about Herod at the Israel Museum, Jerusalem) may be part of the explanation. What is less clear is whether the impressive monumental archaeology has yet led to any truly meaningful revision (beyond the attempts in Schwartz 2001, and above), or whether we should still prefer the standard older accounts of Schalit (1969) and Richardson (1996).

Josephus' account is at its most detailed for the period from Herod to the destruction of Jerusalem, and much non-archaeological scholarship has been concerned with details of its interpretation. Palestine was an anomalous province after Herod's death: Gabba (1999) provided the most authoritative attempt to work out the complications (see also Labbé 2012). Important questions, though, remain open: the view I expressed above, that Palestinian Jews before 66 CE lived for most purposes under the authority of Jewish law, administered by the high priests, is merely a hypothesis, requiring a full reassessment (Cotton 2002 provides a start). The roles of the descendants of Herod in the governance of the province have been explored by Julia Wilker (2007).

My social-historical account of sectarianism's role in post-Herodian Jewish society is based on Schwartz (2001), but the structure of the argument was informed by the work of Baumgarten (1997) who, in my view, misdated the high point of sectarianism to the second century BCE. Indeed, in the most recent scholarship there is an emerging tendency to place even the origins of the phenomenon later than this. Much of the scholarship on the Dead Sea scrolls is concerned with small details of textual reconstruction and interpretation but recently the larger issues of whether the scrolls constitute a sectarian library at all, and whether they are even related to the archaeological site of Qumran, have received much attention. John Collins (2010) provides an account of these controversies.

CHAPTER 4

Martin Goodman (1987) began a still lively debate about the causes of the Jewish rebellions against Rome: in that work he gestured towards a structural-functionalist approach to the question (the Jews did not fit in the Roman Empire). Some of his critics argued that he did not go far enough (Shaw 1989; Avidov 2009; S. Schwartz 2010, and above) but meanwhile Goodman has changed his mind and characterized the initial breakdown of Roman–Jewish relations as essentially accidental (2007; critique: S. Schwartz 2009b). As far as the Great Revolt itself is concerned, the field has been divided between methodology-oriented interpreters of Josephus (S. Cohen 1979; Price 1992) and those who rely, consciously or not, on historical models (Rajak 1983; Goodman 1987; Gambash forthcoming).

The debate about the impact of the 'destruction' is a very old one in Jewish historiography: historians in the nineteenth century – influenced both by traditional Jewish ideas and by Mommsen's view – adopted above – that the Jewish nation was deconstituted in 70 – regarded it as the end of the Jewish 'commonwealth', or of the Jewish nation as a political agent, and the beginning of the Jewish community as a purely religious entity. Zionist historians of the early and mid-twentieth century regarded the Jews' loss of 'nationhood' in Palestine as a gradual process that began only in the fourth century, and so tended to minimize the impact of 70. My debate (here and in S. Schwartz 2013) with J. Klawans (2012) and D. Schwartz (2012) updates the old debate.

The crucial advances in the understanding of the Bar Kokhba Revolt have all come through archaeology, with the discovery and publication of the Bar Kokhba letters (P. Murab. and P. Yadin), the die-link studies of Leo Mildenberg (1984), the discovery of the controversial Tel Shalem arch, which Eck used to advocate a maximalist approach to the revolt (1999; critique in Bowersock 2003), and finally the recent excavations in Jerusalem which have shown that construction of a Roman city at the site preceded Hadrian's visit in 130 (Wexler-Bdolah 2009). All of these have rendered older accounts, based on the folklore-tinged stories in rabbinic literature, obsolete.

CHAPTER 5

There is now a full history – thorough, cautious, sceptical and sophisticated – of the Palestinian rabbis which, though it is not easy reading, constitutes the *summa* of the minimalist view advocated above (Lapin 2012). But it is well worth reading the best maximalist accounts, too (Miller 2006; Schremer 2010). I have said little about Babylonian rabbinism, or Babylonian Jews more generally. The topic is exceptionally difficult; little is known about the western provinces of the Parthian and Sasanian Empires, and much of that little concerns the Christians of northern Mesopotamia, not the Jews of Babylonia and their neighbours. Some scholars now believe the key to the Babylonian Talmud lies in medieval Zoroastrian literature. Some of us have yet to be convinced, but the curious may wish to consult Shai Secunda's new book (2013).

At one time scholars understood the patriarchate as a strong, stable institution, and their accounts tended to be descriptive, static and constitutional. The cautious analysis of the evidence in Levine (1979) and Jacobs (1995) enabled the more dynamic and non-constitutional accounts in S. Schwartz (1999), Stern (2003), S. Schwartz (2004) and Lapin (2012). Appelbaum (2012) tries to account for the dynasticism of the patriarchs. Geoffrey Herman (2012) provides the most detailed analysis to date of the patriarchs' Babylonian counterparts, the exilarchs.

CHAPTER 6

Jewish historians have recently been following the lead of general historians in thinking of late antiquity, especially in the East, as a period of florescence, though quite distinct in feel from the High Roman Empire. This tendency probably began with J. Cohen's compelling observation (1979) that for all their hostile rhetoric, the constitutions of the Christian emperors, until well into the reign of Theodosius II, were surprisingly favourable to the Jews (cf. Linder 1987 – the essential corpus of Roman legislation about the Jews). This fits with archaeological evidence for prosperity and cultural dynamism throughout Syria but most strikingly in the Jewish areas of Palestine, and elsewhere in the Roman Empire (note especially extensive synagogue construction, beginning 350 CE, surveyed in Levine 2005). Archaeology and literature of the period preserved in the Cairo Genizah gave the impression of something of a Jewish revival in late antiquity, at least until the mid-sixth century. Some went further: a tendency – not embraced in this book – to regard Christian–Jewish relations as essentially friendly, indeed, to argue that Christianity and Judaism were not even fully differentiated until nearly the end of antiquity, has gained ground as a result of the influential publications of Becker and Reed (2003) and Boyarin (2004).

Signs of a backlash are beginning to appear. Most important is Leibner 2009, providing a detailed argument that settlement in a core Jewish area of Galilee declined in population (and prosperity?) in the course of the fourth century and did not recover. Though this is clearly not the whole story (Bar 2004), it does suggest that S. Schwartz (2001) needs some refinement. Pulling against this tendency is the opposite one, to argue that signs of demographic thriving and prosperity in Syria–Palestine continued through the plague outbreaks of the mid-sixth century, the Persian conquest of 614, and the Muslim conquest of 638 (Avni 2011). These continuing uncertainties, combined with the fact that many sixth- and seventh-century texts, both Jewish and Christian, especially in more 'modest' genres, like saints' lives and 'popular' apocalypses, have not yet even been mined for basic information, meaning that the field is sure to remain dynamic. The essays collected in Bonfil *et al.* (2012) constitute a good start to this project. Special benefits will accrue to those willing to learn languages outside the comfort zones traditional to the field, in particular Jewish Aramaic, for Christian scholars, Christian Aramaic for Jewish scholars, and Arabic for everyone.

References

Abu El-Haj, N. (2012). *Genealogical Science: The Search for Jewish Origins and the Politics of Epistemology*. Chicago.

Adan-Bayewitz, D. (2008). 'Preferential Distribution of Lamps from the Jerusalem Area in the Late Second Temple Period'. *BASOR* 350: 37–85.

Adan-Bayewitz, D. and M. Aviam (1997). 'Iotapata, Josephus, and the Siege of 67: Preliminary Report on the 1992–94 Seasons'. *JRA* 10: 131–65.

Albright, W. (1957). *From the Stone Age to Christianity*. Baltimore.

Alon, G. (1977). *Jews, Judaism and the Classical World*. Jerusalem.

Ameling, W. (2003). 'Jerusalem als hellenistische Polis: 2 Makk 4, 9–12 und eine neue Inschrift', *Biblische Zeitschrift* 47: 105–11.

(2004). *Inscriptiones Iudaicae Orientis II, Kleinasien*. Tübingen.

Anderson, B. (1983). *Imagined Communities: Reflections on the Origins and Spread of Nationalism*. London.

Aperghis, G. G. (2004). *The Seleukid Royal Economy: The Finances and Financial Administration of the Seleukid Empire*. Cambridge.

Appelbaum, A. (2012). 'Rabbi's Successors: The Later Jewish Patriarchs of the Third Century'. *JJS* 63: 1–21.

Ariel, D. and J.-P. Fontanille (2012). *The Coins of Herod: A Modern Analysis and Die Classification*. Leiden.

Asad, T. (1993). *Genealogies of Religion: Discipline and Reasons of Power in Christianity and Islam*. Baltimore.

Aslanov, C. (2012). 'Romanos the Melodist and Palestinian *Piyyut*: Sociolinguistic and Pragmatic Perspectives', in Bonfil *et al.*, pp. 613–28.

Aviam, M. (2004). *Jews, Pagans, and Christians in the Galilee: 25 Years of Archaeological Excavations and Surveys*. Rochester, NY.

Avidov, A. (2009). *Not Reckoned Among the Nations: The Origins of the So-Called 'Jewish Question' in Roman Antiquity*. Tübingen.

Avigad, N. (1973). *Beth Shearim III, Catacombs 12–23*. Jerusalem.

Avi-Yonah, M. (1976). *The Jews under Roman and Byzantine Rule*. Oxford.

Avni, G. (2010). 'The Conquest of Jerusalem by the Persians: An Archaeological Assessment'. *BASOR* 357: 35–48.

(2011). '"From Polis to Madina" Revisited – Urban Change in Byzantine and Early Islamic Palestine'. *Journal of the Royal Asiatic Society* 21: 301–30.

Baer, Y. (1950). 'The Origins of the Organization of the Jewish Community in the Middle Ages'. *Zion* 15: 1–41 (in Hebrew).

Baker, C. (2011). 'A "Jew" by Any Other Name?'. *Journal of Ancient Judaism* 2: 153–80.

Baker, R. (2012). 'Epiphanius, *On Weights and Measures* 14: Hadrian's Journey to the East and the Rebuilding of Jerusalem'. *ZPE* 182: 157–67.

Baltrusch, E. (2002). *Die Juden und das Römische Reich*. Darmstadt.

(2009). 'Herodes und das Diaspora-Judentum', in L.-M. Günther (ed.), *Herodes und Jerusalem*, Stuttgart, pp. 47–60.

Baly, D. (1984). 'The Geography of Palestine and the Levant in Relation to its History', in *CHJ* 1: 1–24.

Bar, D. (2004). 'Population, Settlement and Economy in Late Roman and Byzantine Palestine (70–641 AD)'. *Bulletin of the School of Oriental and African Studies* 67: 307–20.

(2005). 'Rural Monasticism as a Key Element in the Christianization of Palestine'. *HTR* 98: 49–65.

Barclay, John (1996). *Jews in the Mediterranean Diaspora: from Alexander to Trajan (323 BCE–117 CE)*. Edinburgh.

Bar-Kochva, B. (1989). *Judas Maccabaeus: The Jewish Struggle against the Seleucids*. Cambridge.

Bar Nathan, R. and D. Sklar-Parnes (2007). 'A Jewish Settlement in Orine between the Two Revolts', in J. Patrich and D. Amit (eds.), *New Studies in the Archaeology of Jerusalem and Its Region: Collected Papers*. Jerusalem, pp. 57–64 (in Hebrew).

Barag, D. (2012). 'Alexander Jannaeus – Priest and King', in A. Maeir, J. Magness and L. Schiffman (eds.), *'Go Out and Study the Land (Judges 18:2): Archaeological, Historical and Textual Studies in Honor of Hanan Eshel*. Leiden, pp. 1–5.

Baras, Z. (1982). 'The Persian Conquest and the End of Byzantine Rule', in Z. Baras, S. Safrai, Y. Tsafrir and M. Stern (eds.), *Eretz Israel from the Destruction of the Second Temple to the Muslim Conquest*, Jerusalem, pp. 300–49 (in Hebrew).

Baron, S. (1942). *The Jewish Community: Its History and Structure to the American Revolution*, volume I. Philadelphia.

(1952–93). *A Social and Religious History of the Jews*. 18 volumes. New York.

Baumgarten, A. (1997). *The Flourishing of Jewish Sects in the Maccabean Era: An Interpretation*. Leiden.

Becker, A. and A. Reed (2003). *The Ways That Never Parted: Jews and Christians in Late Antiquity and in the Early Middle Ages*. Tübingen.

Beer, M. (1982). 'On the Havurah in Eretz-Israel in the Amoraic Period'. *Zion* 47: 178–85 (in Hebrew).

Belkin, S. (1940). *Philo and the Oral Law: The Philonic Interpretation of Biblical Law in Relation to the Palestinian Halakah*. Cambridge, MA:

Bellemore, J. (1999). 'Josephus, Pompey and the Jews'. *Historia* 48: 94–118.

Ben-Ami, D. and Y. Tchekhanovets (2011). 'The Lower City of Jerusalem on the Eve of Its Destruction, 70 CE: A View from Hanyon Givati'. *BASOR* 364: 61–85.

Ben-David, C. (2006). 'Late Antique Gaulanitis: Settlement Patterns of Christians and Jews in Rural Landscape', in A. Lewin and P. Pellegrini (eds.), *Settlements and Demography in the Near East in Late Antiquity: Proceedings of the Colloquium, Matera 27–29 October 2005* Pisa and Rome, pp. 35–50.

Ben-Dov, J. (2008). 'New Contexts for the Book-Find of King Josiah'. *JBL* 127: 223–39.

Ben-Sasson, H. (1976). *A History of the Jewish People*. Cambridge, MA.

Berkowitz, B. (2006). *Execution and Invention: Death Penalty Discourse in Early Rabbinic and Christian Cultures*. New York.

Bickerman, E. (1978). 'The Generation of Ezra and Nehemiah'. *PAAJR* 45: 1–28.

Bickermann, E. (1979/1937). *Der Gott der Makkabäer: Untersuchungen über Sinn und Ursprung der makkabäischen Erhebung*. Berlin (published in English as *The God of the Maccabees: Studies on the Meaning and Origin of the Maccabean Revolt*. Leiden).

(1984). 'The Babylonian Captivity', in *CHJ* 1: 342–58.

Bijovsky, G. (2007). 'Numismatic Evidence for the Gallus Revolt: The Hoard from Lod'. *IEJ* 57: 187–203.

Bikerman, E. (1935). 'La charte séleucide de Jérusalem'. *REJ* 100: 4–35.

Blenkinsopp, J. (1987). 'The Mission of Udjahorresnet and Those of Ezra and Nehemiah', *JBL* 106: 409–21.

(2009). *Judaism: The First Phase: The Place of Ezra and Nehemiah in the Origins of Judaism*. Grand Rapids, MI.

Bohak, G. (2008). *Ancient Jewish Magic*. Cambridge.

Bonfil, R., O. Irshai, G. Stroumsa and R. Talgam (eds.) (2012). *Jews in Byzantium: Dialectics of Minority and Majority Cultures*. Leiden.

Boustan, R. (2005). *From Martyr to Mystic: Rabbinic Martyrology and the Making of Merkavah Mysticism*. Tübingen.

Bowersock, Glen (1983). *Roman Arabia*. Cambridge, MA.

(1994). 'Roman Senators from the Near East', in G. Bowersock (ed.), *Studies on the Eastern Roman Empire*. Goldbach, pp. 141–60 (originally 1984).

(2003). 'The Tel Shalem Arch and P. Nahal Hever/Seiyal 8', in Schäfer, pp. 171–80.

(2012). *Empires in Collision in Late Antiquity* (The Menahem Stern Jerusalem Lectures). Waltham, MA.

(2013). *The Throne of Adulis: The Red Sea Wars on the Eve of Islam*. New York.

Boyarin, D. (2004). *Border Lines: The Partition of Judaeo-Christianity*. Philadelphia,

(2009). 'Rethinking Jewish Christianity: An Argument for Dismantling a Dubious Category (to which is Appended a Correction of my *Border Lines*)'. *JQR* 99: 7–36.

Bradbury, S. (1996). *Severus of Minorca: Letter on the Conversion of the Jews*. Oxford.

Brettler, M. (1995). *The Creation of History in Ancient Israel*. London.

Briant, P. (2002). *From Cyrus to Alexander: A History of the Persian Empire* (tr. Peter Daniels). Winona Lake, IN.

Bringmann, K. (1983). *Hellenistische Reform und Religionsverfolgung in Judäa: eine Untersuchung zur jüdisch–hellenistischen Geschichte (175–163 v.Chr.).* Göttingen.

Brody, R. (1998). *The Geonim of Babylonia and the Shaping of Medieval Jewish Culture.* New Haven, CT.

Broshi, M. and I. Finkelstein (1992). 'The Population of Palestine in Iron Age II'. *BASOR* 287: 47–60.

Brown, J. P. (1995–2001). *Israel and Hellas*, 3 volumes. Berlin.

Brown, P. (2012). *Through the Eye of a Needle: Wealth, the Fall of Rome and the Making of Christianity in the West, 350–550 AD.* Princeton.

Brubaker, R. (2004). *Ethnicity without Groups.* Cambridge, MA.

Brumann, C. (1999). 'Writing for Culture: Why a Successful Concept Should Not Be Discarded'. *Current Anthropology* 40, Supplement: 1–13.

Brunt, P. A. (1977). 'Josephus on Social Problems in Roman Judaea', *Klio* 59: 149–53.

Cameron, A. (1976). *Circus Factions: Blues and Greens at Rome and Byzantium.* Oxford.

Canella, T., (2006). *Gli Actus Silvestri: Genesi di una leggenda su Costantino imperatore.* Spoleto.

Carlebach, E. (2011). *Palaces of Time: Jewish Calendar and Culture in Early Modern Europe.* Cambridge, MA:

Chalcraft, D. (ed.) (2007). *Sectarianism in Early Judaism: Sociological Advances,* London.

Clarysse, W., S. Remijsen and M. Depauw (2010). 'Observing the Sabbath in the Roman Empire: A Case Study'. *SCI* 29: 51–57.

Clements, R. (1989). *The World of Ancient Israel: Sociological, Anthropological, and Political Perspectives.* Cambridge.

Cohen, G. (1995). *Hellenistic Settlements in Europe, the Islands, and Asia Minor,* Berkeley, CA.

(2006). *Hellenistic Settlements in Syria, the Red Sea Basin, and North Africa.* Berkeley, CA.

Cohen, J. (1979). 'Roman Imperial Policy toward the Jews from Constantine until the End of the Palestinian Patriarchate'. *Byzantine Studies/Etudes Byzantines* 3: 1–29.

(1999). *Living Letters of the Law: Ideas of the Jew in Medieval Christianity.* Berkeley, CA.

Cohen, M. (1994). *Under Crescent and Cross,* Princeton.

Cohen, S. (1979). *Josephus in Galilee and Rome: His Vita and Development as a Historian.* Leiden.

(1981). 'Epigraphical Rabbis'. *JQR* 72: 1–17.

(1984). 'The Significance of Yavneh: Pharisees, Rabbis, and the End of Jewish Sectarianism'. *HUCA* 55: 27–53.

(1993). '"Those Who Say They are Jews and Are Not": How Do You Know a Jew in Antiquity When You See One?' in S. Cohen and E. Frerichs (eds.), *Diasporas in Antiquity.* Atlanta, GA, pp. 1–45.

(1998). 'The Conversion of Antoninus', in P. Schäfer (ed.) *The Talmud Yerushalmi and Graeco-Roman Culture*. Tübingen, pp. 141–71.

(1999a). *The Beginnings of Jewishness*. Berkeley, CA.

(1999b). 'The Rabbi in Second Century Jewish Society', in *CHJ* III: 922–90.

(2006). *From the Maccabees to the Mishnah*. Louisville, KY.

(2008). 'Common Judaism in Greek and Latin Authors,' in F. Udoh (ed.), *Redefining First Century Jewish and Christian Identities: Essays in Honor of Ed Parish Sanders*. Notre Dame, IN, pp. 69–87.

Collins, J. (2010). *Beyond the Qumran Community: The Sectarian Movement of the Dead Sea Scrolls*. Grand Rapids, MI.

Colorni, V. (1964). *L'uso del Greco nella liturgia del giudaismo ellenistico e la Novella 146 di Giustiniano* (Estratto dagli Annali di storia del diritto 8 [1964]). Milan.

Conybeare, F. (1910). 'Antiochus Strategos' Account of the Sack of Jerusalem in AD 614'. *English Historical Review* 25: 502–17.

Coogan, M. (1976). *West Semitic Personal Names in the Murašu Documents*. Missoula, MT.

Cotton, H. (1993). 'The Guardianship of Jesus Son of Babatha: Roman and Local Law in the Province of Arabia'. *JRS* 83: 94–108.

(1998). 'The Rabbis and the Documents', in M. Goodman (ed.), *Jews in a Graeco-Roman World*, Oxford, pp. 167–79.

(1999). 'The Languages of the Legal and Administrative Documents from the Judaean Desert'. *ZPE* 125: 219–31.

(2002). 'Jewish Jurisdiction under Roman Rule: Prolegomena', in M. Labahn and J. Zangenberg (eds.), *Zwischen den Reichen: Neues Testament und Römische Herrschaft*. Tübingen, pp. 13–28.

(2003). 'The Bar Kokhba Revolt and the Documents from the Judaean Desert: Nabataean Participation in the Revolt (P. Yadin 52)', in Schäfer, pp. 133–52.

(2007a). 'The Administrative Background to the New Settlement Recently Discovered near Givat Shaul, Ramallah-Shu'afat Road', in J. Patrich and D. Amit (eds.), *New Studies in the Archaeology of Jerusalem and Its Region: Collected Papers*. Jerusalem, pp. 12–18.

(2007b). 'Private International Law or Conflicts of Laws: Reflections on Roman Provincial Jurisdiction', in R. Haensch and I. Heinrich (eds.), *Herrschen und Verwalten. Der Alltag der römischen Administration in der Hohen Kaiserzeit* Cologne, pp. 134–55.

(2008). 'Continuity of Nabataean Law in the Petra Papyri: A Methodological Exercise', in H. Cotton, R. Hoyland, J. Price and D. Wasserstein (eds.), *From Hellenism to Islam: Cultural and Linguistic Change in the Roman Near East*. Cambridge, pp. 154–74.

Cotton, H. and M. Wörrle (2007). 'Seleukos IV to Heliodoros: A New Dossier of Royal Correspondence from Israel'. *ZPE* 159: 191–205.

Cowey, J. and K. Maresch (2001). *Urkunden des Politeuma der Juden von Herakleopolis (144/3–133/2 v. Chr.) (P. Polit. Iud.)* (Papyrologica Coloniensia 29). Wiesbaden.

Dąbrowa, E. (2010). *The Hasmoneans and Their State: A Study in History, Ideology, and the Institutions*. Kraków.

Dan, Y. (1984). *The City in Eretz-Israel during the Late Roman and Byzantine Periods*. Jerusalem (in Hebrew).

Danby, H. (1933). *The Mishnah*. Oxford.

Dandamaev, M. and V. Lukonin (1989). *The Culture and Social Institutions of Ancient Iran*. Cambridge.

Davies, P. (2007). *The Origins of Biblical Israel*. Sheffield.

De Ste Croix, G. (1981). *The Class Struggle in the Ancient Greek World*. London.

de Vries, H. (2008). 'Introduction', in H. de Vries (ed.), *Religion: Beyond a Concept*, New York, pp. 1–98.

Dench, E. (2005). *Romulus' Asylum: Roman Identities from the Age of Alexander to the Age of Hadrian*. Oxford.

Dothan, T. (1982). *The Philistines and Their Material Culture*. New Haven, CT.

Dusinberre, E. (2003). *Aspects of Empire in Achaemenid Sardis*. Cambridge.

Eck, W. (1999). 'The Bar Kokhba Revolt: The Roman Point of View'. *JRS* 89: 76–89.

  (2003). 'Hadrian, the Bar Kokhba Revolt, and the Epigraphic Transmission', in Schäfer, pp. 153–70.

Eckhardt, B. (2012). '"An Idumean, That Is, A Half-Jew": Hasmoneans and Herodians between Ancestry and Merit', in B. Eckhardt (ed.), *Jewish Identity and Politics between the Maccabees and Bar Kokhba*. Leiden, pp. 91–115.

Ehrlich, C. (1996). *The Philistines in Transition: A History from ca. 1000–730 BCE*. Leiden.

Endelman, T. (2009). 'Jewish Self-Identification and West European Categories of Belonging: From the Enlightenment to World War II', in Gitelman, pp. 104–30.

Engels, J. (2010). 'Macedonians and Greeks', in J. Roisman and I. Worthington (eds.), *A Companion to Ancient Macedonia*. Oxford, pp. 81–98.

Eshel, H. (2007). 'Hellenism in the Land of Israel from the Fifth to the Second Centuries BCE in Light of Semitic Epigraphy', in Y. Levin (ed.), *A Time of Change: Judah and Its Neighbors in the Persian and Early Hellenistic Periods*. Edinburgh, pp. 116–24.

Eshel, H., B. Zissu and G. Barkay (2010). 'Sixteen Bar Kokhba Coins from Roman Sites in Europe'. *INJ* 17: 91–7.

Feintuch, Y. (2011). 'External Appearance versus Internal Truth: The Aggadah of Herod in Bavli Bava Batra'. *AJS Review* 35: 85–104.

Feldman, J. (2006). '"A City that Makes All Israel Friends": Normative *communitas* and the Struggle for Religious Legitimacy in Pilgrimages to the Second Temple', in M. Poorthuis and J. Schwartz (eds.), *A Holy People: Jewish and Christian Perspectives on Religious Communal Identity*. Leiden, pp. 109–26.

Feldman, L. (1993). *Jew and Gentile in the Ancient World*. Princeton.

Feliks, Y. (1990). *Agriculture in Eretz Israel in the Period of the Bible and Talmud*. Jerusalem.

Finkelstein, I. (2008). 'Jerusalem in the Persian (and Early Hellenistic) Period and the Wall of Nehemiah'. *Journal for the Study of the Old Testament* 32: 501–20.

Finn, R. (2006). *Almsgiving in the Later Roman Empire: Christian Promotion and Practice (313–450)*. Oxford.

Fishman-Duker, R. (2012). 'Images of Jews in Byzantine Chronicles: A General Survey', in Bonfil *et al.*, pp. 777–98.

Fleischer, E. (1975). *Hebrew Liturgical Poetry in the Middle Ages*. Jerusalem (in Hebrew).

(1984/5). 'Le-fitron she'elat zemano u-meqom pe'iluto shel R' Elazar berrebi Qilir'. *Tarbiz* 54: 383–428.

Fonrobert, E. and M. Jaffee (eds.) (2007). *Cambridge Companion to the Talmud and Rabbinic Literature*. Cambridge.

Foss, C. (1995). 'The Near Eastern Countryside in Late Antiquity'. *JRA suppl.* 14: 213–34.

(1997). 'Syria in Transition, AD 550–750: An Archaeological Approach'. *DOP* 51: 189–269.

Fraade, S. (2009). 'The Temple as a Marker of Jewish Identity before and after 70 CE', in L. Levine and D. Schwartz (eds.), *Jewish Identities in Antiquity: Studies in Memory of Menahem Stern*. Tübingen, pp. 237–65.

Frankel, J. (1981). *Prophecy and Politics: Socialism, Nationalism, and the Russian Jews*. Cambridge.

(2009). *Crisis, Revolution, and Russian Jews*. Cambridge.

Frankel, R. (2001). *Settlement Dynamics and Regional Diversity in Ancient Upper Galilee: Archaeological Survey of Upper Galilee*. Jerusalem.

Fredriksen, P. (2010). *Augustine and the Jews: A Christian Defense of Jews and Judaism*. New Haven, CT.

Fried, L. (2006). 'The Am Ha'ares in Ezra 4:4 and Persian Imperial Administration', in Lipschits and Oehming, pp. 123–45.

Gabba, E. (1999). 'The Social, Economic, and Political History of Palestine, 63 BCE–CE 70', in *CHJ* III: 94–167.

Galsterer, H. (1986). 'Roman Law in the Provinces: Some Problems of Transmission', in M. Crawford (ed.), *L'impero romano e le strutture economiche e sociali delle province*. Como, pp. 13–27.

Gambash, G. (forthcoming). *Rome and Provincial Resistance: The Rule and the Exception*. Cambridge.

Gambetti, S. (2009). *The Alexandrian Riots of 38 CE and the Persecution of the Jews: A Historical Reconstruction*. Leiden.

Garcia Martinez, F. and E. Tigchelaar (1997–8). *The Dead Sea Scrolls Study Edition*. 2 volumes. Leiden.

Garitte, G. (1960). *La Prise de Jérusalem par les Perses en 614* (CSCO 202–3). Louvain.

Garnsey, P. (1984). 'Religious Toleration in Classical Antiquity', in W. Sheils (ed.), *Persecution and Toleration* (Studies in Church History 21). Oxford, pp. 1–27.

Gera, D. (1998). *Judaea and Mediterranean Politics, 219–161 BCE*. Leiden.

(2009). 'Olympiodoros, Heliodoros and the Temples of Koile Syria and Phoinike'. *ZPE* 169: 125–55.

Gerstenberger, E. (2012). *Israel in the Persian Period: The Fifth and Fourth Centuries BCE* (tr. S. Schatzmann). Leiden.

Gibbon, E. (1983). *The Decline and Fall of the Roman Empire*, Book I. New York (originally published 1776).

Gil, M. (1992). *A History of Palestine, 634–1099*. Cambridge.

(2006). 'The Apocalypse of Zerubbabel in Judaeo-Arabic'. *REJ* 165:1–98.

Gitelman, Z. (ed.) (2009). *Religion or Ethnicity? Jewish Identities in Evolution*. New Brunswick, NJ.

Gitler, H. and O. Tal (2006). *The Coinage of Philistia of the Fifth and Fourth Centuries BC: A Study of the Earliest Coins of Palestine*. New York.

Goodblatt, D. (1994). *The Monarchic Principle: Studies in Jewish Self-Government in Antiquity*. Tübingen.

Goodenough, E. (1935). *By Light, Light: The Mystic Gospel of Hellenistic Judaism*. New Haven, CT.

(1953–68). *Jewish Symbols in the Greco-Roman Period*, 13 volumes. New York.

Goodman, M. (1983). *State and Society in Roman Galilee, AD 132–212*. Totowa, NJ.

(1987). *The Ruling Class of Judaea: The Origins of the Jewish Revolt against Rome*. Cambridge.

(2002). 'Current Scholarship on the First Revolt', in A. Berlin and J. Overman (eds.), *The First Revolt: Archaeology, History, Ideology*. London, pp. 15–24.

(2006). *Judaism in the Roman World: Collected Studies*. Leiden.

(2007). *Rome and Jerusalem: The Clash of Ancient Civilizations*. New York.

Goodman, M. and P. Alexander (2010). *Rabbinic Texts and the History of Late Roman Palestine*. Oxford.

Gordon, R. (ed.) (1995). *'The Place Is Too Small for Us': The Israelite Prophets in Recent Scholarship*. Winona Lake, IN.

Grabbe, L. (1998). *Ezra-Nehemiah*. London.

(2008). *A History of the Jews and Judaism in the Second Temple Period*, volume 2: *The Coming of the Greeks*, Edinburgh.

(ed.) (2011). *Enquire of the Former Age: Ancient Historiography and Writing the History of Israel* (European Seminar in Historical Methodology 9; Library of Hebrew Bible/Old Testament Studies 554). Edinburgh.

Grabbe, L. and O. Lipschits (2011). *Judah between East and West: The Transition from Persian to Greek Rule* Edinburgh.

Graf, D. (1984). 'Medism: The Origin and Significance of the Term'. *Journal of Hellenic Studies* 104: 15–30.

Grégoire, H., and M.-A. Kugener (1930). *Vie de Porphyre, évêque de Gaza, par Marc le Diacre*. Paris.

Grosdidier de Matons, J. (1977). *Romanos le Mélode et les origins de la poésie religieuse à Byzance*. Paris.

Gruen, E. (1993). 'Hellenism and Persecution: Antiochus IV and the Jews', in P. Green (ed.), *Hellenistic History and Culture*. Berkeley, CA, pp. 238–74.

(1998). *Heritage and Hellenism: The Reinvention of the Jewish Tradition.* Berkeley, CA.

(2002). *Diaspora: Jews amidst Greeks and Romans.* Cambridge, MA:

Günther, L.-M. (2005). *Herodes der Grosse.* Darmstadt.

Gussmann, O. (2008). *Das Priesterverständnis des Flavius Josephus.* Tübingen.

Habicht, C. (1976). 'Royal Documents in 2 Maccabees'. *HSCP* 80: 1–18.

Hachlili, R. (1998). *Ancient Jewish Art and Archaeology in the Diaspora.* Leiden.

(2009). *Ancient Mosaic Pavements: Themes, Issues and Trends.* Leiden.

Hall, J. (2002). *Hellenicity: Between Ethnicity and Culture.* Chicago.

Haran, M. (1983). 'Book-Scrolls at the Beginning of the Second Temple Period: The Transition from Papyrus to Skins'. *HUCA* 54: 111–22.

(1985). 'Bible Scrolls in Eastern and Western Jewish Communities from Qumran to the High Middle Ages'. *HUCA* 56: 21–62.

Harker, A. (2008). *Loyalty and Dissidence in Roman Egypt: The Case of the Acta Alexandrinorum.* Cambridge.

Hengel, M. (1974). *Judaism and Hellenism: Studies in Their Encounter in Palestine during the Early Hellenistic Period.* Philadelphia.

(1989). *The Zealots: Investigations into the Jewish Freedom Movement in the Period from Herod I until 70 AD.* Edinburgh.

Herman, Gabriel. (1987). *Ritualised Friendship and the Greek City.* Cambridge.

Herman, Geoffrey. (2012). *A Prince without a Kingdom: The Exilarch in the Sasanian Era.* Tübingen.

Herr, M. D. (2009). 'The Identity of the Jewish People before and after the Destruction of the Second Temple: Continuity or Change?', in L. Levine and D. Schwartz (eds.), *Jewish Identities in Antiquity: Studies in Memory of Menahem Stern.* Tübingen, pp. 211–36.

Hezser, C. (1997). *The Social Structure of the Rabbinic Movement in Roman Palestine.* Tübingen.

Himmelfarb, M. (1990). 'Sefer Zerubbabel', in D. Stern and M. Mirsky (eds.), *Imaginative Narratives from Classical Hebrew Literature.* Philadelphia.

Hirschfeld, Y. (1992). *Judaean Desert Monasteries in the Byzantine Period.* New Haven, CT.

(2004). *Excavations at Tiberias, 1989–1994.* Jerusalem.

(2007). 'New Excavations in Roman, Byzantine and Early Islamic Tiberias', in J. Zangenberg, H. Attridge and D. Martin (eds.), *Religion, Ethnicity, and Identity in Ancient Galilee: A Region in Transition.* Tübingen, pp. 207–29.

Hirschfeld, Y. and D. Ariel (2005). 'A Coin Assemblage from the Reign of Alexander Jannaeus Found on the Shore of the Dead Sea'. *IEJ* 55: 66–89.

Holum, K. (2004). 'Caesarea's Temple Hill: The Archaeology of Sacred Space in an Ancient Mediterranean City'. *Near Eastern Archaeology* 67: 184–99.

Hopkins, K. (1991). 'Conquest by Book', in M. Beard *et al.* (eds.), *Literacy in the Roman World.* JRA Suppl. 3: 133–58.

Horbury, W. and D. Noy (1992). *Jewish Inscriptions of Graeco-Roman Egypt.* Cambridge.

Horowitz, E. (1998). 'The Vengeance of the Jews was Stronger than their Avarice'. *Jewish Social Studies* 4: 1–39.

Horsley, R. and J. Hanson (1999). *Bandits, Prophets and Messiahs: Popular Movements in the Time of Jesus*. Harrisburg, PA.

Hume, David (1957). *The Natural History of Religion*, Stanford, CA.

Ilan, T. (1987). 'The Greek Names of the Hasmoneans'. *JQR* 78: 1–20.

Irshai, O. (2009). 'Jewish Violence in the Fourth Century CE – Fantasy and Reality: Behind the Scenes under the Emperors Gallus and Julian', in L. Levine and D. Schwartz (eds.), *Jewish Identities in Antiquity*, Tübingen, pp. 391–416.

Isaac, B. (1984). 'Judaea after 70', *JJS* 35: 44–50.

(1990). *The Limits of Empire: The Roman Army in the East*. Oxford.

(1998). *The Near East under Roman Rule*. Leiden.

Jacobs, M. (1995). *Die Institution des jüdischen Patriarchen*. Tübingen.

Jacobson, D. (2007). 'The Jerusalem Temple of Herod the Great', in N. Kokkinos (ed.), *The World of the Herods*. Stuttgart, pp. 145–76.

Jaffee, M. (2001). *Torah in the Mouth: Writing and Oral Tradition in Palestinian Judaism*. New York.

(2007). 'Rabbinic Authorship as a Collective Enterprise', in Fonrobert and Jaffee, pp. 17–37.

Japhet, S. (2009). *The Ideology of the Book of Chronicles and Its Place in Biblical Thought*. Winona Lake, IN.

Johnson, S. R. (2004). *Historical Fictions and Hellenistic Jewish Identity: Third Maccabees in Its Cultural Context*. Berkeley, CA.

Jones, A. H. M. (1931). 'The Urbanization of Palestine'. *JRS* 21: 78–85.

Jonnes, L. and M. Ricl (1997). 'A New Royal Inscription from Phrygia Paroreios: Eumenes II Grants Tyriaion the Status of a Polis'. *Epigraphica Anatolica* 29: 1–29.

Kahane, M. (2006). 'The Halakhic Midrashim', in S. Safrai, Z. Safrai, J. Schwartz and P. Tomson (eds.), *The Literature of the Sages: Second Part, Midrash and Targum*. Assen, pp. 3–105.

Kaizer, T. (2008). 'Introduction', in T. Kaizer (ed.), *The Variety of Local Religious Life in the Near East in the Hellenistic and Roman Periods*. Leiden, pp. 1–36.

Kanter, S. (1980). *Gamaliel II, the Legal Traditions*. Chico, CA.

Kasher, A. (1985). *The Jews in Hellenistic and Roman Egypt*. Tübingen.

(1988). *Jews, Idumaeans and Ancient Arabs: Relations of the Jews in Eretz-Israel with the Nations of the Frontier and the Desert During the Hellenistic and Roman Era (332 BCE–70 CE)*. Tübingen.

(1990). *Jews and Hellenistic Cities in Eretz-Israel*. Tübingen.

Kasher, A. and E. Witztum (2007). *King Herod, A Persecuted Persecuter: A Case Study in Psychohistory and Psychobiography*. Berlin.

Katzoff, R. (1995). 'Polygamy in P. Yadin?'. *ZPE* 109: 128–32.

Katzoff, R. and B. Schreiber (1998). 'Week and Sabbath in Judaean Desert Documents'. *SCI* 17: 102–14.

Kaufmann, Y. (1937). *Toldot Ha-Emunah Ha-Yisre'elit*. 4 volumes. Jerusalem.

Kennedy, H. (1985). 'From Polis to Madina: Urban Change in Late Antique and Early Islamic Syria'. *Past & Present* 106: 141–83.

Klawans, J. (2012). *Josephus and the Theologies of Ancient Judaism*. Oxford.

Kloner, A. and B. Zissu (2003). 'Hiding Complexes in Judaea: An Archaeological and Geographical Update on the Area of the Bar Kokhba Revolt', in Schäfer, pp. 181–217.

Kloner, A., D. Regev and U. Rappaport (1992). 'A Hellenistic Burial Cave in the Judaean Shephelah'. *Atiqot* 21: 27*–50*.

Kochavi, M. (1972). *Judaea, Samaria and the Golan: Archaeological Survey, 1967–8.* Jerusalem.

Kokkinos, N. (1998). *The Herodian Dynasty: Origins, Role in Society and Eclipse.* Sheffield.

Konstan, D. (1997). *Friendship in the Classical World.* Cambridge.

Kraay, C. (1980). 'Jewish Friends and Allies of Rome'. *American Numismatic Society Museum Notes* 25: 53–7.

Kraemer, R. (2009). 'Jewish Women's Resistance to Christianity in the Early Fifth Century: The Account of Severus, Bishop of Minorca'. *JECS* 17: 635–65.

Kreissig, H. (1970). *Die Sozialen Zusammenhänge des Judäischen Krieges.* Berlin.

Kushnir-Stein, A. (2008). 'Reflection of Religious Sensitivities on Palestinian City Coinage'. *INR* 3: 125–36.

 (2009). 'Coins of Tiberias with Asclepius and Hygieia and the Question of the City's Colonial Status'. *INR* 4: 94–108.

Labbé, G. (2012). *L'Affirmation de la puissance romaine en Judée.* Paris.

Lapin, H. (1995). *Early Rabbinic Civil Law and the Social History of Roman Galilee: A Study of Mishnah Tractate Baba Mesi'a'.* Altanta, GA.

 (2001). *Economy, Geography, and Provincial History in Later Roman Palestine.* Tübingen.

 (2011). 'Epigraphical Rabbis: A Reconsideration'. *JQR* 101: 311–46.

 (2012). *Rabbis as Romans: The Rabbinic Movement in Roman Palestine, 100–400 CE.* Oxford.

Le Roux, P. (2004). 'La romanisation en question'. *Annales. Histoire, Sciences Sociales* 59: 287–311.

Leibner, U. (2009). *Settlement and History in Hellenistic, Roman, and Byzantine Galilee.* Tübingen.

 (2012). 'The Beginning of Jewish Settlement in Galilee in the Second Temple Period: Historical Sources and Archaeological Discovery'. *Zion* 77: 437–70 (in Hebrew).

Lemche, N. (1988). *Ancient Israel: A New History of Israelite Society.* Sheffield.

Levine, L. (1974). 'The Jewish–Greek Conflict in First Century Caesarea'. *JJS* 25: 381–97.

 (1975). *Caesarea under Roman Rule.* Leiden.

 (1979). 'The Jewish Patriarch (Nasi) in Third Century Palestine'. *ANRW* II.19.2: 649–88.

 (1996). '"The Status of the Patriarch in the Third and Fourth Century: Sources and Methodology", *JJS* 47: 1–32.

(2005). *The Ancient Synagogue: The First Thousand Years*, 2nd edition. New Haven, CT.

(2012). *Visual Judaism in Late Antiquity: Historical Contexts of Jewish Art*. New Haven, CT.

Lewis, S. (2006). *Ancient Tyranny*. Edinburgh.

Lieber, L. (2010). *Yannai on Genesis: An Invitation to Piyyut*. Cincinnati.

Lieberman, S. (1942). *Greek in Jewish Palestine*. New York.

(1950). *Hellenism in Jewish Palestine*. New York.

(1975). 'Response to the Introduction by Professor Alexander Marx', in J. Goldin (ed.), *The Jewish Expression*. New Haven, CT, pp. 119–33 (first published 1948).

Liebeschuetz, J. H. W. G. (2001). *The Decline and Fall of the Roman City*. Oxford.

Lightfoot, J. L. (2003). *Lucian on the Syrian Goddess*. Oxford.

Linder, A. (1987). *The Jews in Roman Imperial Legislation*. Detroit.

Lipschits, O. (2006). 'Achaemenid Imperial Policy, Settlement Processes in Palestine, and the Status of Jerusalem in the Middle of the Fifth Century BCE', in Lipschits and Oehming, pp. 19–52.

Lipschits, O. and M. Oehming (eds.) (2006). *Judah and the Judeans in the Persian Period*. Winona Lake, IN.

Luraghi, N. (2006). 'Traders, Pirates, Warriors: the Proto-History of Greek Mercenary Soldiers in the Eastern Mediterranean'. *Phoenix* 60: 21–47.

Ma, J. (2000a). *Antiochos III and the Cities of Western Asia Minor*. Oxford. (reprinted 2005).

(2000b). 'The Epigraphy of Hellenistic Asia Minor: A Survey of Recent Research (1992–1999)'. *AJA* 104: 95–121.

(2007). 'Review of Aperghis'. *Hermathena* 182: 182–8.

(2012). 'Relire les *Institutions des Séleucides* de Bikerman', in S. Benoist (ed.), *Rome, a City and Its Empire: The Impact of the Roman World through Fergus Millar's Research*. Leiden, pp. 59–84.

(forthcoming). 'The Restoration of the Temple in Jerusalem by the Seleukid State: II Macc. 11.16–38'.

McLaren, J. (1998). *Turbulent Times? Josephus and Scholarship on Judaea in the First Century CE*. Sheffield.

McLynn, N. (1994). *Ambrose of Milan: Church and Court in a Christian Capital*. Berkeley, CA.

Magness, J. (2002). *The Archaeology of Qumran and the Dead Sea Scrolls*. Grand Rapids, MI.

(2005). 'The Date of the Sardis Synagogue in Light of the Numismatic Evidence'. *AJA* 109: 443–75.

(2009). 'Did Galilee Experience a Settlement Crisis in the Mid-Fourth Century?' in L. Levine and D. Schwartz (eds.), *Jewish Identities in Antiquity*, Tübingen, pp. 296–313.

Manning, J. (2003). 'Demotic Law', in R. Westbrook (ed.), *A History of Ancient Near Eastern Law*. Leiden, pp. 819–62.

(2010). *The Last Pharaohs: Egypt under the Ptolemies*. Princeton.

Mason, S. (1989). 'Was Josephus a Pharisee? A Re-examination of *Life* 10–2'. *JJS* 40: 31–46.

(2007). 'Jews, Judaeans, Judaizing, Judaism: Problems of Categorization in Ancient History'. *JSJ* 38: 457–512.

Mattingly, D. (2011). *Imperialism, Power, and Identity: Experiencing the Roman Empire*. Princeton.

Meshorer, Y. (1982). *Ancient Jewish Coinage*, 2 volumes. New York.

Mildenberg, L. (1984). *The Coinage of the Bar-Kokhba War*. Aarau.

Millar, F. (1983). 'The Phoenician Cities: A Case Study in Hellenisation'. *PCPS* 209: 55–71.

(1993). *The Roman Near East, 31 BC–AD 337*. Cambridge, MA.

(2005). 'Last Year in Jerusalem: Monuments of the Jewish War in Rome', in J. Edmondson, S. Mason and J. Rives (eds.), *Flavius Josephus and Flavian Rome*. Oxford, pp. 101–28.

Millar, F., E. Ben-Eliyahu and Y. Cohn (2013). *Handbook of Jewish Literature from Late Antiquity*. Oxford.

Miller, S. (2006). *Sages and Commoner in Late Antique Erez Israel*. Tübingen.

(2010). 'Stepped Pools, Stone Vessels, and Other Markers of "Complex Common Judaism"'. *JSJ* 41: 214 43.

Mittag, P. (2006). *Antiochos IV. Epiphanes: eine politische Biographie*. Klio Beihefte, new series 11. Berlin.

Modrzejewski, J. (1997). *The Jews of Egypt, from Ramses II to Emperor Hadrian*. Princeton.

Moore, G. F. (1927–30). *Judaism in the First Centuries of the Common Era: The Age of the Tannaim*. 2 volumes. Cambridge, MA.

Morgan, K. (ed.) (2003). *Popular Tyranny and its Discontents in Ancient Greece*. Austin, TX.

Münz-Manor, O. (2010). 'Liturgical Poetry in the Late Antique Near East'. *Journal of Ancient Judaism* 1: 336–61.

Nau, F. (1927). 'Deux episodes de l'histoire juive sous Théodose II (423 et 438) d'après la vie de Barsauma le Syrien'. *REJ* 84: 184–206.

Netzer, E., (2006). *The Architecture of Herod, the Great Builder*. Tübingen.

Neusner, J. (1970). *Development of a Legend: Studies on the Traditions Concerning Yohanan ben Zakkai*. Leiden.

(1981). *Judaism: The Evidence of the Mishnah*. Chicago.

(1982). *The Talmud of the Land of Israel: A Preliminary Translation and Explanation*, 35 volumes. Chicago.

Newman, H. (1997). 'Jerome and the Jews'. PhD dissertation, Hebrew University. Jerusalem.

Niehoff, M. (1999). 'Alexandrian Judaism in the Nineteenth Century', in A. Oppenheimer (ed.), *Jüdische Geschichte in hellenistisch-römischer Zeitalter: Wege der Forschung: Vom alten zum neuen Schürer*. Munich, pp. 9–28.

Niemeier, W.-D. (2001). 'Archaic Greeks in the Orient: Textual and Archaeological Evidence'. *BASOR* 322: 11–32.

Nippel, W. (1995). *Public Order in Ancient Rome*. Cambridge.

Nongbri, B. (2008). 'Dislodging "Embedded" Religion: A Brief Note on a Scholarly Trope'. *Numen* 55: 440–60.

Noy, D. (1993–5). *Jewish Inscriptions of Western Europe*. 2 volumes. Cambridge.

Oppenheimer, A. (2007). *Rabbi Judah Ha-nasi*. Jerusalem (in Hebrew).

Ortner, S. (ed.) (1999). *The Fate of 'Culture': Geertz and Beyond*. Berkeley and Los Angeles.

(2006). *Anthropology and Social Theory: Culture, Power, and the Acting Subject*. Durham, NC.

Ostrer, H. (2012). *Legacy: A Genetic History of the Jewish People*. New York.

Otto, W. (1913). *Herodes*. Stuttgart.

Papoutsakis, M. (2007). 'The Making of a Syriac Fable: From Ephrem to Romanos'. *Le Muséon* 120: 29–75.

Pastor, J. (1997). *Land and Economy in Ancient Palestine*. London.

Patrich, J. (2009). 'Herodian Entertainment Structures', in D. Jacobson and N. Kokkinos (eds.), *Herod and Augustus*. Leiden, pp. 181–213.

Pearce, L. (2006). 'New Evidence for Judeans in Babylonia', in Lipschits and Oehming, pp. 399–412.

Penslar, D. (2001). *Shylock's Children: Economics and Jewish Identity in Modern Europe*. Berkeley, CA.

Porten, B. (1996). *The Elephantine Papyri in English: Three Millennia of Cross-Cultural Continuity and Change*. Leiden.

Price, J. (1992). *Jerusalem under Siege: The Collapse of the Jewish State, 66–70 CE*. Leiden.

Pritchard, J. (1969). *Ancient Near Eastern Texts Relating to the Old Testament*. Princeton.

Pucci Ben Zeev, M. (2005). *Diaspora Judaism in Turmoil, 116/117 CE: Ancient Sources and Modern Insights*. Leuven.

Raban, A., edited by M. Artzy, B. Goodman and Z. Gal (2009). *The Harbour of Sebastos (Caesarea Maritima) in Its Roman Mediterranean Context* (BAR International Series 1930). Oxford.

Raban, A. and K. Holum (eds.) (1996). *Caesarea Maritima: A Retrospective after Two Millennia*. Leiden.

Rabinovitz, Z. (1965). *Halakhah and Aggadah in the Liturgical Poetry of Yannai*. Tel Aviv.

Rajak, T. (1983). *Josephus: The Historian and His Society*. London.

(2002). *The Jewish Dialogue with Greece and Rome: Studies in Cultural and Social Interaction*. Leiden.

Rajak, T. and D. Noy (1993). 'Archisynagogoi: Office, Title, and Social Status in the Greco-Jewish Synagogue', *JRS* 83: 75–93.

Rappaport, U. (1969). 'Les Iduméens en Égypte'. *Révue de Philologie* 43: 73–82.

(1982). 'John of Gischala: From Galilee to Jerusalem'. *JJS* 33: 479–93.

(1990). 'The Hellenization of the Hasmoneans'. *Tarbiz* 60: 477–503.

Rechter, D. (2002). 'Western and Central European Jewry in the Modern Period', in M. Goodman, J. Cohen and D. Sorkin (eds.), *Oxford Handbook of Jewish Studies*. Oxford, pp. 376–95.

Regev, E. (2005). *The Sadducees and Their Halakhah*. Jerusalem.

(2011). 'Royal Ideology in the Hasmonaean Palaces in Jericho'. *BASOR* 363: 45–72.

(2012). 'The Hasmoneans' Self-Image as Religious Leaders'. *Zion* 77: 5–30.

Reich, N. J. (1933). 'The Codification of the Egyptian Laws by Darius and the Origins of the "Demotic Chronicle"'. *Mizraim* 1: 178–85.

Reif, S. (2000a). 'The Damascus Document from the Cairo Genizah: Its Discovery, Early Study and Historical Significance', in J. Baumgarten, E. Chazon and A. Pinnick (eds.), *The Damascus Document: A Centennial of Discovery*. Leiden, pp. 109–31.

(2000b). *A Jewish Archive from Old Cairo: The History of Cambridge University's Genizah Collection*. Richmond, UK.

Richardson, P. (1996). *Herod, King of the Jews and Friend of the Romans*. Edinburgh.

Rives, J. (2005). 'Flavian Religious Policy and the Destruction of the Jerusalem Temple', in J. Edmondson, S. Mason and J. Rives (eds.), *Flavius Josephus and Flavian Rome*. Oxford, pp. 145–66.

Rocca, S. (2008). *Herod's Judaea: A Mediterranean State in the Classical World*. Tübingen.

Rosman, M. (2010). 'The Authority of the Council of the Four Lands Outside Poland-Lithuania', in A. Teller, M. Teter and A. Polonsky (eds.), *Social and Cultural Boundaries in Pre-Modern Poland* (Polin vol. XXII). Oxford, pp. 83–108.

Rustow, M. (2008). *Heresy and the Politics of Community: The Jews of the Fatimid Caliphate*. Ithaca, NY.

Rutgers, L. (1995). *The Jews in Late Ancient Rome: Evidence of Cultural Interaction in the Roman Diaspora*. Leiden.

(1997). 'Interaction and Its Limits: Some Notes on the Jews of Sicily in Late Antiquity'. *ZPE* 115: 245–56.

(1998). 'Some Reflections on the Archaeological Finds from the Domestic Quarter on the Acropolis of Sepphoris', in H. Lapin (ed.), *Religious and Ethnic Communities in Later Roman Palestine*. Bethesda, MD, pp. 179–95.

Saenz-Badillos, A. (1993). *History of the Hebrew Language*. Cambridge.

Safrai, Z. (1995). *The Jewish Community in the Talmudic Period*, Jerusalem (in Hebrew).

Sand, S. (2009). *The Invention of the Jewish People*. London.

Sanders, E. P. (1992). *Judaism: Practice and Belief, 63 BC to AD 66*. Philadelphia.

Sanders, E. P., A. Baumgarten, A. Mendelson and B. Meyer (eds.) (1980–3). *Jewish and Christian Self-Definition*. 3 volumes. Philadelphia.

Sandwell, I. (2007). *Religious Identity in Late Antiquity: Greeks, Jews and Christians in Antioch*. Cambridge.

Sartre, M. (2001). *D'Alexandre à Zénobie: Histoire du Levant antique IVe siècle av. J.-C.–IIIe siècle ap. J.-C.* Poitiers.

Schäfer, P. (1981). *Der Bar Kokhba-Aufstand: Studien zum zweiten jüdischen Krieg gegen Rom*. Tübingen.

(ed.) (2003). *The Bar Kokhba War Reconsidered*. Tübingen.

Schalit, A. (1969). *König Herodes*. Berlin.

Schiffman, Z. (2011). *The Birth of the Past*. Baltimore.

Schofield, A. and J. Vanderkam (2005). 'Were the Hasmoneans Zadokites?' *JBL* 124: 73–87.

Schorsch, I. (1994). *From Text to Context: The Turn to History in Modern Judaism*. Hanover, NH.

Schremer, A. (2010). 'The Religious Orientation of Non-Rabbis in Second-Century Palestine: A Rabbinic Perspective,' in Z. Weiss, O. Irshai, J. Magness and S. Schwartz (eds.), *'Follow the Wise': Studies in Jewish History and Culture in Honor of Lee I. Levine*. Winona Lake, IN, pp. 319–41.

Schwartz, D. (1990). *Agrippa I: The Last King of Judaea*. Tübingen.

(1994). 'Josephus on Hyrcanus II', in J. Sievers and F. Parente (eds.), *Josephus and the History of the Greco-Roman Period*. Leiden, pp. 210–32.

(2008). *2 Maccabees*. Berlin.

(2012). 'Introduction', in D. Schwartz and Z. Weiss (eds.), *Was 70 CE a Watershed in Jewish History? On Jews and Judaism before and after the Destruction of the Second Temple*. Leiden, pp. 1–19.

Schwartz, J. (1986). *Jewish Settlement in Southern Judaea from the Bar Kokhba Revolt to the Muslim Conquest*, Jerusalem.

Schwartz, S. (1990). *Josephus and Judaean Politics*. Leiden.

(1993a). 'John Hyrcanus I's Destruction of the Gerizim Temple and Judaean–Samaritan Relations'. *Jewish History* 7: 9–25.

(1993b). 'A Note on the Social Type and Political Ideology of the Hasmonean Family'. *JBL* 112: 305–9.

(1999). 'The Patriarchs and the Diaspora'. *JJS* 50: 208–222.

(2000). 'King Herod, Friend of the Jews', in J. Schwartz, Z. Amar and I. Ziffer (eds.), *Jerusalem and Eretz Israel: Arie Kindler Volume*. Tel Aviv: pp. *67–*76.

(2001). *Imperialism and Jewish Society, 200 BCE to 640 CE*. Princeton.

(2002a). 'Historiography on the Jews in the 'Talmudic Period', 70–640 CE', in M. Goodman, J. Cohen and D. Sorkin (eds.), *Oxford Handbook of Jewish Studies*. Oxford, pp. 79–114.

(2002b). 'Rabbinization in the Sixth Century', in P. Schäfer (ed.), *The Talmud Yerushalmi and Graeco-Roman Culture*, volume III. Tübingen, pp. 55–69.

(2004). 'Big-Men or Chiefs? Against an Institutional History of the Palestinian Patriarchate', in J. Wertheimer (ed.), *Jewish Religious Leadership: Image and Reality*, volume I. New York, pp. 155–73.

(2005). 'Hebrew and Imperialism in Jewish Palestine', in C. Bakhos (ed.), *Ancient Judaism in Its Hellenistic Context*. Leiden, pp. 53–84.

(2006). 'Political, Social and Economic History of Palestine, 70–235 CE', in *CHJ* IV: 23–52.

(2007). 'Conversion to Judaism in the Second Temple Period: A Functionalist Approach', in S. Cohen and J. Schwartz (eds.), *Studies in Josephus and the Varieties of Ancient Judaism: Louis H. Feldman Jubilee Volume*. Leiden, pp. 223–36.

(2009a). 'Euergetism in Josephus and the Epigraphical Culture of First Century Jerusalem', in H. Cotton, R. Hoyland, J. Price and D. Wasserstein (eds.),

From Hellenism to Islam: Cultural and Linguistic Change in the Roman Near East. Cambridge, pp. 75–92.

(2009b). 'Sunt Lachrymae Rerum'. *JQR* 99: 56–64.

(2010). *Were the Jews a Mediterranean Society? Reciprocity and Solidarity in Ancient Judaism.* Princeton.

(2011). 'How Many Judaisms Were There? A Critique of Neusner and Smith on Definition and Mason and Boyarin on Categorization'. *Journal of Ancient Judaism* 2: 208–38.

(2013). 'Was There a Common Judaism after 70?' in R. Boustan and A. Reed (eds.), *Envisioning Judaism: Studies in Honor of Peter Schäfer on His Seventieth Birthday.* Tübingen.

(forthcoming). 'Finkelstein the Orientalist', in W. V. Harris (ed.) *Finley and Politics.*

Secunda, S. (2013). *The Iranian Talmud.* Philadelphia,

Shahar, Y. (2003). 'The Underground Hideouts in Galilee and their Historical Meaning', in Schäfer, pp. 217–40.

Shatzman, I. (1991). *The Armies of the Hasmoneans and Herod.* Tübingen.

(2005). 'On the Conversion of the Idumaeans', in M. Mor (ed.), *For Uriel: Studies in the History of Israel in Antiquity Presented to Professor Uriel Rappaport.* Jerusalem, pp. 213–41.

(2007). 'Jews and Gentiles from Judas Maccabaeus to John Hyrcanus according to Jewish Sources', in S. Cohen and J. Schwartz (eds.), *Josephus and the Varieties of Ancient Judaism: Louis H. Feldman Jubilee Volume.* Leiden, pp. 237–65.

Shaw, B. (1989). 'Review of Goodman'. *JRS* 79: 246–7.

(1993). 'Tyrants, Bandits, and Kings: Personal Power in Josephus'. *JJS* 44: 176–204.

Sherwin-White, S. and A. Kuhrt (1993). *From Samarkhand to Sardis: A New Approach to the Seleukid Empire.* London.

Sievers, J. (1990). *The Hasmoneans and Their Supporters: from Mattathias to the Death of John Hyrcanus I.* Atlanta, GA.

Simon, M. (1986). *Verus Israel: A Study of the Relations between Christians and Jews in the Roman Empire (135–425)* (tr. H. McKeating). Oxford.

Simon-Shoshan, M. (2012). *Stories of the Law: Narrative Discourse and the Construction of Authority in the Mishnah.* Oxford.

Simonsohn, S. (1975). 'The Hebrew Revival among Early Medieval European Jews', in S. Lieberman (ed.), *Salo Wittmayer Baron Jubilee Volume on the Occasion of His Eightieth Birthday,* Jerusalem, pp. 831–58.

Sklar-Parnes, D., Y. Rapuano and R. Bar-Nathan (2004). 'Excavations in North East Jerusalem – A Jewish Site Between the Revolts'. *New Studies on Jerusalem* 10: 35–41.

Smallwood, E. M. (1981). *The Jews under Roman Rule, from Pompey to Diocletian.* Leiden.

Smith, J. Z. (1982). 'Fences and Neighbors: Some Contours of Early Judaism', in *Imagining Religion: From Babylon to Jonestown.* Chicago, pp. 1–18.

Smith, Mark (2000). *The Origins of Biblical Monotheism.* Oxford.

Smith, Morton (1952). 'The Common Theology of the Ancient Near East'. *JBL* 71: 135–47.

(1971). *Palestinian Parties and Politics that Shaped the Old Testament.* New York.

Snodgrass, A. (2006). *Archaeology and the Emergence of Greece.* Edinburgh.

Spielman, L. (2010). 'Sitting with Scorners: Jewish Attitudes toward Roman Spectacle Entertainment from the Herodian Period through the Muslim Conquest'. PhD dissertation, Jewish Theological Seminary. New York.

Stemberger, G. (1993). 'Zwangstaufen von Juden im 4. bis 7. Jahrhundert: Mythos oder Wirklichkeit?' in C. Thoma, G. Stemberger and J. Maier (eds.), *Judentum – Ausblicke und Einsichten: Festgabe für K. Schubert zum siebzigsten Geburtstag.* Frankfurt, pp. 81–114.

(2000). *Jews and Christians in the Holy Land: Palestine in the Fourth Century.* Edinburgh.

Stern, D. (2004). 'Anthology and Polysemy in Classical Midrash', in D. Stern (ed.), *The Anthology in Jewish Literature.* Oxford, pp. 106–39.

Stern, E. (1982). *Material Culture of the Land of the Bible in the Persian Period.* Warminster.

(ed.) (1993). *New Encyclopedia of Archaeological Excavations in the Holy Land,* 4 volumes. Jerusalem.

Stern, S. (2003). 'Rabbi and the Origins of the Patriarchate'. *JJS* 54: 193–215.

Stökl Ben Ezra, D. (2003). *The Impact of Yom Kippur on Early Christianity.* Tübingen.

Stolper, M. (1985). *Entrepreneurs and Empire: The Murašu Archive, the Murašu Firm, and Persian Rule in Babylonia.* Leiden.

Strack, H. and G. Stemberger (1996). *Introduction to the Talmud and Midrash.* Edinburgh.

Strange, J., T. Longstaff and D. Groh (2006). *Excavations at Sepphoris,* volume I, *University of South Florida Probes in the Citadel and the Villa.* Leiden.

Sukenik, E. (1932). *Ancient Synagogue of Beth Alfa: An Account of the Excavation Conducted on Behalf of the Hebrew University.* London.

Sullivan, R. (1990). *Near Eastern Royalty and Rome, 100–30 BC.* Toronto.

Swartz, M. (1996). *Scholastic Magic: Ritual and Revelation in Early Jewish Mysticism.* Princeton.

Syon, D. (2006). 'Numismatic Evidence of Jewish Presence in Galilee before the Hasmonean Annexation'. *INResearch* I: 21–4.

Talgam, R. (2012). 'Constructing Identity through Art: Jewish Art as a Minority Culture in Byzantium', in Bonfil *et al.*, pp. 399–454.

Talgam, R. and Z. Weiss (2004). *The Mosaics of the House of Dionysos at Sepphoris* (Qedem 44). Jerusalem.

Tate, G. (1992). *Les campagnes de la Syrie du nord du IIe au VIIe siècle: un exemple d'expansion démographique et économique à la fin de l'antiquité.* Paris.

Tcherikover, V. (1959). *Hellenistic Civilization and the Jews.* Philadelphia.

Toher, M. (2001). 'Nicolaus and Herod in the *Antiquitates Iudaicae*'. *HSCP* 101: 427–48.

Tsafrir, Y., and G. Foerster (1997). 'Urbanism at Scythopolis–Beth Shean in the Fourth–Seventh Centuries'. *DOP* 51: 85–146.

Tuplin, C. (2011). 'The Limits of Persianization: Some Reflections on Cultural Links in the Persian Empire', in E. Gruen (ed.), *Cultural Identity in the Ancient Mediterranean*. Los Angeles, pp. 150–82.

Ussishkin, D. (2008). 'Excavations at Betar, the Last Stronghold of Bar Kokhba'. *Qadmoniot* 136: 108–12 (in Hebrew).

van Bekkum, W. J. (2010). 'The Future of the Ancient *Piyyut*', in Goodman and Alexander, pp. 217–33.

Van de Mieroop, M. (1997). *The Ancient Mesopotamian City*. Oxford.

Van Seters, J. (1983). *In Search of History: Historiography in the Ancient World and the Origins of Biblical History*. New Haven, CT.

Vidal-Naquet, P. (1980). 'Interpreting Revolutionary Change: Political Divisions and Ideological Diversity in the Jewish World of the First Century AD'. *Yale French Studies* 59: 86–105.

Von Falkenhausen, V. (2012). 'The Jews in Byzantine Southern Italy'. In Bonfil et al., 297–316.

Wallace-Hadrill, A. (2008). *Rome's Cultural Revolution*. Cambridge.

Ward-Perkins, B. (2005). *The Fall of Rome and the End of Civilization*. Oxford.

Weiss, Z. (2010). 'From Roman Temple to Byzantine Church: A Preliminary Report on Sepphoris in Transition'. *JRA* 23: 196–219.

Wellhausen, J. (1878). *Prolegomena zur Geschichte Israels*. Berlin.

Wexler-Bdolah, S. (2009). ''Al Ha-kesher shebeyn Rehov Ha-'Amudim (ha-Kardo) Ha-Mizrahi shel Yerushalayim Veha-Legyon Ha-'Asiri Ha-Romi Le-Or Hafirot Rihvat Ha-Kotel', in D. Amit, G. Stiebel, O. Peleg-Bareket (eds.), *Hiddushim Be-Arkhiyologiyah shel Yerushalayim U-Sevivoteha*. Jerusalem, pp. 19–27.

Wickham, C. (2006). *Framing the Early Middle Ages*. Oxford.

Wiesehöfer, J. (1996). *Ancient Persia: from 550 BC to 650 AD*. London.

(2009). 'The Achaemenid Empire', in I. Morris and W. Scheidel (eds.), *The Dynamics of Ancient Empires*. Oxford, pp. 66–98.

Wilker, J. (2007). *Für Rom und Jerusalem: Die herodianische Dynastie im 1. Jahrhundert n. Chr.* Frankfurt am Main.

Will, E. (2003). *Histoire politique du monde hellénistique*. Paris.

Williams, M. H. (2008). 'Lessons from Jerome's Jewish Teachers: Exegesis and Cultural Interaction in Late Antique Palestine', in N. Dohrmann and D. Stern (eds.), *Jewish Biblical Interpretation and Cultural Exchange: Comparative Exegesis in Context*. Philadelphia, pp. 66–86.

Wills, L. (1995). *The Jewish Novel in the Ancient World*. Ithaca, NY.

Wolff, H.-J. (1978). 'Römisches Provinzialrecht in der Provinz Arabia'. *ANRW* II.13: 763–806.

Wolfson, H. (1947). *Philo: Foundations of Religious Philosophy in Judaism, Christianity, and Islam*. Cambridge, MA.

Woolf, G. (1994). 'Becoming Roman, Staying Greek: Culture, Identity and the Civilizing Process in the Roman East'. *PCPS* 40: 116–43.

(1998). *Becoming Roman: The Origins of Provincial Civilization in Gaul.* Cambridge.

Yadin, A. (2004). 'Goliath's Armor and Israelite Collective Memory'. *Vetus Testamentum* 54: 373–95.

Yahalom, J. (1985). *The Poetic Language of the Early Palestinian Piyyut.* Jerusalem (in Hebrew).

Yerushalmi, Y. (1982). *Zakhor: Jewish History and Jewish Memory.* Seattle.

Ziosi, F. (2012). 'Roma e gli Ebrei in Rivolta'. Dissertation, Scuola Normale Superiore di Pisa.

Zissu, B. (2000–2). 'The Geographical Distribution of Coins from the Bar Kokhba War'. *INJ* 14: 157–67.

Zuiderhoek, A. (2009). *The Politics of Munificence in the Roman Empire: Citizens, Elites and Benefactors in Asia.* Cambridge.

Index